# Fire in My Ears

## A Novel

## Susan Schneider

Copyright 2013 by Susan Schneider

ISBN-13:9781484807255
ISBN-10:1484807251

To all the teachers, parents, and even grandmothers, who spend all their energy setting children on happy paths.

"What fire is in mine ears? Can this be true?"

*Much Ado About Nothing*
William Shakespeare

*Fire In My Ears*

One

When I was a child in the middle of the American 1950s, I feared that my mother's side of the family was a pack of crazy people. They were nothing like the families that were on television every night or the ones that lived on my street. I never mentioned them or my opinion of their mental health to anyone because I didn't want to be lumped together with lunatics. Their behavior made me uneasy, so I kept it to myself, safely unaddressed. I had plenty of opportunity to observe them up close because every Sunday they would gather at my house to spend the day with my grandmother Mary who lived with me and my parents and brother David most of the time.

Unlike my aunts and uncles and their families, my family lived in a house in suburbia. When my parents had married right after the war, they moved away from the city neighborhoods where they had grown up, and I used to think that maybe it was living in apartments that were almost as miniature and cramped as my model doll house that had caused the relatives to act in ways much larger and more exaggerated than regular people when they visited. It was like some pressure built up during the six days between visits, and then it was released as they drove down my block, and they exploded into huge three-dimensional cartoons when they got to my house.

In warm weather, Uncle Morty would arrive first, early in the morning. He'd come alone, without his wife Rose, before anyone had even left their beds, to wash his car in our driveway and make breakfast for himself in our kitchen. In fact the sound that often stirred me from my sleep was the loud hum of steadily running water. I could check that it was Uncle Morty simply by sitting up and kneeling at the window next to my bed. His light blue Ford would be below me, covered with lather, and he'd be leaning over working on a hubcap with a rag, a cigar clamped between his teeth and a straw fedora tilted back off his forehead. The green hose would be running, and a stream of water would be coursing down the driveway into the street. I'd watch silently from my secret observation post as he eventually picked up the hose and twisted the brass nozzle. His cigar would shift from left corner of his mouth to the right and back again as he tested the effect of various intensities of mist on the triangle of lawn between the flagstone path and the concrete driveway. Finally satisfied, he'd turn the water on the car and the soap would run off in sheets. I knew he'd be inside brewing coffee any minute. My grandmother, lying in her bed set at a right angle to mine would shift and begin to work herself slowly to a sitting position, eager to see her oldest child, Morty.

Grandma Mary, called Bubby by her thirteen grandchildren, seemed to me to be an ancient human being, from another century and another country, and another way of life. I'd been told often about how beautiful Bubby had been when she was young, and even the self-effacing Bubby herself would talk to me about her youthful beauty when she told me stories every night, but there was no way I could see it. Bubby had a certain smell about her, not repulsive exactly, but on the edge of moldy and sour, with a veil of the lavender soap she had used since the day she got married. Her skin was like silky crepe clinging to her bones in some places and draping away in others, a lot like the fabric my mother had hung on the living room windows. She was paralyzed on her left side, the result of a stroke she'd had in her sixties, and every picture of her shows an embarrassed woman hiding her useless crumpled left fist. The shame of her infirmity was clearly stamped onto her deeply lined forehead and eyes that never looked directly into the camera. The answer to, "How are you?" was, "Still living," with apologies, like her surviving as long as she had was a mistake, an oversight in God's bookkeeping. I can remember watching her standing in front of the wooden counter in the kitchen, preparing food. Her white hair would be caught up in clear plastic combs with her pink scalp glowing where her hair parted, and she'd be paring apples or potatoes in her own special way. "Come, Sarah," she used to invite me. "I'll show you how I can still cook." She would clamp one into her bad hand and strip away the peel with careful deliberate passes using the knife held in her good hand. If it were apples, they were turned into big rectangular apple cakes made with cookie dough and sprinkled sugar that would fill the house with the warm welcoming aroma of cinnamon. And if it were potatoes, they were grated for potato pancakes fried in peanut oil and rich fragrant onions for Morty and the rest of the children.

Other aunts and uncles and cousins would arrive as the day wore on, until the house was filled to a pulsing, growling rumble. The cousins would tumble out of the car snarling at each other after their long ride from the Bronx, and advance in waves on my house and yard like an army of ants that devours everything in its path. The aunts and uncles stayed primarily in the kitchen, squeezed into two yellow leather bunk seats, one on either side of the long oak table. If it were winter, the radiator that was far under the table, up against the wall, would hiss and sputter periodically, as if it were commenting on the proceedings. Aunt Ruthie always claimed the end seat, clutching her oversize purse as if it had something of real value in it, and refused to slide in when her sisters and brothers arrived. They ate huge meals there, but not all together like Norman Rockwell had it. Aunt Esther, a tiny woman whose hair color changed weekly, might be bent over a bowl of my mother's mushroom and barley soup, looking like someone was getting ready to steal it from her at any moment. Next to her, her husband, Uncle Jack, had already eaten his soup and a plate of boiled chicken, and was cracking walnut shells, one against another. He was the only one who didn't smoke, which made me wonder how he could stand to sit in the smeared air with the rest of them. The smoke always made me stay just on the other side of the door that led to the living room; I was infrequently noticed. The rare times I was ever addressed, it was with annoyance. "Sarah! Get away from that door, already. Go play with your cousins."

Uncle Milt never ate anything unless his wife, Aunt Ruthie served it to him, but she was usually clinging to her end seat, chain smoking, and unwilling to move. Uncle Milt, too small and wiry to ever really be hungry, spent his time in the far corner of the bunk seat, wedged against the wall, probably resting his feet on the radiator, spouting one-liners that even I could see were utterly stupid. No one laughed or even paid any attention to him. Being ignored never acted as a deterrent, of course.

Aunt Jean would be yelling at her husband, the meek but handsome Uncle Solly, to, "Get those kids away from me!" One of their daughters might have wandered into the kitchen to whine, and Aunt Jean, the youngest sister, didn't think anyone but herself was her responsibility. I tried to avoid Uncle Solly because he pinched my cheeks by grabbing my skin between his thumb and first finger and rotating it like he was trying to screw it off. My mother always excused him by explaining that he had been wounded in the Battle of the Bulge and had made her a wallet while he was recuperating in a hospital that she still used.

"He has a metal plate in his arm. That's why he doesn't drive." It was the explanation for anything he said or did, or didn't say or do. The metal plate hadn't weakened his fingers, I thought. But did my mother mean that there's always a key from the past that untangles present behavior?

My mother's real name was Rivka, but no one called her that except Uncle Morty. When Aunt Jean had been very little, she called her older sister Rikki, and that name stuck. My friends had mothers named Helen or Selma or Beatrice, and I loved that my mother had such a young trendy name. I was sure it was part of what set her off from her family and prevented her from being part of their burlesque show every Sunday. Rikki never sat with her sisters on the yellow bunk seats, but stationed herself in front of the stove frying potato pancakes or brewing pots of coffee in her vacuum pot. She listened to their raucous talk and laughed in the right places. But she was mostly an observer like me. It might have been more than her name, though. She once told me that when she took a summer job at a camp for poor children, she met other young people working there who came from rich families that sent their children to college and went to the ballet and the opera, and that summer had changed her life: she knew she would never be like her sisters and brothers, and she never was. Of course, it's impossible to escape your past completely, and I sometimes saw my mother's face looking like it was being torn in two by vicious winds, as she fought with herself to be of her family and not be of her family.

Someone always brought along Aunt Rose, Uncle Morty's wife. But she never sat in the bunk seats with the rest of them. She was a sister-in-law, an interloper, a veritable stranger. She'd been married to Uncle Morty for over thirty years by the time I was watching them interact with each other at her house every Sunday. But she was always referred to by her maiden name, Rose Aronsky, spoken as if it were one word, which, in fact, I thought it was. Aunt Rose was fat, with dimpled hands like a child's, and she wore floral pattern dresses with narrow belts made of the same silky slippery fabric that slid up over her round middle. She pulled them down into place almost constantly. She stood the whole time she was there, right in front of the sink, and washed dishes as her sisters-in-law and brothers-in-law finished with them. She had little fat feet that looked to me like they were trying to escape from their shoes. Blobs of flesh protruded through oval shaped design elements around the toes, and wide slabs of it gushed up around the straps that buckled across the top. Every once in a while, she would eat something from one of the plates that accumulated on the counter, her pinky extended gracefully from her fat dimpled hand, but she never actually sat down with a plate of her own. She always said everything twice, as if she had to echo herself to feel like she was in a conversation.

"It's a pity; it's a pity," she would intone, scraping uneaten pot roast into the garbage pail. No one would ever answer her, or maybe someone would say,

"G'wan, g'head there." Your opinion of us is unwelcome, this meant. I never understood why they were mad at Aunt Rose, or why she continued to come every week to be the object of such derision, or why her husband Morty ignored it. But I was always uncomfortable watching it.

The truth is Uncle Morty, in spite of his benign oval face, had a dark and mysterious side. He had once had a business in Cuba, and he used to travel there for at least a week every month to keep an eye on things. Later, of course, when Castro took over, the business was lost and he never went back. But his time in Cuba wasn't spent exclusively at his factory. Morty had another family there, sort of like a life in a parallel universe. There was a woman and children, one of my cousins whispered as we set up the dollhouse furniture on the green and white floor tiles of the basement playroom, "And everyone knows about them, even Aunt Rose." I wasn't sure whether to believe it. It was a story just as unlikely, I thought, as the scary tales of Jerry the Ghost that the older children made up to frighten the younger ones, right before they shut off the lights and screamed. But maybe if it were true, it explained why someone else had to bring Aunt Rose, not her own husband, and why Uncle Morty didn't seem to care that she ate scraps off other peoples' plates and carried on conversations with herself. After Castro came, when Cuba was essentially vaporized for Americans, I imagined the other family lined up against a high chain link fence, their fingers curled through it, maybe a small son and a daughter about my age. They'd be facing north, with their blue eyes that were just like Uncle Morty's, squinting toward New York through hundreds of miles of air, waiting for their father to come and rescue them. But of course, since none of the adults talked out loud about these children, neither did I.

The last aunt and uncle to arrive were my mother's brother Mike and his wife Marly. Uncle Mike's real name was Moses, but his sisters and brother called him Mayshe. But since her real name was Marlene, it seemed like the two of them were a small troupe of at least five separate players. They glided down the street in their long black Cadillac, a new one every year, and parked it across the end of the driveway. I thought it looked like an ocean liner moored to a small pier. Their son Daniel always rode in the front with his father, and Aunt Marly sat in the back, wearing lots of rings and necklaces, her red hair swept up into an elegant French knot as if she were going to a ball right after their visit with the family. Whenever she lit one in her succession of Pell Mell cigarettes, she would stick out the tip of her tongue and remove a fleck of tobacco with two fingers tipped with bright orange nails. Her perfume billowed in clouds around her and seemed to encase her in a fortress of safety from the family. There was something elegant and trashy about her at the same time. Uncle Mayshe was a rich businessman with manicured nails and a sparkly pinky ring on each pudgy hand. He'd sell anything, even Aunt Marly's jewelry right off her if someone complimented it. Sometimes he'd roll a fifty dollar bill off a large wad he'd fished out his pocket and send someone out to the Chinese restaurant, with the off-hand command, "Hey, get me some Chinks." I didn't know what his reference meant, but I somehow knew it was a word I shouldn't use or ask about. "Marly drinks," Aunt Ruthie would remark just under her breath to Aunt Esther, who would nod without even turning her head, and add, "And she goes with men, any men."

"I heard she goes with women, too," Aunt Esther would counter, with a satisfied sneer. These were old stories, repeated every Sunday and not news to anyone. If Aunt Marly heard, she didn't react. She was an outsider too, like Aunt Rose, a sister-in-law who was never really accepted. By the time Uncle Mayshe, Aunt Marly and Daniel arrived, the noise would have risen to a furious pitch, like a phonograph record that is turned steadily louder and I would have ducked further into the living room, afraid to be too close, but also afraid to leave them to their own devices.

Periodically, one sister and her husband and children would be missing from the gathering for an interval of a week or even longer. Uncle Morty once stopped coming for several years. This meant that there had been a fight. I heard snatches of the substance of these fights during the week when I quietly listened to my mother's side of a phone conversation with one of her sisters. I would play quietly on the floor, watching the smoke from my mother's cigarette scroll softly toward the ceiling, forgotten in its ashtray, and my mother would repeat indignant retorts of the offending sister to the sympathetic one. These roles switched often. She could be reporting to Esther about Jean or to Ruthie about Esther. The substance of their arguments was never completely clear to me, but I knew whom not to expect the following Sunday.

The only uncle who never appeared was Uncle Sidney. I had no clear idea where he was, but my grandmother always cried quietly if his name came up, clutching the side of her face like she was trying to peel it off, so I figured he had died. Cousin Danny announced one day to the rest of the cousins that Uncle Sidney wasn't dead at all. It was an autumn day, when the cold first begins to drill through children who are used to summer weather and think it will continue forever, and the cousins were spending their time in the backyard, jumping in piles of raked yellow maple leaves. "He's in a nut hospital. He's crazy," he announced with authority just before he made a spectacular running leap into the stack of foliage they had just amassed for him. "My father used to visit him," he said as he surfaced and threw a handful of leaves at his cousins.

"No. That must be wrong, " I said.

"Sarah, you're so stupid," he snorted. My other cousins went right on throwing leaves at each other, as if it were perfectly ordinary to hear of a psychotic uncle. It was a story that I put with the tales of Uncle Morty's other family. Why wouldn't my mother have gone to visit him too, after all, if it were true? I never asked about him. Thinking of him as the dead uncle was less complicated.

While their parents interrupted each other raucously in the kitchen, or one or another would occasionally speak to my grandmother in Yiddish, the language she understood best, as she sat quietly in her straight-backed kitchen chair, the cousins had the run of the rest of the house and the yard. I knew they must have eaten at some point during the day, but I knew too that they were never called in to sit at the table together. It always seemed strange to me. My immediate family ate dinner together every night at 7:00 when my father came home from the city with his suit jacket flung over his shoulder and his tie loosened, just like the publicity photos of Frank Sinatra. The table was always set, with a tablecloth, folded napkins, and properly placed silverware. We always started with precisely sectioned grapefruit halves, then meat, potatoes and a vegetable, with a salad on the side. If the potatoes were French fries, my brother David and I counted them out so neither got extras. But these Sunday meals were different. The children were simply handed chunks of this or that, a chicken leg, a slice or two of seeded rye bread, a wedge of salami, if they wandered into the kitchen to report an offense one of their cousins or sisters or brothers had done to them.

Then suddenly, the adults would remember what a long ride it was back to the Bronx, and they'd scream shrilly to their children who had, by that time, worked themselves into an exhausted frenzy, "We're leaving. Are you hungry?" They'd set off all at once, emptying all the cookies from the cabinet by the kitchen door into lunch bags, "for the ride." The house would deflate instantly, almost grow smaller, in fact, and settle into silence as its over-stretched walls resumed their original form, until my mother took out her vacuum cleaner. Her lips would be pursed as if the memories of the day disturbed her, somehow. She must have known that the nastiness and character assassination that passed for sisterly and brotherly love in her family should have been stopped, or at least pointed out. But their neurotic layers had been painted on so thickly by then that she must have felt unable to act. Or maybe she just regretted that she wasn't oblivious to it all, the way they all seemed to be. The roar the vacuum made as she guided it around the empty spaces her sisters and brothers had just vanished from rivaled any jet engine in decibels. My father would appear from his basement workshop smelling like sawdust or paint, dressed in the soft plaid flannel shirt and blue jeans that were his weekend uniform, singing about having the world on a string or maybe dancing in the dark, and my grandmother would begin to shuffle slowly toward the stairs.

On these Sundays when my grandmother's whole family came to see her, there was cacophony and dissonance everywhere, but especially in the kitchen. As the day wore on, my aunts and uncles became caricatures of themselves. My mother and her three sisters thought of their sisters-in-law as strangers, and with the exception of my father who intentionally backed off, they considered their husbands as necessary appendages, sort of like silent partners. The brothers thought of their wives the same way. They teased and derided the idiosyncrasies of those Others in ways that were clever and funny, but the mood always grew nastier as the visit wore on, like a slowly wakening beast that realizes how hungry it is and finally roars with anger and frustration. By the end of their visit, they were stinging each other with merciless humor, without rational thought, intent only on finding the known weaknesses for their barbs. I sometimes laughed at the antics, but even as a nine-year-old, I always understood the hurtful intentions.

I remember how apart my grandmother was from the proceedings. Her children came to see her every week, but they barely included her in the goings-on. They scarcely spoke to her, even ignoring her to the point that I wondered what had created such animosity toward her.  But my clearest memory of these marathon visits is how much of an outsider I felt in my own house in the midst of the curling and looping noise my mother's family created around me.  I often left the games my cousins were playing in the backyard or the basement and lurked by the door into the kitchen, listening carefully as the scenario at the table surged on like the Wizard of Oz twister.  When they left, I felt like we, my parents, my brother, my grandmother and I, could change back into our selves, and resume our normal roles in our normal average family.  The carping, gossiping nastiness would be put away for a week, and my father would come away from whatever project had been occupying all day, enter the kitchen and sit in his usual place at the bunk seats.  I thought my father must have felt like a remote and maybe even bemused observer too.  No one ever said a word about how different my mother's family was from other families.  In fact, except for the television families, I didn't have a clear idea of what other families were like.  I felt, though, that it couldn't be possible that my family was like others.  Everything about them seemed extreme.  It was almost as if they were painted in electrified primary colors, pulsing along their outlines, brighter and more shocking to look at than normal people.  They were the kind of grotesque creatures that used to be featured in circus sideshows, but instead of physical oddities, theirs were emotional and conversational. One Sunday I saw my father roll his eyes and whistle a sigh of relief right after the kitchen door closed behind them, and when our eyes met, some understanding passed between us.  He knew, too.

None of my aunts or uncles or cousins ever seemed aware of themselves as unusual or strange back then, nor did my mother ever see them as anything but a bubbling loving stew of a family.  But they were strange, filled with some kind of dangerous anger that escaped in short eruptions like steam bursting from my mother's pressure cooker. And the most unsettling thing about them was their urgent secretiveness. They all had plenty to say, but no one ever asked anyone for an opinion, and nothing was ever discussed or deliberated over, and their overwhelming need was to keep outsiders out. It is easy to see why a child would have sensed that any questions about them should be left unasked: the answers would be too terrifying.

And even now, nearly half a century after those clamorous all day sessions, the reverberations are still around. The children, grand-children and great grand-children of those aunts and uncles who mistakenly thought they were close and loving and dear to each other are neither happy, nor healthy, nor comfortable in this world. They are jealous, insular, suspicious and unable to love each other or anyone else. They divide the world into "family" and "strangers" and have open resentment for the first and hostile distance from the second. And if they ever search for the cause of their miseries, when they try to peel off all the layers of the onion to find where the stink originates, they will have to look beyond those aunts and uncles who were squeezed together every Sunday. The keys are in the stories, and in particular, in one story that was made on one single day, from way back before any of them was born. They will need all those stories that Mary entrusted to me, her granddaughter, in her apologetic accented voice every night as we two were lying in our twin beds.

The tales my grandmother told did not always unfold in a neat chronological narrative, but if I reshuffled them, they did follow Mary's life. Some were as golden as the fairy tales from the storybooks in the bookcase that separated our beds, complete with happily-ever-after endings. These painted pictures rivaled any of the children's movies that I was taken to see at the local theater. There was the one about the neighbor in her little shtetl who raised geese that were always escaping their pen and terrorizing the villagers, or the recounting of a wedding that had three accordion players and everyone got a headache and stayed in bed late the next day. Both my grandmother and I laughed ourselves to sleep on those nights. But some stories were so dark and grim and overhung with horror that I dared not question their veracity.

Eventually, the telling took on an almost frenzied pace, and the events followed one another in an uninterrupted straight path that aimed itself at some fast approaching target. I never knew in advance if the nightly bedtime story would send me into a delicious slumber or a fearsome nightmare. But I understood that Mary needed to explain what had happened, and I needed to be the grandchild who listened.

Now, all these years later, I understand what was behind my grandmother's need to tell the story of her life: she was atoning, apologizing for it. She saw the unhealthy, unhappy beings her children were with a clarity that I've only acquired lately. As she sat, mostly silently, at that kitchen table, she must have been trying to figure what part of their relentless nastiness she was responsible for. And when she saw how their misery was replicated in the next generation, and probably anticipated its reappearance in the one that would follow, she must have been filled with remorse. It had all started in one instant, when she made one decision that set her on the path her life took, and she was filled with regret. That decision was like a pebble thrown into a pond, with the resulting ripples disturbing the surface and even the life below the surface. Somewhere along the line, she came to see in me, her sometimes roommate, the possibility of redeeming her past, and in one small portion of her progeny, preventing its damage, calming the ripples.

She wanted to enable me to avoid the mistakes she knew she had caused, and she determined that telling me her complicated and painful tale was the way to do that.

But why me? Was it simply that we were roommates, like college girls from disparate backgrounds who are assigned to the same dorm room and end up best friends for life? Or did she see something in me that made her believe I alone, apart from my cousins, could benefit from her atonement for that singular decision she had made? I don't know the answer. But as I retell her story, I feel grateful that I know it.

Two

Although Mary never described her childhood home in graceful flowing English, I came to understand the look and feel of the place by transposing the Yiddish flecked language into scenes I knew from school lessons or stories I had read. I became so accustomed to translating her phrasing into clear English that I stopped realizing I was doing it. I put together a view of that world that is as accurate as I can get it. It became clear that the climate and landscape of nineteenth century rural Belarus, then a part of Russia, conspired to turn people towards each other. It was flat, horizontal, and punctuated with white birches like a Japanese artist had conceived of it, and created it with brushes and black ink. In the far distance, forests could be seen that had been growing bigger and darker since the beginning of time. Around the perimeter of many towns, enthusiastic rivers burbled on their way past, carrying carp and pike from one settlement to the next. After the spring mud, the summer world could sometimes seem green and fragrant, but usually it was covered with dust. In the winter, it was frozen and rutted as if an icy hand had touched it and brought every form of life to a shocking halt.

The people lived in close proximity to this land of black earth, with mere inches of uninsulated walls between them and the outside. They crowded together, sometimes with their animals, in tiny wooden huts with straw roofs, many half sunken into the ground, and found that the regular rhythm of devout religious life provided answers to questions about their existence that they had no time to ask. In the towns that were filled with Jews whose families had lived there for hundreds of years, the inhabitants were safeguarding their souls until the Messiah came. Those with inquisitive spirits suffered. My grandmother told me about neighbors who read a lot of secular books, asked each other questions about their limited little lives that had no easy answers, and quietly or with loud fervor left for Palestine, or St. Petersburg, or someplace where they could find like-minded companions. Mostly, no one left. The definition of life was the one they were living. If some years it was harder, that was just how it was. When the pogroms came, and they did as reliably as the seasons, the people either hid well and survived, or they did not hide well enough and were slaughtered. Spring always seemed to promise that life was getting easier. But even the people who clung to each other from habit and necessity did not always cling happily.

And then, one night, the stories that my grandmother had always told me in a casual offhand way took on a more seriously intentioned tone. The moment was so clearly a turning point in my life, so much a life-changing transition that I can look back on it from the broad perspective that adulthood provides and remember it with crisp clarity. "Sarah, my Sarah, I want to tell you about my life. Do you want to listen? I want, I need, to explain things."

We were lying in the dark of our shared room. I had begun to slip out of the day, but was instantly awake. The warm comfort of sleepiness fled, replaced by a sharp awareness, like a freshly washed blackboard that was ready for the lesson of the day that would be written there. "Do I, Bubby? That would be the best present I could think of." I puffed up my pillow, leaned it higher against the headboard, and settled myself back, almost sitting upright. I knew that this formal request was the beginning of something new, something important. The fact that it was nighttime, that neither of us could see the other's face, and that the whole enterprise was implicitly secret gave it the air of a solemn undertaking. And then, without any other explanation, Mary began to tell me about her childhood. What a tightrope she walked, trying to explain to a nine-year-old what an adult would be appalled by. She must have tried to wait until I was older, but somehow knew she was running out of time.

"I remember one day, Sarah, the icy edges of the puddles around my house were finally melting, and I was outside the door of the house, just seeing how my new boots that my father had given me would feel outside, and waiting for something to happen, even though I knew it never would. Do you think anyone else in my family had new boots? Only me! I remember I was feeling pretty special for a while. The door was open a little because my mother said she wanted to let the winter smell out. I could hear my parents talking, and I could even see my mother holding her broom in one hand and a rag in the other. They didn't know I was there, I think, or maybe they did." She paused, seeming to survey the scene in her head, as if she was trying to get it to come into sharp focus.

"My father was talking, in a nervous voice, like almost he was afraid to tell my mother something. 'I'm taking Mary with me, Hannah.' He busied himself with papers he was pushing into his old leather case so that my mother could not drill into his eyes and discover the discomfort this discussion caused him. She knew it was time for him to travel to the forestland that his sister managed for a minor nobleman. There had been a decree from Tsar Nicholas the last year that made it illegal for Jews to buy, sell, manage or lease rural property. But Aunt Leah's nobleman was almost a nobody, low enough to ignore the tsar's broad rules. He was also too lazy to manage the forest himself, and too involved with his "other passions," as Aunt Leah explained it, to pay close attention to her comings and goings. As long as no one called attention to him or complained, things could go on as always.

"Right away, my mother started to scream. 'How are you taking her again? You know I need her here! She's supposed to help me! Look at this place!'

"I studied my mother's face through the open door. It was pinched and pale, and she swept her hand around the room she had been cleaning when my father came to collect the documents he needed and make his announcement. She leaned against the broomstick, bending the bundle of straw that was knotted to the bottom. My mother, I knew, was pregnant again. Some of the neighbors called a change of life baby a happy miracle. But for Mama, there was no joy. I was supposed to be the last. She wanted grandchildren, not motherhood again.

"'And what about her lessons?' My mother's face was red; I knew this was going to be a big fight, and I couldn't decide if I should come inside and shush them, or run to the river to escape from them. 'Mrs. Goldshtain says she has no idea what the rest of the girls are learning. You can't keep taking her with you! She can't read a word, and she'll never learn.'

"'I'm not interested in your opinion, Hannah.' He screamed at her in a new shrill voice, like he was trying to convince himself and her at the same time. 'I said I'm taking my daughter, so get one of the others to help you. Where is Fanny? Where is Tova?' I remember I looked around, sort of searching for my sisters too. But Mama was still screaming, just shrieks with no words, and she was holding the rag to her head, like she had a terrible pain. My sympathy went back and forth between my parents. I knew my mother needed my help. I was the youngest then, and before Dvorah was born, I was supposed to be the child who took care of her parents as they aged. Every family had a child who knew that was her destiny. It was understood. But I knew my father liked me best and a trip with him was a prize designed just for me. I would spend time being the center of the world, worshipped, and I would escape from my life of drudgery.

"'Fanny is helping me already. She watches the oven. She brings the bread to the market. Never mind where Tova is! She's busy! Why must you take Mary again? And where is she, anyway? She's supposed to be embroidering the ladies' mantels. I told her to hem the. . . . Oy, what's the use.' My mother was so sad, suddenly, deflated like a balloon when the air flies out; I wanted to run to her. So I came back inside the house, but as soon as I shut the door, I knew I didn't want to be there, either. I knew I was the root of my parents' quarrel. And coming into the house was no escape from that knowledge. Its two dark rooms gave no peaceful place of safety. The low ceilings were like a heavy weight on my crowded family, like they were a threat of some kind. My parents' arguments embarrassed me, especially when I knew I was the cause."

I pictured my grandmother standing just inside the door of a hovel, like the one Snow White found herself in after her stepmother had tried to poison her, but not as cheerful. I could see in my mind's eye my grandmother's new boots, made of soft black leather, a special gift from her father Mendel and at the same time, the clear symbol of her mother Hannah's disdain, and in a quick flashback, I could see the young Mary painstakingly fastening the whole stiff row of buttons with a button hook. I watched the imaginary earlier scene unspool as my grandmother stepped out of the house to try the new boots out on the cobblestones of the market square. The muddy icy ruts outside her own door would be no test of them, I knew my grandmother would have thought, and she would have needed to get out of her mother's sight to see if the boots would click loudly enough to make anyone notice.

When she said before that she was waiting for something to happen, I knew it wasn't quite true. It would have been more accurate to say she was waiting to make something happen. Mary's mother would have been scandalized to know that one of her daughters was trying to attract attention. I had been told how my grandmother had been scolded by her own mother more than once to stop tossing her curls over her shoulder and behave herself. "'Who are you?'" Bubby would quote her mother. "'The only thing you should be staring at is the ground. You look for trouble, Mary, and I promise it will find you. Are you listening to me, Mary?'" When my grandmother told me about those moments, it was with a sort of pride. She loved being her father's favorite in those early days. But really, what kind of young woman was this Mary? Where did she get the idea that she was exempt from the life that everyone around her was living? There was something dangerous there, something dangerous in her beauty. I only sensed this truth vaguely, then. But looking back at it after my own mother's death, I shudder.

"My father's eyes lit up every time he looked at me, and he always said there was nothing to criticize me for. Those new boots had followed satin ribbons, and silk embroidery thread. My mother could not criticize the gift of embroidery floss, I knew. Even at ten, my needlework was the envy of everyone. I made a challah cover that my mother used every Friday night. Even my sisters had to admit that the stitching was precise and the word Shabbos was cleverly sewn in beautiful blue silk threads that my brother Simon had printed for me to copy."

I suddenly realized that my grandmother didn't need to know how to read or write to find herself bathing in the glow of praise that was showered upon her. There had never been a story of Mendel having anything to praise his other daughters about. Mary's sisters, both older and far plainer, Fanny with a wandering eye, and Tova too scrawny, got quiet scorn from their father in every story.

This piece of my grandmother's tale had an eerie echo in the next generation. Once, when my mother and I were waiting our turn at the checkout desk in the library, my mother began telling me how her parents derided and criticized their daughters. Aunt Esther, she remembered, was, "too stupid, like a cow," for school, and Aunt Ruthie was never going to find a husband because, "she has poppy eyes," and Aunt Jean, "could never pull her face away from a mirror," and she herself was, "blind, with four eyes, from reading all the time." I don't know what prompted those revelations, but I remember they created a chill down my spine. What parents spoke to their children that way? Of course, I couldn't find the words to question her. I knew she'd realize she was vilifying her parents, and that would stop her cold.

As to my grandmother's brothers, I had been told, were always reading and studying in the shul. They were totally inexplicable to their father. Once, Mary had told me about how disappointed her father had been that his sons were not interested in learning about his work in Aunt Leah's forest business. "We were walking together, my father and me, on a Saturday after shul, and he said he wanted to talk about something he was puzzled about. 'What's so important in the books?' he asked me, like a little girl would know answers. 'The world is beautiful, fragrant and welcoming. Louis and Simon are beginning to smell like parchment and ink, and even, God forbid, urine. Are they too busy learning to even bathe properly? Look how I look, my Mary. I am always precise in my grooming. My shirt,' he said with pride, smoothing down the front, 'is always crisply starched, and white as new snow. I demand this of Hannah, your wonderful mother, who never complains about tasks that are rightly hers. And my beard,' he continued, 'is trimmed neatly, even though some neighbors and my observant sons are scornful. Let them sneer,' he mumbled righteously to himself. 'The new century is coming, and the old ways will surely give way to fresh new ideas. Businessmen such as I will sweep past the old rabbis who are too bent over their books to even notice the new scents in the air.' I always listened to my father's ranting with adoration. When I was your age, Sarah, I thought my father was surely the most wise, most modern, and most admirable in the whole village, or maybe even the whole region."

And it was clear to Mary that Mendel's feelings about her were mutual.

"I was the rosy, shiny queen of the house. New boots were the least he could give me. Anyone listening to his argument with my mother about taking me with him on his trip to inspect the forest knew he would take me in the end, whether my mother liked it or not. 'One day, my revered ancient aunt will die, she should rest in peace, and leave to me alone her connection to the nobleman's forest, or so she has promised.' I knew that he relished two weeks alone with me his beautiful and adoring daughter. Hannah, he must have thought, would have to manage.

"The baby that was coming, a mistake even he had to admit privately to me, was the cause of Hannah's temper tantrum. But in the long run, my father rationalized, if it turned out to be a girl, this would be the child who could comfort Hannah in her old age. She would be the one to carry the water from the well, sweep out the two rooms that are our house, light the oil lamp that Hannah likes near her bed, bring home the butter and rye flour from the Monday market, and the fish from the Thursday market, and all the other chores that shape our lives. 'None of these responsibilities suit you, Mary, my beauty. For you, Mary, I will find a handsome, rich man. But not too soon. Neighbors are already arranging marriages for their daughters that were only a few years older than you. But what's their rush? A girl like you, my Mary, whose smile reveals even white pearls, who swims with abandon in the river, whose eyes are on fire with the thrill of just being alive, you have time before you must trade for the solemnity of being a wife.' My father said that he liked the sparks that I threw off and he would always edge near enough to me to inhale what he called, 'my rosy young fragrance.' I used to pretend that he was embarrassing me, but underneath, I loved it. 'I'm not ready to even think about giving you up,' he would say. 'Being near a beauty like you, Mary, makes me feel vigorous, like a stallion, and optimistic! You remind me of myself in my younger years.' I was quite sure that everything he said about me was true, and that being favored was exactly what I deserved."

Any adult hearing his blandishments to his daughter would have been shocked. Now, in the twenty-first century, they'd certainly call Child Protective Services! This man was seducing his daughter, without question. How alarming that my grandmother would even tell a nine-year old this stuff. No wonder there had been nightmares. But how compelling her reasons must have been. She must have felt thunderous guilt that she had abandoned her mother and allowed herself to be elevated by her father, and she must have seen her poisoned family as God's perfect justice.

"Then, he just turned away from my mother and said, 'Come, my sweetest child. We'll go to the forest and inspect Aunt Leah's trees. Get ready.' I remember that I looked at my mother to measure her reaction. I wanted her nod of approval, but Mama pursed her lips as she turned sharply away and continued sweeping. Papa took the loaf of dense black bread and a block of cheese from the table and strode out of the house, not even bothering to close the door. He began to load the small wagon with the food and a thick blanket. He always took a prayer book too on his trips away from the village. It wasn't that he was so devout, but it was better be safe than sorry, he always said. I was torn between pleasing my mother by staying home and helping her with the drudgery that was her life, or escaping for two weeks with my father. Going to the forest with him would be an enchanting adventure. As the cart jogged along in the rutted path, he would spin out magical tales of golems and spirits and dead ancestors who could work miracles from the beyond. He would tell me about the future too, how my life would be when I was all grown up and married to a rich man who would buy me jewels and build me a big house with ten rooms and shiny wooden floors. This man would worship me, my father promised, because I was so beautiful with such clear eyes, and silky hair that fell in ringlets almost to my waist. 'And you'll never have to cut it, my beauty, even if the rabbi says you must.' As I thought about the trip, it was easy to decide which parent to please. I watched my father through the open door, grabbed a thick shawl from its hook on the wall, and tried to kiss my mother goodbye. But she jerked away from me.

"'We'll be back soon, Mama, and I'll do all your work then while you rest.' I tried to assure my mother, but I knew my voice was too bright and my eyes were on my father the whole time. I had no sincerity, and it was as obvious to my mother as her bitter exhaustion. I always chose my father, every chance I got, and this time was no different.

"And then the deluded father and his adored daughter were gone."

My grandmother finished the story as if the people in it were not her and her parents, but some fictional characters in a book. She didn't say good night, sleep sweetly, have dreams of gold or any of her usual loving expressions. She fell instantly asleep, leaving me to sort through the significance of what I had heard, and to wonder what journey the two of them seemed to have embarked on. I was too young to understand the unease I felt.

Even now, when I understand her motive, that desire to clear her conscience of all the damage she had caused, I feel a ripple of anxiety. I wonder if she could have, would she have made different choices in the life she had begun to tell me about? I watched my aunts and uncles every Sunday and I knew what they were like. Did my grandmother really wish they had turned out to be other people? Did she not like her children? The advantage of hindsight is not enough.

Three

I had heard that story about the trip in the forest before, but my grandmother had never called it the story of her life before. It had always been more casual. It was not one of the terrifying ones that Bubby sometimes told as we lay in adjoining twin beds in the dim light in my room, but it wasn't exactly happy either. Yes, Mary got to go on an exciting journey with her father, but what about Hannah? I wanted to ask how the family managed without Mendel and Mary. What did they eat if the travelers had taken the bread and cheese? And what about how tired Leah was? What about the new baby that was coming? But I knew that questions were not part of our routine. Bubby was going to sleep, moaning softly every so often, and there was no point in bothering her. So I turned over on my side and looked at the wallpaper next to my bed that was slightly illuminated by the hall light that shone through the half opened door. The wallpapering job was one of my father's weekend projects, and I could remember perfectly when it had gone up. Years after, when I grew up and went off to college, I took with me a cabinet that had been part of that childhood bedroom. It eventually had a place in the garage, where my husband stored old hoses and watering cans. When it was carried to the curb finally, it seemed like a precious remnant of my father finally reaching its end. I almost rescued it, and if it had been a little less mildewed, I would have.

My other grandmother, Sarah, the one I'm named after, had named my father Joseph, but he was never called anything but Joe. In fact, when he joined the Navy, he began signing official papers with his nickname, and by the time I came along, Joe was his legal name. It was a name that was perfect for a man who preferred plaid flannel shirts and olive drab work pants or jeans to the suit with the white shirt and tie he wore to his job in the city. On his dresser, a pile of white plastic collar stays grew by two as each day of the week passed, but on Saturday, they all disappeared. Joe would emerge from the bedroom dressed for weekend schemes, singing loudly, or whistling a popular song or an old tune from the war years. He would bound down the stairs, eager to get busy working with his hands. Joe took great pleasure in building things. During the week after dinner, he'd sit in the living room with the TV on, but he'd ignore it. I could almost see the plans for the next project taking shape in his mind. Sometimes he would make a note about how much lumber or how many rolls of wallpaper or cans of paint he would need. He always licked the pencil point before he began writing, and furrowed his brow as he began listing supplies.

After breakfast on Saturdays, he would disappear to the lumberyard as if it were his playground. He'd be gone for hours, and when he came back, the car would be laden with the elements of the new enterprise. Pieces would be tied to the roof, secured with the rope he always had available in the trunk or poking out the rear window with a red ribbon on the end flapping importantly in the breeze. If they were on the roof, his arm would be settled akimbo in the open window, winter or summer, with his hand gripping the purchases on the roof as if he alone could prevent their tearing free and scattering across the road. He would stack the goods in the garage or ferry them down the basement steps to his workshop. I would hear the buzz of saws ripping through wood, or drills and hammers at work preparing the project at hand for installation. A house full of my mother's relatives on Sunday would serve as no deterrent to his activities. He would go on with his work as if the place were his empty glorious universe. In recalling my father, it is impossible for me to reconcile this vigorous young man with the fact of his death at age fifty of a massive heart attack. Life unfolds at funny angles.

The wallpaper in my room had begun with a plan my mother had dreamed up. I remember watching as Rikki held her hand out, palm down, against the wall to indicate where a new chair rail should be installed. Joe snapped open his yellow carpenter's ruler and measured the distance from the floor, marking it with a flat pencil he stored behind his ear. I sat on the top edge of my headboard, observing the scene. The headboards and footboards of the twin beds in my room made of oak, carved deeply with country scenes. I sometimes ran my finger through the scenes of people cavorting in quaint European market places as if Bruegel had put them there. But I loved to balance on the top rail, my bare heels against the carved people anchoring me. From that vantage, I could see my father set up the pasting table in the hallway just outside the bedroom.

He scooped paste mix into an old blue crockery bowl and added water. He stirred it around with a thin wooden stick and brushed it on pre-cut lengths of wallpaper. He folded the lengths gently, paste to paste, and waited for them to set up. I suspect that my father knew I was inspecting every move he made, but he did not interrupt my thoughts, nor did I intrude on his. When he was ready, he opened the paper, leaving a small folded section at the bottom and applied the strip to the wall and coaxed out the air bubbles with a stiff narrow brush. Then he opened the bottom fold, trimmed the excess with a single-edge razor, and finished with a wooden mini-roller along the seams. I hopped off my headboard perch for a closer examination of the pattern.

The paper had a pink background, and was covered with columns of pieces of furniture. They didn't look photographic or even very accurate, but rather whimsical as if they had originated in the dream of a cartoonist. There was a chair with an ornate wooden frame and a plush seat covered with a complicated calico pattern. There was a roll-top desk with dozens of cubbyholes and compartments. There was a Victorian loveseat with a sensually carved back and legs that seemed able to walk off. My favorite item was a chandelier with many upturned arms each of which ended in a tiny elaborately decorated lampshade. All the furniture was depicted head-on facing out and stacked up in columns, and all of it seemed to invite the viewer to pop in and use it. The best part was that as Joe worked his way around the room adding additional lengths of paper, the pattern repeated endlessly as if my room had become a spectacular miniature used furniture store. My father used up the remaining lengths of paper by covering an old cupboard, the same cupboard that had gone out with the trash, more than fifty years after it had been the last piece of the project, which was then installed next to the small bookcase. I knew I would never get tired of living amid that paper, lying in my bed next to it, or tracing the various pieces with my finger while my grandmother lay in her bed a few feet away. The wallpaper and my father were inextricably bound, and even as a nine-year-old, that was clear to me.

Studying that wallpaper usually had a calming effect on me, especially after one of my grandmother's troubling tales. My thoughts wandered from the wallpaper back to the young Mary and her father Mendel as they made their way across the Belarusian landscape in the open cart. I could picture the two of them as their old horse pulled them toward the forest. I could almost smell the horse and feel the spring breezes as the pair rambled along the rutted paths. What did a forest inspector really do? Trees in forests grew without anyone having to look at them. I wanted to ask Bubby more about her father's job, but I could hear her breathing and I knew she was asleep. I should have asked what exactly happened on that trip. How did they sit? Where did they sleep?

How did Mendel keep warm? It was relentlessly disturbing, and now, there would be no answers. The stories always left me with more questions than answers. Bubby seemed so proud that her father loved her better than her sisters and brothers, but that made me uneasy. Once, while my mother was brushing my black curly hair into the ponytail that would tame it, I asked my mother which child she loved more. Rikki acted shocked at the mere idea of having a favorite.

"Parents love all their children equally, Sarah," my mother would pronounce as if she were reciting from a rulebook. But I knew it wasn't true. Even though Bubby's story was distressing to me as a child, there was no mistaking the truth of it. And I had met Bubby's siblings once. It was during the summer, when Bubby had been staying with Aunt Ruthie in a bungalow in Rockaway and they had all come to visit and spend the day at the beach. I remember that I watched the tide of people from this older generation coming and going between the front porch of the bungalow where Bubby rocked gently in a wooden rocking chair, and the kitchen where Aunt Ruthie in her floral housecoat with the snap closure prepared a thick beef stew that was completely wrong for a summer meal. Their shoes made scratchy noises because of the ubiquitous sand that was tracked on to the patterned linoleum floor of the bungalow.

The truth was that there was a chasm of space between Bubby and her family even though they were no more than ten feet apart the whole day. Fanny and Tova giggled with each other while they sat on the porch and ignored their sister Mary as if her chair were empty. They weren't paralyzed like Bubby, I remember explaining to myself, and that's why they weren't including her. Their husbands must have died years ago, I supposed. There were stories my mother told about visiting the aunts by subway when she was a little girl, and these often ended with a comparison of Bubby's brothers-in-law to her husband. They were kindly, generous to their families even in their poverty, and her own father was stingy, critical and cold. And the aunts always made a point of saying they weren't going to visit anymore, because their sister and her husband were nasty to each all day; he would remark on how young and vigorous one of their neighbors looked compared to his wife, and she would scream at him to go live with her.

But those stories explained nothing about the chill I was seeing on that porch. I hardly knew any details about my grandmother's sisters, because no one ever mentioned them. Louis and Simon ignored their sister too. Soon after they had arrived, they had gone for a walk with Uncle Milt who was delighted that he had a new audience for his old jokes. Their wives, they explained when Aunt Ruthie demanded to know why they weren't there, had gone to the bungalow colony in, "the Ketskills," where their children stayed in the summer with the grandchildren. Aunt Ruthie mumbled something nasty in Yiddish under her breath, but it was purposely loud enough for her uncles to hear. I caught some of it, about a black year being wished on them. Simon and Louis flinched, and quickly stepped off the porch onto the sidewalk with Uncle Milt. They nearly tripped over a group of little girls that included my cousin Stacie that was crouched there playing jacks in front of the porch. Aunt Ruthie burst into a stream of criticism at the girls.

"What are you sitting in the middle of the sidewalk for? Can't you see people are falling all over you?" The girls barely looked up from their ball and jacks. Their thin arms and legs were tangled together in one impenetrable jumble of sundresses, shorts and sandals.

I knew that the site of the game didn't upset Aunt Ruthie. The girls played there constantly for the whole three months that they spent with their families in the bungalows during the summer. It was the wives of Louis and Simon as well as Fanny and Tova that had called up the invective. Aunt Ruthie didn't like that these people hardly ever showed up to visit their invalid sister, and now that they were finally there, they had some nerve to ignore her.

But why didn't Bubby ever call her sisters or brothers, I wondered? Bubby had once been incredulous that the phone worked in Yiddish. Now she knew it worked in any language. I had demonstrated and had offered to place any call she wanted. But Bubby wasn't really interested.

"Maybe tomorrow, my darling," she had promised vaguely. But now that I thought about it, maybe Mary's attitude had been not so much vague and as seething silently. I knew she would never call them or anyone.

"They'll call me if they are interested to talk," Bubby had pronounced on another occasion. It was as if she planned to not like anyone, just in case they might not like her. She was carefully protected. Of course, my mother had been no different, as the years had unspooled. She, too, waited for calls rather than make them. In her long widowhood, she lost touch with people one by one, content to sit fuming and angry, just like her mother had done fifty years earlier.

I turned over in my bed again. Bubby's sisters and brothers didn't like her. I knew it must have something to do with their father's ancient favoritism for his daughter Mary. He did not do her any good, I thought to myself, and drifted into a deep sleep. In fact, he didn't do anyone any good. But who knows if that was his fault, exclusively.

Four

Many of the stories that my grandmother told me were repeated often. Sometimes I would ask for a particular story that I found funny, like the one about the night that was so cold that Hannah brought a neighbor's untended goat into the house so she wouldn't freeze. I also liked stories that were nearly unbelievable, like the one about Mary and her friend Rivka going swimming in the river wearing just their underclothes. I couldn't picture Bubby being so young and carefree. Children can only see people as they are at the moment. The old lady in the bed next to me was hobbled by paralysis and ruled by her fears, regrets and loneliness and bent with guilt as much as age. The thought of her being a child able to run across a field to a river with a companion was both a delight and troubling. I could see that the scene seemed as vivid to Bubby as if it had happened last week. But here she was, old and fragile. How could a life swirl by so quickly?

Some of the stories were scary, like the one about my grandmother and her older sisters being followed as they came home from the mill by some Russian boys who teased them in a language they did not understand. I had heard plenty about the danger that the Russians posed to the Jews, and youth was no protection. But the sisters got back home safely with the flour, and I thought that scary stories with happy endings were sometimes fun. But there was one story that Bubby only told once, and even that time it was left unfinished. It was as if Bubby had fallen into the past and forgotten that her listener was her young granddaughter. Only at the last second did she remember that she was an old lady trapped in old broken body and speaking to a child who couldn't possible understand, and would only be frightened by it. She trailed off vaguely, as if she was falling asleep, and I knew I must never bring it up again. But just remembering the incident Bubby had begun to share was enough to leave me scared by the mystery of it all over again. I wish I had been able to question her about exactly what had happened. But I couldn't, and now I have only a fragmentary understanding of a crucial moment.

The story began as many of them did. "Sarah, my darling, do you want to hear about when I was a girl?" Even if I was just on the verge of sleep, I was instantly alert. I loved being transported back sixty years to a world that had vanished, and I knew that Bubby was depending on me to listen.

"Definitely yes, Bubby. Which one tonight?" I sat up and positioned my pillow against the headboard. I leaned back against the pillow and folded my hands together on top of the blanket.

"I'll tell you about the time I went swimming in the river," said Bubby.

"With Rivka? When you both left your skirts and blouses by the bush? I love that one." I closed my eyes and began to picture the riverbank where the river curved a bit around the rise in the land.

"No, not that time. I'll tell you about the time I went by myself."

"Bubby! You went swimming alone? That's dangerous, you know. You should always swim with a buddy."

Mary ignored my admonition. Her voice was different when she began speaking again. It was nearly hollow, and I felt like the temperature of the room had dropped abruptly. My window rattled a bit, as if some storm had suddenly risen in protest. I turned to look at my grandmother's face, but the room was too dark.

"It was a very hot summer in this story I'm telling now," began Bubby. "Rivka and I were really too big to go swimming. But I wanted to go anyway. Mrs. Goldshtain wouldn't let Rivka go; I didn't even ask her. Everything would be different if she had come, but I knew she would never, so I didn't even ask her."

Bubby's voice had gotten so low and raspy, like her throat had dried up, or closed down even. I knew she was remembering something painful.

"Rivka died that fall. It was terrible." Bubby stopped talking for a while. Maybe that was the story? My mother was named for Bubby's friend Rivka, so I thought the story was going to be about how Rivka had died. So I waited for Bubby to continue. But Bubby was silent for so long that I thought she must have fallen asleep. I pulled my pillow down flat on the bed, and turned on my side to begin to go to sleep myself. The story of Rivka's death must be terrible, I thought. How could a young person die? Wasn't death supposed to come after your grandchildren are all grown up? And here was Bubby, all these years later, still so sad about Rivka that she couldn't even talk about it.

"I was sitting in the doorway of our house. I was repairing something, a blouse maybe. Yes, it was a blouse Mama wore on Shabbos. Very clean. Very beautiful." Bubby had started to talk again but she was talking into the air now. I lay perfectly still and Bubby's voice floated over me darkly. Outside, the wind picked up and roared like a chorus of wailing witches. I shivered as I waited for Bubby to go on.

"The doorway made a little shadow, but it was so hot. I remember I had a handkerchief tied around my neck. I took it off and dipped it into the pail of water that my little sister Dvorah had brought from the well. Where were the others? I don't remember. But Dvorah was getting big by then, and she always brought the water. No, sometimes a water man came."

I could hear the strain as Bubby tried to remember accurately. The story seemed so important that she needed to tell it perfectly, as if any aberration in the truth would puncture it. She seemed to want to present it like it a complete framed picture, so that when it was out in the open, someone could lift it and remove it the way the garbage men lifted and removed the pail from the side of the house and deposited it into their truck to be ground to pulp and forgotten.

"I tied the handkerchief around my neck again and tried to go back to the blouse. But the water from the handkerchief dripped down my chest, dripped between my breasts. It didn't make me cooler, though. It just made me want to be wet all over my body. 'Mama, I'm going to the river!'"

It was so eerie. Bubby had slid back to the hot doorway of her childhood home. She was calling to her mother, telling her she was going to the river. She wasn't in the room with me, lying in her bed next to me, and she wasn't old or sick or argued over by her children. She was an eighteen year old beauty with water dripping down the inside of her clothes on her way to the river to cool off, her sewing dropped into the dust next to the three-legged stool she had been sitting on and it was 1900.

"I was only going to step into the river up to my knees. I could tuck my skirts up into my waistband, through my legs. That way, if someone passed by, it would look fine. I was going to go around the bend of the river, beyond where I swam with Rivka, because sometimes no one would be that far from the village. It was so hot, suffocating, I could only think of the water. The heat was ringing in my ears, like a choir of evil spirits, and I had to escape from them."

I wanted to bolt out of my bed, run down the stairs, and be with my parents who were drinking their coffee at the kitchen table and murmuring quietly to each other as they always did after the children and Mary went to bed. But there was no way to escape the story. It pulled me in as hard as it pushed me out, and I knew I could not leave Bubby alone with her harrowing memory. I somehow knew that I was about to learn what had happened to my grandmother that had enabled her to leave her parents, her suffering mother and her adoring father, and never see them again, never speak to them again, and, in her ignorant illiteracy, never write to them or read a word from them again. It was something I had quietly never understood, nor ever had the nerve to ask about. And here it was, the explanation, about to drop into my lap.

"I don't remember when I sat down to take off my boots. But I was barefoot when I walked along the edge until the tree. All the boys used to climb out on that tree and crawl along the branch that stuck out over the water and then let go and splash into the river laughing. But no one was there. "Good,' I said out loud to no one. I grabbed the trunk and swung around it to the far side. You couldn't get to that part of the river any other way. The bushes were too thick there."

Bubby had begun to sound different again. Now her voice was full of pleasure and daring, and I could hear that she was smiling as she spoke. She actually laughed at the next piece. "I took off my skirts and blouse, and my shift too! I tossed them onto the tree branch, one at a time! I never missed, either. Everything hung there just like the wash hanging on the line on Tuesday mornings when Tova finishes rinsing and wringing."

I sucked in my breath. I could hear Bubby's glee, but this was wrong, bad, and sure to come to no good. What was Bubby thinking? Swimming naked in the river? In public without her clothes? How could she do such a thing? I could not understand my grandmother's delight at such a transgression.

"I was a good swimmer, you know. Rivka's brother taught us, Rivka and me. But I was the best. So I began to swim, and the heat of that day melted off me. I dove under the water again and again, and the river combed my hair back over my head and away from my shoulders like a silky wind. I swam down the river a way, and then back to the tree with my clothes hanging like flags. It was silent there. But then it wasn't."

This last sounded different. Bubby's voice had gone hollow. Everything after that was whispered, and I had to strain to hear it. And there were so many silences, punctuated by soft moaning sighs that I thought Bubby was having an attack, and that I should get her the bottle of pain pills that she needed periodically. But I was afraid to interrupt, afraid to move, afraid of the story.

"Someone was swimming there next to me. I began to make my way to the tree, to get to my clothes. But my hair was in my eyes, and the person, the man, was holding me, stroking me, sighing in my ear. I could feel his legs against my legs. I couldn't swim away. I couldn't. I couldn't. I tried to scream. But I was screaming only in my head. And by then I was so cold." Then Bubby stopped talking. But the moaning continued, like she was being tortured by spasms of pain.

I was weeping by then, and my legs were trembling. I don't remember what I thought my grandmother was describing. But if I was making any noise, Bubby didn't hear it, because she was trapped in her memory, paralyzed by it, and unable to unwrap its grip from her mind. Then she found her voice, and it was a shocked young woman that spoke.

"The man held me from behind, so I wouldn't see him. But I knew who it was. He called me 'Mary, my beauty,' and I knew. I denied it. I shook my head. I kept trying to push the wet hair away from my face to see that what I knew was wrong. But it wasn't wrong. The voice whispered to me, 'Mary, my beauty,' and I knew. 'We'll get combs for your hair,' and I knew. 'No,' I said. 'Let go of me,' I said. I said it over and over. But it was only in my head that I spoke. My mouth couldn't speak."

Her father? I did not know how to understand this. At nine, I had no understanding that a father might be evil enough, or sick enough, to grope his daughter, or worse. But then Bubby's voice went on, even more spectral than before.

"I tried to fight him. But he was strong, stronger than I was. And he was naked, with nothing to get in his way, and he had his legs wrapped around me. And then we were close to the bank of the river, and he could stand there, and he held me and twisted me around to face him. He was on fire, his face was different, his mouth was open, and his eyes were squeezed shut. 'Mary, my beauty,' he said. And then we fell onto the mud and he was on top of me and pushing against me, forcing me." The moaning began again. But when it stopped this time, the voice was different. It was angry, seething with resolve that I had never heard before from my grandmother.

"Then he gasped suddenly because he saw who he was and who I was, and he was scared. He pushed himself away from me and stood up, and he groaned and he began to run away. I watched him. His hair was hanging in his face, and he was skinny and the mud was streaked across his shoulder. He looked back as he ran, naked, saying 'No, no, it was a mistake, an error, a mistake.' And he ran to his clothes and jerked them on. All the time he was saying, 'No, a mistake,' and shaking his head like a madman. I watched him. And when he was gone, I crawled from the mud back into the water. I didn't think of anything. I swam back to the tree, and I pulled my blouse and my shift and my skirts off the branch, and I put them on. But I didn't think of anything, no, nothing. Empty." Mary was sneering then, in the bedroom she shared with me, her nine-year-old granddaughter. Then her voice became Bubby's voice, the one that I recognized, the one that had asked earlier if I wanted to hear a story of her girlhood. "I'm sorry," she said. For a while she was silent, but then I heard her breathing change, and I knew my grandmother was sleeping.

Never, never would I speak of that story to anyone. I thought it must have been a nightmare my grandmother had been having. She probably wasn't even really awake when she told it. It was all a terrible mistake, like my great-grandfather had said in the story. It had not really happened, I was sure, and I had been told it by mistake, surely. The best thing to do, I decided, was to try to forget it. I turned over, concentrated on the wallpaper in the dim light, and used the hem of my blanket to dry my face. I tried to focus on the morning that would come eventually, but the hot day in my grandmother's past did not easily relinquish its hold. It was a long time before sleep finally came.

I don't know exactly what Mendel did to his daughter. Was it a rape? Did he come to his senses before that happened? But, really, what's the difference? What he did was so unspeakable, so utterly without the possibility of forgiveness, that the specific anatomical explanation is meaningless. In a moment in time, he tore away from my grandmother any sense that there was beauty or trust in the world. And since beauty was the one pillar that supported her and kept her nose above the fetid air that described life in

a shtetl in Belarus in the first years of the twentieth century, essentially he killed her. It

would have been easy to leave.

## Five

Every once in a while, I would hear my mother on the phone, feverishly making arrangements with one of her sisters about Bubby. I never thought that sharing my room with my grandmother was unusual or intrusive. I felt grown up and helpful when I helped her to the bathroom, or brought her some juice for a pill. And I loved when she tried to help me brush my hair, even though she wasn't really good at it with only one had that worked. It was not that different from Susie and Amy Miller who lived two houses down and shared their bedroom, or Laura and Sherrie Gordon whose house around the corner I could see from my window. But apparently, there was something wrong with it, because sometimes, they would pack up all her stuff in shopping bags, and take her to stay with a different aunt for three or four weeks.

Then my dresser would have one empty drawer where Bubby's bloomers, as she called them, and her two nightgowns and small stack of stockings had been kept. The shawl that lay folded at the foot of her bed, and Bubby's pink sweater that hung on the back of a kitchen chair would be gone, and the closet would have extra space where her three cotton chintz housedresses and her one navy blue dress up outfit had hung. And the glass container that held her teeth at night would be gone from the night table between our beds. It seemed almost like a death had taken place, but there was no mourning or even discussion about the emptiness that had come to take Bubby's place. The phone conversations leading up to these trips away were tense and accusatory.

"I'm not interested in your money problems. Stop spending money every time that blouse man, what's his name, Eli, steps into your house and you'll have money.

Anyway, I'll send her with money just like I always do, and Mayshe will send a check too. It's your turn. I want her out of Sarah's room for a month, at least."

I could not hear Aunt Ruthie's side of the conversation, but I could hear that my aunt was screaming. I could almost see her dark eyes wide open, nearly popping out of her face, and her mouth open side enough for a clear view of every tooth. My mother had tipped the phone away from her ear, and the anger was unmistakable.

"Then you call Esther and tell her to come and get Mama's things. Or call Jean. That would make a refreshing change, wouldn't it?" My mother spoke to her sister through clenched teeth, and the sarcasm was acid. My mother's nostrils flared as she listened to Aunt Ruthie's reply, and then she screamed into the phone in Yiddish and banged the receiver down into its cradle. She raked both hands through her black hair, and I thought for a second she would rip out thick hanks and throw them angrily on the floor.

My eyes widened and filled with tears. I remembered Bubby's last visit to Aunt Jean's house, but I put off thinking about it, hoping the memory would finally die if I didn't dwell on it. I ran downstairs and turned on the TV in the living room and raised the volume to drown out the memory of my mother's fight with her sister. Where was Bubby, anyway, I thought frantically? Leaving the TV blasting, I dashed to the front door and pulled it open. There, wrapped in her gray overcoat held closed by its one huge button, with a floral silk scarf around her head and knotted snugly under her chin, sat my grandmother in a webbed folding chair having a conversation with Mrs. Watson, the grandmother who lived with her family next door. Mrs. Watson had graduated from Wellesley College in 1903 and I thought she spoke in Eleanor Roosevelt's voice. My grandmother was illiterate and she was so embarrassed by her English that she rarely spoke to anyone outside her family. Mrs. Watson had given my grandmother an embroidered handkerchief for Christmas the previous year, and Bubby had just pulled it out of the edge of her sleeve to show Mrs. Watson how she cherished it. The likelihood of their being friends was so comical to me that I momentarily forgot the argument between my mother and Aunt Ruthie. The April air was just beginning to shake off the sharp winter temperatures, but it was too chilly for me to be outside without a coat listening to Bubby telling Mrs. Watson that she had lived through another winter. I bounced up the one step just as my mother yanked open the yellow front door from the inside. I remembered the angry conversation I had fled.

"Why is that TV so loud, Sarah? And why is it even on in the afternoon?" I could see that my mother was still caught up in her fiery mood. I went inside past my mother who had begun to shut the door behind her.

"I'll fix it. Look," I glanced backward over my shoulder and started for the living room. "Bubby thinks she's having a conversation with Mrs. Watson. Isn't she so cute?" My mother followed my gaze, and instantly her face softened.

"Yes, I guess she's cute." My mother started to shut the door gently, but had second thoughts. "Hello, Mrs. Watson. How are you? Mama, come in for a cup of tea. It's getting cold. Would you like to come in, Mrs. Watson?"

"Oh, gracious no. I was just going inside myself. I'll be seeing you, Mary."

"God bless you, Kate. Yes, I'll see you. God bless you." She pulled a half-shredded tissue from her paralyzed fist and dabbed at her eyes that were running from the nippy air. Then she began the difficult task of rising from the chair, stepping up into the house and removing her coat and scarf. I changed my mind about adjusting the TV volume and held open the storm door and helped my grandmother steady herself. She looked at me fleetingly, and with her face, her eyes especially, she said, "Don't worry, Sarah. I'll tell you, and you'll understand why everyone is angry and spiteful and you'll escape from the past. Don't worry, because everything will be fine." She conveyed this message to me in an instant, without uttering a word, but I trusted her. I shut the front door behind her and followed her to the kitchen.

By the time we had made our way into the kitchen, the tea was ready. The TV was off, and my mother was peeling potatoes for dinner. The sound of cold water running into a large glass bowl in the sink filled the room. My mother dropped the peeled potatoes into the bowl as she worked her way through the pile. I saw that the rage had drained away from her face, but her eyebrows were drawn together and her forehead was creased into worried grooves. I could not ask what was wrong. What I understood about the phone argument was that it was about my grandmother, and there was my grandmother sitting right in the same room on one of the yellow bunk seats quietly sipping tea through a small cube of sugar she held between her front teeth. I also knew that my grandmother would be leaving to visit one of her other daughters soon, although which one and why were unknowns. I looked at the two women. One was peeling and one was sipping. Each was absorbed in her own thoughts. I wandered out of the kitchen and when I was safely alone I decided to review what I had seen and heard outside Aunt Jean's apartment, in the hope that it would somehow be less stinging this time.

My grandmother had been living with my family for months, and there was a plan that she would visit with Aunt Jean for a week. It would be a short stay because Aunt

Jean's apartment was really too small for Bubby to move in. Uncle Mayshe had come out to get her on a Thursday, I remembered, because he complained about missing his regular Thursday business stops. He called Aunt Marly twice and demanded to know where she had been earlier in the day.

"You never go to the beauty parlor on Thursday! You go on Friday! You're a liar, Marly, and I know where you were." Uncle Mayshe banged down the phone, and immediately called back and screamed at his wife again. He paced up and back as far as the phone cord allowed, but he reminded me of a wild animal confined to a too small cage. I couldn't figure out what animal he was like, because he was pudgy and bulky, and every caged animal I'd seen at the Bronx Zoo was sleek. I tried to concentrate instead on helping my grandmother with her gray coat, but the fight was filling up the room and preventing her from finding the entry to the sleeve.

"Stop carrying on Mayshe," snapped Rikki with annoyance. "She might have changed her appointment. What are you screaming for? You're upsetting Sarah and Mama." I was beginning to lose my breath as I tried to understand why my uncle was screaming, why Bubby was leaving, and why my mother was so short tempered. "Just get in the car and take Mama to Jean. You'll soon be back in your own house and you can scream at Marly all night."

I walked with Bubby to Uncle Mayshe's long black car, and guided her into the front seat. My grandmother's face was clouded and her papery skin was almost as gray as her coat. "I'll see you Sunday, Bubby. It's only a few days from now."

"Okay, my darling. Everything is fine." Bubby's face and her words didn't match, I thought. But seconds later, Uncle Mayshe and my mother appeared from the kitchen door, so there was no time for me to soothe her or even find out what was wrong. Did she understand that she was unwelcome at Aunt Jean's? Did she feel like she was being thrown out of my house? Was she worried about inconveniencing her son Mayshe? Or was it just Uncle Mayshe's fight with his wife? Uncle Mayshe swung into the car, waved at his sister without looking at her, and the car glided off. He ignored me like I wasn't there. I watched until they turned the corner and were gone. My mother had already gone back into the house.

But everything was not fine. On Friday, I picked up the ringing phone and before I even said hello, Aunt Jean was screaming.

"You come and get her! I can't have her here! The teeth, the half eaten cubes of sugar, the moaning all night. I can't take it! You have a house and this apartment is too small for five people." Aunt Jean had not even waited to hear whom she was talking to.

"Aunt Jean, it's Sarah. Do you want to talk to my mother?"

"Oh, Sarah." Aunt Jean's voice changed. "How are you, black-eyed Sarah? Yes, I want to talk to your mother. Put her on."

When my mother picked up the extension upstairs, I tried to stay on the line and listen. But my mother knew I would try that.

"Wait a second, Jean. Hang up, Sarah. This doesn't concern you."

After her conversation with Aunt Jean, there was a tumultuous flurry of calls to Aunt Esther and Aunt Ruthie, and back to Aunt Jean. I could only hear my mother's side, but I was able to understand that my grandmother was coming back to us earlier than planned. My mother was still huffing angrily hours later as she began to set the table for dinner. But I was secretly relieved. Bubby couldn't be having fun with her other grandchildren, I knew. No one had to tell me who was her favorite grandchild. And no one else was interested in the nightly stories. I knew that my mother loved Bubby and even liked that she mostly lived with us. But she also resented that her sisters never relieved her.

On Saturday morning, David, my parents, and I set off early to collect Bubby. The parkway was empty.

"Look, kids," announced my father. "We're the first family on the road today." I slid forward on my seat and peered out the windshield. It was true; the road was completely empty on both sides. But what did that mean? Was it good? Was it dangerous? I was edgy and uncomfortable because my mother was silent and distant. My father's cheerfulness was incongruous. Was he really pleased about being the first on the road? Was he trying to coax a smile from his pursed lipped wife? Were we almost at Aunt Jean's? My brother was bouncing up and down on the edge of the seat, attempting to annoy me. But I was too far into my own apprehension to react.

And then we crossed a river on a long bridge that made a turn mid-way across, and we were suddenly there. While my father and brother waited with the car in front of the big apartment building, my mother and I took the elevator to the seventh floor. The ride was silent. But my mother's face was alive with commentary about our task. Her nostrils flared periodically. Her teeth were clenched. Her eyes were narrow behind her sunglasses, which she did not remove even though we were inside. I reached for her hand, but she was unresponsive. It was like I was riding with a cold mannequin of my mother rather than the warm breathing person.

As the elevator door opened, I could hear an explosion of screaming and crying in the hallway. Bubby was sitting outside Aunt Jean's apartment on a metal folding chair. Next to her on the floor were two shopping bags. Pouring from one was a tangle of clothing and the other held a pillow that had burst the seam of the bag. Bubby was holding her good hand to her face and she was wailing. My younger cousin Melissa was wedged in the door to the apartment and sobbing noisily. Inside the apartment, Aunt Jean was carrying on shrilly.

"I told you to close that door, Melissa. I'm coming over there to smack your face." They hadn't seen us yet.

"But Ma. Aunt Rikki isn't here yet. And Bubby is crying." Melissa was trembling, and she clearly couldn't decide if she should obey her mother and close the door or risk her mother's wrath and stay with her grandmother. Seconds later Aunt Jean appeared for an instant, her blond hair flying in every direction like it was on fire, and in one motion she yanked her daughter's arm, smacked her face and slammed the door. Melissa's wails were muffled behind the door, but Bubby's increased their volume. Other apartment doors cracked open, and then closed silently.

I could feel all the blood drain out of my face. The hallway began to spin. My mother leaped forward to her mother, all her earlier anger dissolving instantly. She wrapped her arms around her sobbing mother, and began talking over her shoulder to the closed apartment door.

"Jean, you selfish bitch! What kind of monster are you? You put your mother out the door? You bitch!" For a moment, her voice became a snarl, but the situation forced her to put those feelings aside and fix things.

"Sarah, can you hold these two bags?" Her tone was calm, and I instantly understood that we were a team that was going to save Bubby.

I gathered the two bags in my arms and held them tightly in front of me. I pushed the button for the elevator with my nose, and the three of us burst into giggles. When the doors opened, we bundled inside. Just as we began to descend, through the round glass window I caught a glimpse of Aunt Jean's door opening just wide enough for an arm to reach out and retrieve the folding chair. The window went black, and I wondered if I had imagined the arm, or if it had really happened. Bubby's ragged breathing evened, and by the time the elevator door opened on the ground floor, my family had returned to its regular roles. My father and brother were waiting in the car at the curb, and we began our drive home.

No one talked about the scene that I had witnessed. No one offered me an explanation of Aunt Jean's horrible actions. Her family was absent from the Sunday meetings for several months, but no one made clear why, or why they were back when they finally returned. It was as if the whole miserable affair had never taken place. I found myself wondering if I had made it up, or dreamed it after one of Bubby's more frightening stories. I surreptitiously examined Aunt Jean's face as she sat laughing on the bunk seat with her sisters and brothers. It looked like it had always looked: carefree, pretty, and satisfied. And my mother handed her a plate of potato pancakes to pass along, just one sister handing a dish to another sister. Bubby sat in her regular place at the head of the table, watching her children, her face a calm mask.

And now, a year later, there was talk of another visit. It was like we were on a terrifying carousel being looped past the same scenes over and over, but with no memory of having been there before. And it seemed to me as if I was the only one who

remembered the mistakes, but I was also the only one who had no power to fix anything.

Six

When Joe came home that night, he wasn't his cheerful self. He wasn't whistling any popular tunes, and there was no wink with the usual, "How's my Sarah?" greeting. Rikki turned off all the simmering pots on the stove, and began fixing things before she even knew what the problem was. "Tell me what happened, Joe, and I'll tell you what we'll do," Rikki promised, walking toward her husband.

"It's nothing. They're just stupid," my father muttered, applying his usual explanation for anyone's outrageous behavior. "There's no emergency. The carpool is breaking up. They don't want to drop me downtown anymore, and they think they can make better time going home on the Triboro." I had been leaning over the table, setting out the plates and napkins, but I paused, unsure whether this news was a family disaster or just some parent talk that really wouldn't change anything. I heard Bubby hobbling down the hall on her way to the kitchen, and I abandoned the table and scooted backwards off the bunk seat to go help her negotiate. It had already been a day of mysterious anxieties, and I seized the opportunity to remove myself from any new tension. But the hallway wasn't far away, and my parent's conversation continued clearly.

"You don't mean they're breaking up. You mean they kicked you out!" Rikki's rage mounted instantly to vein pulsing frenzy.

"They're right, Rikki. They will get to work faster, and they'll get home faster. I'll figure something out. Let's just have dinner, okay? What have you got?" Joe's voice was a tired calm, unfamiliar to me.

"The nerve!" Rikki went on, ignoring her husband's attempt to lower the intensity of her anger. "What, you never went out of your way for them?" Bubby and I were making our way to the table, but Rikki was flailing around the kitchen, banging down plates and silverware and nearly knocking her mother off her unsteady feet. "Well, right after dinner, we're going out to buy a second car. Where's David, Sarah? Get him down here; we have to eat right away." The fury went out of her voice as soon as she had articulated the plan. She was in charge, and having her strategy lined up created the serenity in her that even her husband's efforts to diffuse things could not equal. My face relaxed cautiously; it didn't seem like a catastrophe. But I couldn't understand why my father's friends were rejecting him. No wonder he seemed blue. It was just like when the girls across the street had instantly folded up their doll wardrobe cases when I began walking up their driveway toward their porch where they had been playing. "We have to go in. We can't play now," was their greeting. It might have been true and there was nothing overt to be angry at or hurt by. But I imagined that my father felt the same way now that I had. I was glad that Rikki had a scheme. It was much better than a sad silent father and an enraged sputtering mother.

Rikki and Joe left right after dinner for the car dealership. I washed the dishes and Bubby went up to bed. I was just getting ready to get into my bed when my parents got back, so I went to sit on the top step to hear the exciting news. "We're a two car family, Sarah! We bought a Renault. It's a little French car, very cute, Sarah, and we'll pick it up tomorrow. Daddy can come and go on his own schedule now, and the hell with those so-called friends. I knew we couldn't trust them." Rikki's voice was lilting, like a happy bird's song, and Joe was smiling indulgently behind her. All would be fine, I thought. I stood up and went back to my room where Bubby was already tucked into her bed.

"Good night, Bubby. Do you feel okay? Daddy got a new car. Everything will be fine, now." My relief tumbled out all at once like a sigh. The question of which of her daughters Bubby would soon be going to visit was forgotten for the moment, obliterated by the carpool crisis and the new car. It became one of the myriads of unsettled unsolved moments of my family's life.

"Should I tell you a happy story, my Sarah?" I clicked off the overhead light, and climbed into bed.

"Yes. I'd like a happy story. Definitely."

"This one is about a fire," Bubby began.

"But I thought you said a happy story, Bubby. A fire isn't happy."

"This one was happy, because in this one, I saw Avram the first time." I could hear that Bubby was smiling as she spoke the name Avram. I knew that was my grandfather's name, but that whole subject was another mystery, maybe the biggest one, swirling with cloudy information and half-explanations. Maybe Bubby would clear it all up this very night, I hoped. As far as I could conclude, my grandfather was a sort of ghost who attended every family gathering invisibly, sitting on a nearby chair, imagined only by me. No one acknowledged him, referred to him, or even remembered that he had ever existed. In fact, I had no sure idea if he was even dead or alive. There were no stories about his funeral or his grave, and no one ever lit a memorial candle for him on Yom Kippur, so he was likely still somewhere. But I just did not know. Rikki offered practically nothing on the subject of her father.

"My father was a very religious man, Sarah," she answered all my questions about him. It was the neat explanation for any specific questions posed, and it closed the subject.

"What did your father do, Ma?"

""What games did you play with your father, Ma?"

"Why did your family come to America from London, Ma?"

"Why isn't your father in any of your wedding pictures," was one question, however, that was left unasked. I knew that his piety was not the answer for that one, and I also knew that if Rikki had wanted to tell me why Uncle Morty was in her wedding pictures, walking her down the aisle in her beautiful satin dress, she would have. Something had broken the line that should have stretched from the happy moment my grandparents met to now, and I had little hope that anyone would ever explain the interruption.

I settled back against my headboard as Bubby transported me back to her village in Belarus in tsarist Russia.

"This story I'm telling happened in the summer, Sarah. The land was dry that year; the rains didn't come. The thatch on the roofs was flaking on the edges, it was so dry. The roads were dust. I remember that when I walked with Rivka on Shabbos in the afternoon, we left a cloud of brown in the air behind us. The dust was in our hair, even in our mouths. The part of the river where we used to swim was just a trickle of water, sometimes with bare spots between puddles. But I never went there after. . . . I never went there. Rivka told me it was dry, and then she was trying to convince me that she could teach me the letters, that it wasn't too late for me. Her mother had showed all the girls, but I didn't want to learn. In that time, I was as dry inside as the land. Rivka said I was still beautiful, but I knew she was wrong. What could reading fix? Nothing. God had dried up that river, and I alone understood. Soon the whole town and then all the forests and then the whole world. It was the opposite of Noah. A punishment. Oy, yi, yi, that punishment!"

Bubby stopped talking. I waited in the silence for what was supposed to have been a happy story, but Bubby was back to the one too awful to look at again for even a second. "Bubby, maybe we should just go to sleep," I offered. But my grandmother didn't even hear me, because she went back to the story as if I had not spoken.

"The next morning, there was smoke. It started in a shed where they made the horseshoes. The forge was hot, too hot for the dry roof, and suddenly everyplace there was fire. In a minute, the houses next door were burning. People were screaming, oy, I remember, 'Help, help, fire!'"

My grandmother had slipped back in time, back to her tinder dry village, where buildings that wouldn't have stood up if they weren't leaning on each other were igniting one another like a dark secret being passed along. The story was turning out to be another nightmare builder. What was happy about the town in flames?

"Everyone was running away, screaming. My mother was holding the candlesticks with one hand, I remember, and Dvorah's hand with the other. 'Go to the hill, Mary,' she was screaming. 'Where is Tova? Where is Fanny? Run away, Mary! Stop looking!' The neighbors poured out of their houses like children running out of the school when the lessons are over, but the screaming wasn't joyful. No, because it was like a pogrom without Cossacks on horses. And the fire was grumbling and growling like a wolf in the forest, angry and demanding attention from us."

"Did the fire department come, Bubby?" I asked, fairly sure that there was no such thing. I really needed to hear a happy ending.

"And then my brother Louis grabbed the dairyman's horse. Herschl was his name, the neighbor. The horse was resting from the deliveries, but when the roaring of the fire started, he was fighting with his reins, trying to run away too. Herschl wasn't near; I didn't see him. So Louis boosted himself onto the horse. I was watching, because Louis never did anything like that. He studied Torah, Louis, just studied. But the fire called him out of the shul. And while my mother was screaming for me to run away, I was watching Louis riding on a horse, out of the village, and away from the fire. Was he escaping? Stealing Herschl's horse to escape? I remembered then the hill, and lifted up the bottom of my skirt to run with the others."

"Where did Louis go, Bubby?" Mary ignored the question, because she was barely aware of me or their bedroom or the fact that she was an old crippled woman. She was a young woman running from a fire in her village, and I sensed that the fire was the first thing that had pierced my grandmother's consciousness since the devastating incident with her father at the river. She had not mentioned him again to me, and it seemed like she had not been aware of his whereabouts since that unspeakable day at the river. I would not have been shocked to learn that he was rarely home anymore.

"Everyone was on the hillside when I got there. Rivka was near her mother, and I ran to them, all the time looking back to the smoke that was boiling up like milk that you forget on a stove. 'Louis rode away on Herschl's horse,' I whispered to Rivka; I was ashamed to say it. She couldn't hear me; all the women were wailing. Rivka's aunt was screaming for her little son. But I didn't scream even once. I watched, only watched.

"And while I was watching, suddenly, Louis came back. I saw the horse coming closer along the road, with my brother on his back, and then the fire brigade from Beshankovichi just behind him. It was only a mile away, Beshankovichi, only up the river a little way, but it was bigger than my village, and they could put out fires with their pumper. There were six horses pulling that wagon, six, and many men, many. The women's wails became praises, and clapping, and then we sat on the ground to watch."

I felt like I was watching in my head an episode from one of the western movies that my brother liked. The posse had arrived to save the day, and the music changed from dirge to triumphal. I pictured all the women spreading out their skirts as they lowered themselves to the ground and gathered their children around them to observe the spectacle of their men and the neighboring villagers pumping what little water there was from the river and handing buckets dipped out of wells along lines of strong and ready rescuers.

"And then I saw Avram."

It was a simple statement, but Mary's voice was entirely different. It had wonderment, and sweetness, almost as if sunlight were shining on it. I knew that my grandmother was talking about the grandfather whose name was never spoken, whose picture had somehow been banished, and whose memory did not seem to exist for any of his many children or grandchildren. I lay very still for fear of breaking the spell that my grandmother was under.

"And he was so handsome, like a nobleman, and as I watched him walk toward the hill, closer to me and closer, every other person disappeared. Really! It is true. Every woman, every child, every noise, every smell, all was sucked away like God vacuumed it all up, leaving only Avram walking toward me, me alone, on the side of the hill. And I knew he had come to save me, save me from the fire, from my smoking village, from my father, my mother, my nasty sisters, my stinking brothers, my ignorance, from the future I would have there. So I stood up, straightened my skirt, and walked toward him. For one tiny second, I saw my mother waving her arms at me, like she was trying to collect me, like I was a chicken trying to escape from the slaughterer's blade. But I blinked, and for me, she was gone. Avram spoke to me, but at first I couldn't hear him, because he glowed with a light that came from his eyes, and the light drowned out the voice. Then I realized that he had told me his name, and was asking for mine. But no girl could speak to a man like that. It was forbidden. But I didn't care. My savior had come, so I walked off the hill with him."

I was smiling as I leaned back on my headboard. The carving in the wood usually made it difficult to find a comfortable spot, but this story was so romantic, so unexpected, that I felt like I too was bathed in my grandfather's light. My grandmother's voice resumed, but this time it was more businesslike. "Avram told me about his family, his sister who had just gotten married and gone to Warsaw with her new husband; his studies, because he came from a very religious family and read the Torah every day in the shul; his plans to go the very next week to London to his cousins; he poured out his life. He told me I would come with him, and marry him, and be his partner forever, that he knew he loved me the moment he saw me sitting there. And also he told me I was beautiful." When I think of this story, I can hear my grandmother's voice again, and I know that those last words had been spat out bitterly as if they explained and justified every other piece of Mary's life, every decision, every fault, every liability, every moment of misery and punishment that she had every experienced in her life up to the very moment of lying paralyzed in her granddaughter's room in the middle of the twentieth century. The glow of the story evaporated instantly, and I remembered then that this knight in shining armor was probably still alive somewhere, and I understood that my grandmother considered him guilty of more than brazenly speaking to her on a hillside when they were young. His confirmation of her beauty set up their relationship so that it couldn't help but fail, eventually.

"Later, maybe a week later, after the flames had died and the smoke had blown away, and the people who had no homes were gathered into the houses of their sisters and brothers, and life began again to be familiar and ordinary, I told my mother about Avram. Many people from our village had already left forever. Young men ran from the tsar's army. Jews were taken for 25 years, you know.

"I thought my mother would be sad, but also glad that I too would leave that village, the pogroms, the hard life. But her face got black and pulled itself in, like a roasted eggplant. 'It's a scandal, Mary. I'll tell you, and you'll listen, my daughter.' She said there was a part of his life I didn't know. 'Herschel found out and Bella, his wife, whispered it to me just last week when he came back from delivering milk in Beshankovichi.' Her face opened a little, but her voice was as thin and brittle as the ice that forms on the inside of a window in the dead of winter. 'Everyone there knows, Mary, everyone. Avram's sister,' and here she took a long breath to steady her voice, 'didn't get married and go to Warsaw, Mary. He's a liar, that Avram. His sister was married two years ago, Mary, two. But two weeks ago, just before the fire, her new baby died, Mary, and last week, my daughter, Avram's sister koshered her baby, just like he was a brisket. She put his little dead body on her table, and sprinkled salt all over him, Mary, like she was going to roast him for Rosh Hashanah. And she was taken away, Mary, somewhere, and may you never know where. Some people are saying that the fire was God's answer.' She was screaming by then, and spitting her words right into my face. I wanted to tell her that God must not have been paying attention, because he sent the fire to the wrong village. But I held my temper in. My mother had stopped to catch her breath, but she wasn't done with me yet. 'That's why Avram is going to London, to escape his family's curse. Who can blame him, the coward, for running away. But you can't go with him, Mary, and it's not because you can't arrange your own marriage. I always knew you'd never allow your parents to do that. You can't go with him because his family is crazy, Mary, and he can run to London, but the crazy will go with him! And if you go, the crazy will become part of you, and you'll never be able to escape it, Mary. It will follow you forever!'"

Mary stopped talking, and I heard her sighing and moaning softly. I was torn between wanting to know what happened next to my grandmother, and dreading the information. Then, Mary's moans stopped, and she picked up the story. I braced myself, clutching the edge of my comforter, and hoped that I would soon understand about my grandfather and his whereabouts. "But I didn't care what she said. I already knew from my brother Louis that I had to take a train, because his rabbi was trying to arrange for some of his students to go to America, and I could find out where to go, and how to go, but I would go, I knew I would go. I promised her I would wait two months and no longer for him to get settled with his cousins in London. I would wait for the cooler weather, I told her, right to her fiery face, but I was going, escaping my half burned village and my cursed life there no matter what anyone thought or said."

The story was gushing out of my grandmother like a forgotten faucet, and the speed of her voice underlined her desperate need to flee. I remembered that my father had an expression he often used, "Wherever you go, there you are," which always made me laugh, but my grandmother's words had, in a flash, illuminated its real meaning. I thought of how she sat quietly at the head of the table every Sunday, but I knew she wasn't quiet and content; she was quiet and sad. Was it because leaving to go to London had been a mistake? Or because she hadn't listened to her mother? Did she think that her mother's prediction had been right, that she had looked for trouble and it had found her? Did she think the crazy had become part of her, and then everyone she had brought into the world? At the time, I didn't know what, exactly, caused her unhappiness.

But now I understand, looking back on it all. Bubby had escaped from her life in tsarist Russia, but she brought her misery, her punishment, her constant rebuke, along. She never escaped from herself, from her benighted beauty, from the impulses it instilled when she was a child who didn't think a person as beautiful as she had to learn to read or follow any of the rules society imposes. She always thought that her beauty would pave the way to an easy and protected life. And she had good reason to think that when she was a child. I had heard many accounts of the reactions people had to Mary's glorious childhood beauty. But the understanding of the dangers of this mistake were suddenly clear to me, and it felt odd to know what someone so much older and more experienced obviously never learned. My grandmother had been jealous and insecure her whole life. It was just like the complaints my mother's aunt had voiced years before, about how Mary would scold her husband acidly if he even greeted one of the other women, especially a younger one, with less gray hair, who lived in their tenement. This suspicion was part of the burden my grandmother carried around with her, like luggage chained to her wrist. Mary had bitterness, not wisdom.

After a long pause, Mary resumed talking again. But her voice was exhausted, because her memory of that first happy meeting with Avram led her inevitably to all the misery that followed. "Go to sleep now, Sarah, my darling. I'll tell you about going to London maybe tomorrow. I'm tired now, weary." And then my grandmother was asleep. Her breathing was steady and calm, as it always was after she had disgorged another piece of her life's tale. I was surprisingly calm then too. I felt like it was the first time the elements of my grandmother's life were beginning to add up. I still didn't know enough, but it reminded me of the big jigsaw puzzles that I sometimes worked with my mother. I had formed a corner, found all the interlocking bits of cardboard, and now I could go on to the second corner. Filling in the middle would be easy once the perimeter was in place.

## Seven

We didn't see Aunt Jean and Uncle Solly and their children for the rest of the spring, and then the hot weather brought the usual shift in routines as the aunts and uncles retreated to Rockaway Beach and the world of summer bungalows. Jean and Solly rented on a street distant from her sisters and their families for the first time. But after Labor Day, when everyone packed up their belongings and returned to their city apartments, the clash seemed to mend itself. By the time I had acquired my new school shoes and a new pencil case and lunch box, Jean and Solly reappeared at the Sunday gatherings. No one welcomed them back, remarked on their being missed over the summer, or resolved to never let such a painful rift split the family again. It was as if it had never happened. I looked at their faces as they sat around the big oak table in the kitchen, but they offered no answers.

It was the early fall of Eisenhower's re-election campaign. My mother's sisters and brothers never talked about politics except to make fun of my parents' support of Adlai Stevenson. They were not analytical, but relished the chance to deride someone. "I know why you want him for president. He's a snooty bookworm, Rikki, just like you. What's wrong with the man who beat Hitler?" They never went after my father, for some reason. I knew that the husbands and wives of the siblings had no opinions on anything, or at least that was how it seemed. But the only slightly veiled contempt in which their very presence was held did not lap onto Joe. So if my father liked Stevenson, they figured he was entitled to be wrong, and there was nothing about it that they cared to remark on.

The presidential race was troubling to me because my friend Patty liked Eisenhower too, and went to school sporting an I LIKE IKE button on her corduroy jumper. I had no words to explain to Patty what was wrong. At home, my mother was contemptuous of the president. "He can't complete a sentence. They made him president of Columbia because they didn't know what else to do with him. And then president of the United States! He has no opinions! And Mamie is a drunk. Who could be stupid enough to vote for him?" My father rolled his eyes and chuckled affectionately at her flailing anger. "Relax, Rikki. What are you getting so excited about? Your life will be exactly they same when he's re-elected as it is right now. And my friend Red says Mamie has some condition. His sister-in-law has it too. It's not booze. So just relax, would you?" But my father always calmed my mother's emotions, so I couldn't be sure which one was right.

And now Patty was wearing that button. How could I tell my friend that my mother said she was stupid to be for Eisenhower? And that meant Patty's parents were stupid too. I vowed never to have that conversation. But I felt estranged from my friend, and ill at ease at her house. Even the grilled cheese sandwiches that Patty's mother Celia always put in front of us whenever I was there seemed somehow sour, like there was suddenly a poisonous ingredient toasted in. "I don't really like grilled cheese anymore, Celia. And I think I have to be home soon. Bye Patty," I fibbed, and dashed out the kitchen door, into the breezeway, and down the driveway before my friend and her mother could question me. It was a Republican house, and I had never realized before. Did I notice a new funny smell there, or had it always smelled like that? The greatest loss was that Patty's oldest sister Beverly was engaged, and Patty and I had been allowed to read her *Bride* magazines, and listen in as the invitations were chosen, the flowers were considered, and the wedding gown was fitted. It was like seeing a glorious dream acted out in real life. But now I had to give up my front row seat at that presentation. And worst of all, my mother didn't even notice that I had stopped going to Patty's house. I couldn't have explained that to my mother any more than I could have explained to Patty why I was uncomfortable being her friend. Patty had become an Other, like Aunt Rose Aronsky or Aunt Marly, and Rikki had been the instrument.

I had never been to a wedding. I had never been to a funeral either, but weddings were a more potent loss. When I had been in the second grade, the two girls who lived across the street, Susie and Lulu, were flower girls at their cousin's wedding, and they were allowed to play dress up in their matching gowns once the wedding had taken place. Susie didn't want me to play wedding with them. "You don't really know how weddings look, you know. So how are going to know how to pretend?" My mother had been dismissive. "They are mean. I never liked them. Don't play with them!" And once, when a celebrity's wedding was to be shown on the news, I had not been allowed to stay up and see it. "It's a school night, Sarah. There will be plenty of weddings for you to see."

The collective loss of all the weddings, and the glittery romantic images surrounding them only served to confuse my idea of what marriage was. As usual, I had only my mother's family as examples of what was true. My cousin Veronica was married to Frank. Once, Veronica had been in our kitchen, talking on the phone to her husband. "You can visit your mother any time you want. I'm not involved." Veronica winked at me, as if she were demonstrating a special trick. "That's my decision now, and that's my decision forever, Frank. But you can do whatever pleases you. Just don't even think about going on weekends. What about dinner? Are you picking up anything?" The conversation turned to other matters, but I was left wondering how Frank was supposed to visit his mother if he worked all week, and he wasn't allowed to go on weekends. And was I now supposed to understand something about how to treat a husband's family? And did this explain why my father's family was barely in my life? They all lived in Brooklyn, but I was almost never taken to spend the day with them. I had a grandfather right in Brooklyn, but I had never really spoken to him. And there were a bunch of aunts, uncles and cousins, too, but maybe my father was only allowed to see them during the week? No, that didn't seem possible.

As to other marriages, I also had my Aunt Jean as a model. Uncle Solly adored Aunt Jean, but somehow he couldn't please her. He had a handsome face with even features and softly curly hair with one ringlet that fell across his forehead. But he did not make enough money. She liked to think of herself as gorgeous and glamorous. Her favorite stories were always versions of how people she passed on the street stopped to stare at her. "I'm a knockout. It's just how it is," she would always sigh. Her husband was a war hero, but his wounds made him somehow unmanly. And Uncle Milt, who thought he could endear himself to his wife's family by contributing some nasty gossip, announced one Sunday during Aunt Jean's long absence that while piloting his taxi down Queens Boulevard that week, he had seen her walking into a bar with her boyfriend. That was totally ridiculous, I thought. Boyfriends were for teenagers, not my mother's married sisters. And just because Uncle Milt claimed to have followed them along Queens Boulevard in his taxi, and watched them go into a bar, did that make it true? The whole story had to have been invented by Uncle Milt so that someone would finally pay attention to something he said. "Yeah, yeah," scoffed Aunt Ruthie. "I should listen to you?" I never heard them talk about Aunt Jean's boyfriend again, and once Aunt Jean was back at the Sunday gatherings with adoring Uncle Solly, and I began to wonder if the whole rumor had been some sort of joke that only I did not understand.

Aunt Ruthie and Uncle Milt's marriage was characterized by periods of their going at each other in fiery flare-ups alternating with periods of their ignoring each other in deadly silence. Just before Election Day, on a Thursday, Mrs. Farrington was at our house. She had steel gray hair that was tightly permed and captured into an almost invisible net that encircled her entire head and created a hard brown edge just at her hairline. Her lips were a thin line, and she always cocked her head to the side, trying to hear what was being said. She was the usual babysitter almost every Thursday; that was the day that my mother would take the train into the city to meet my father for a night at the theater. It didn't matter whether my grandmother was there or perhaps visiting with one of her other daughters, Mrs. Farrington was a Thursday regular. Rikki always said that her mother would not be able to take care of two children, and she liked another adult in the house if she and my father were out. On that particular Thursday, Ruthie and Milt's daughter Stacie was there because she would be staying with us for the week, as there had been another vicious fight between her parents. This news was kept from my grandmother because she was making a weeklong visit to Aunt Esther's. It was rare enough for Aunt Esther to find room for her mother in the midst of orderliness and her husband and children, so my mother had insisted that Mary not be told about Ruthie and

Milt's trouble, lest she insist on coming home to comfort Stacie in person. My mother

wanted as little disruption of normal life as possible.

David and I hated Mrs. Farrington for any number of reasons. First, she always

gave us macaroni salad for dinner with all sorts of mysterious things chopped up into it. It

smelled ferocious, and nothing would induce us to eat it. Then, Mrs. Farrington was

nearly deaf, and I had to get right up close to her starchy smell and shout to make her

comprehend what I was saying. The TV was played loud enough to vibrate the windows

and her big old Chevrolet left a wide blotch of grease in the middle of the designated

hopscotch area on the driveway. Why the adults thought that leaving my fragile cousin

Stacie in the care of the dreaded Mrs. Farrington would help was another one of the

puzzles that I couldn't solve. And with Bubby away, matters were even worse, in my

opinion.

I remembered that Thursday because of Stacie's response to her parents' fighting

and being deposited with her younger cousins and Mrs. Farrington. It contributed more

confusion about the nature of marriage. That evening the lingering warmth of the end of

summer snapped, and the chill in the air began in earnest. The light during the day

seemed suddenly different, and early darkness created a shift in mood as everyone began

to turn inward for the coming winter. Stacie, who was barely speaking to anyone,

retreated into the guest room, wearing her older brother's long sleeved striped t-shirt, a

pair of jeans rolled up at the ankles, and fuzzy pink slippers. She had squeezed herself

into a corner of the sofa that opened into a bed that was so uncomfortable that my mother

called it "the prison bed," and she was reading a copy of Seventeen magazine, something

that struck me as enormously sophisticated. Stacie was 14 that year, nearly six years older than I was, but she looked about 12. She never relaxed enough to eat a meal; she was as thin as a girl could get without crumpling. Her hair was very dark, but so fine and thin that it was more like a halo than hair. I knew that getting her to eat Mrs. Farrington's macaroni salad would have been more unlikely than a walk on the moon, something barely even imagined at the time.

I wandered into the guest room to see if I could get Stacie into a frame of mind that might allow her to come downstairs when the shrill, "Dinner is served," call echoed up the stairs. The door was mostly shut, so I tapped it lightly as I pushed it open wide enough to fit through. The noise startled Stacie, and I heard a little gasp escape as Stacie drew her knees tighter to her chest.

"Can I see the cover?" I tested the waters.

"Can you just leave me alone? I'm not in the mood for a chat."

"How long do you think you're staying this time, Stacie?" I tried to make conversation. It was met with a nearly electric silence. I got up and began working my way quietly to the door. I turned and was about to warn Stacie about the time, but I saw that even though Stacie was staring intently at the magazine, big fat tears were sloshing over the rims of her eyes.

Later that night, after we had gone to bed, the moonlight came filtering through the Venetian blinds at my windows, creating stripes of light and dark on my blanket. I looked over at my grandmother's empty bed, and wished longingly that she had been there. I sat up in bed and crouched on my knees pushing the wooden slats aside as I gazed past the Impala, wondering when my parents would be home. Outside, I saw an astonishing sight, one that illuminated the damage that some marriages caused. Stacie, with a thick robe wrapped around her wraithlike body, wearing a pair of old roller skates, the kind that clipped around your shoes, was skating up the block. Her strides were smooth and long, and she was purposeful. She turned her head and looked over her right shoulder once. Her face was as serene and confident as I had ever seen it. As she skated away, it was as if every cruel memory she had in the world had evaporated. Her mother and father and their nasty painful screaming were gone for the moment, and until my parents came home and launched a panicky search that discovered her on a bench at the local park, she was happy. Stacie was brought back to the prison bed in the guest room, fed warm milk, and promised that she could go home in the morning.

As I settled myself back into my bed, I began thinking about marriage again. Of course another marriage that I knew about was Uncle Morty and Aunt Rose's. The specter of those Cuban children gripping that chain link fence floated past me for a second. There was no comfort in thinking about that one, either. But the most mysterious and troubling marriage that I could think of was my grandmother's. Bubby always sat quietly at the head of the table in the kitchen, almost regally, watching and listening to the remarks and banter of her children and their spouses. When they piled into their cars and departed for their own homes, my grandmother shuffled up to her bed, still silent.

To me, the person most conspicuous at these visits was the one who never appeared, was never remembered fondly or even angrily, was never even mentioned at all, was my grandfather. He was half the reason any of them existed at all, wasn't he? Weren't all the bedtime stories leading up to him? One night, I promised myself, I would ask my grandmother about her husband. How had that glorious romantic meeting at the fire and the sugary promises that were made that night fallen away and dropped Mary into the bitter misery she seemed to live in? Why had a marriage that had begun like a fairy tale faded to such misery? Could it possibly have been worse than the one Jean and Solly lived? Or Ruthie and Milt's? Or as deceitful as Morty and Rose's? As mixed in with sly trickery as Veronica and Franks? I would definitely ask. Maybe as soon as Bubby got back from Aunt Esther's. And maybe I would try going back over to Patty's house. If her sister would let us, we could look at all the engagement presents that had arrived, and maybe I could find some new clues to understanding how those happy beginnings could lead to such unhappy middles. Understanding the endings was surely impossible.

Eight

Stacie was taken home the next morning as promised, and my grandmother returned the following Sunday. When I got home from school the next day, I found her sitting outside by the front door. The weather had warmed a bit, as it sometimes does in the fall, seemingly unable to decide whether or not it's ready to bring in the frost and icy rain. The leaves of the crabapple tree on the front lawn were strewn around it waiting for my father to rake them up and burn them in a big metal can he used every fall. I thought of how different the tree was in the spring when it looked like a giant lollypop of pink blossoms.

"Look at how empty the tree is, Bubby!" I said as I sloshed through the leaves across the lawn to my grandmother. "I really like it better when it becomes a giant bouquet. I wish I would be able to wrap it up then and give it to you for a present."

"Ah, Sarah, my sweetest. Then there would be no more tree there the next year. Maybe I'll be gone by then, and you'll need it to remember me by."

"Bubby! I hate when you talk like that. You'll be here next year. You haven't finished the story, and you have to tell me how you got to London, and what it was like there, and how you got to America, and when the children were born, and what my mother was like when she was my age, and where my grandpa is." Children's words sometimes tumble out without attendant thought. But my grandmother's face, which had been adoring her grandchild, froze at the last phrase. She closed her eyes, and with her good hand, she waved me away.

"Go inside, Sarah, go in. I'm tired now."

I backed away from her as if I had been slapped. The mistake in bringing up my grandfather was that it had been done in broad daylight, outside the house, looking right into her face, I decided. The stories could only be told in the embrace of darkness, I realized, when Bubby didn't have to see my reactions, or even remember that I was there listening. Up until that moment, we could both pretend that our nightly exercise was so secret, that maybe it didn't even exist in daylight. I had breeched some divide, and now, I worried, the whole project might end.

"I'm sorry, Bubby. Forget what I said. Let's just remember the flowers from the tree. And how soon the crabapples come after the blossoms fall off. Remember that time you baked them in a pie? Maybe we could do that again. I could pick up all the crabapples that fall off the tree, and you could show me how you make the dough. Okay?" I spoke frantically, dancing around my grandmother's chair, trying to erase the vacant look that had fallen over her face. There was painful silence for a few minutes. Then, Mary's eyes cleared.

"You remember that pie, Sarah? But it was so sour! We couldn't eat it, remember? Maybe we'll make apple cake later. This is apple season, my Sarah. Go see if there are apples in the refrigerator."

I nearly wept with relief, and bounded into the breezeway to the kitchen door. My mother was tossing peeled potatoes into a yellow enamel pot on the stove. "Hi, Sarah. How was school? Do you have homework?" She looked at me and stirred the pot without looking,

"Do we have any apples? Bubby and I want to make apple cake." I ignored my mother's question. I did my school assignments while sitting on the edge of my bed every day, and never needed reminding. Was my mother confused about which child she was talking to?

"Look in the refrigerator, but I'm starting dinner now. Maybe tomorrow would be better for baking projects." The homework question had properly evaporated, I noticed.

"But Bubby's in the mood now. And tomorrow is too long from now. We'll do it fast, and meantime, you can go look at the crabapple tree. All the leaves fell off. Please?"

There was a pause while my mother considered. "Fine. I need to run up to the store for milk anyway. Maybe I'll walk. Go tell her I said it's okay."

I tore out of the kitchen, through the hall and around the corner to the front door before my mother had finished her sentence or had a chance to change her mind. "Bubby!" I called as I pushed open the screen door. "It's okay, we can bake! Let's go in!" But my enthusiasm deflated instantly when I saw her Bubby wiping tears off her cheek. "Don't cry, Bubby, please don't cry. I'm sorry about before. Let's go inside, okay?"

I caught my grandmother's arm with one hand and steadied the chair with my foot. Mary rocked back and forth a few times as she gathered the momentum she needed to stand. "I'm not crying, Sarah, my darling. Maybe something blew into my eye." I knew that wasn't true, but I was happy to put the whole incident behind me. We made our way slowly up the step and into the house. And then, just as we entered the kitchen arm in arm, with its cheerful wallpaper with the pictures of vegetables and roosters, and the savory aromas from the bubbling pot that my mother had left to simmer, and the long empty bunk seats that would fill with aunts and uncles the following Sunday, Bubby stopped and turned to me. "I'll tell you everything, Sarah. I won't die until I finish. Don't worry anymore. But remember, it's our secret, and it's not for anyone else to know. It's for you, because you are the one who will understand." And then she shuffled to the refrigerator and began taking out the apples. I froze into the spot where my grandmother had turned to me. Her words were too cryptic for the nine-year-old me.

I watched as the pile of apples grew on the wooden counter, and I watched my grandmother open a drawer and take out a knife, and I watched as she wedged an apple into her paralyzed hand and began paring it slowly. But I didn't really see any of these activities, because I too was paralyzed in a way. My grandmother's words had been like an anointment of a sort. I had been chosen, elevated, really, to receive something important. And even if I didn't understand then exactly why it had to be a secret, I vowed silently to honor the request. It might be difficult, I knew, never to tell anyone about Bubby's stories, not my mother or father, or any of my cousins, because some of it terrified me, and some of it was too wonderful not to talk about. But I saw my part as sacred, somehow, and drew my responsibility into my heart.

"I promise, Bubby. I'll keep your stories inside me forever." And when I finally moved, it was to bring my hands to my chest, and hug the promise into myself, where it would take root, and grow vines that twisted around and around. Those vines would give forth some flowers as heavenly as the crabapple blossoms, but also some fruit as sour as crabapples themselves. It's only now, after so much time has passed, that I've been able to examine that vine and those flowers and crabapples. Humans endure so much. Why don't they simply curl up and submit to the crushing weight of their lives? I think back at that old lady who was trying to make sense of her life and its consequences, and I don't know how she managed to live to get old. Now, as I review everything she told me, I do understand. And if there was some punishment in place, as she was sure there was, it's well paid off by now.

"Put water in a bowl, please, Sarah, for the apples. And squeeze a lemon in so they won't turn brown." My grandmother was completely involved in slicing apples, as if nothing but baking had happened all day. "And tell me, what did you do in school today?"

Nine

That night, Bubby went to sleep early. It was just that she was too exhausted that there was no story, I tried to convince myself. The next day, it rained furiously all day, and by the time I came home from school, the lawn was littered with the few leaves that had remained on the trees. That night as we turned off the light, Bubby began humming to herself. It wasn't "Raisins and Almonds," one of her favorite Yiddish melodies, or even one of the popular tunes that my father was always singing. It was unfamiliar to me. "What are you singing, Bubby? I never heard that song."

"I heard that song in London, Sarah. I suddenly remembered it just now." The humming stopped, and the room was filled with the pattering of the rain on the windows. "Should I tell you about when I left my home, Sarah?" Bubby's voice was so ordinary, so relaxed, that for one second, I forgot that this was going to be the story of how a young girl left her parents forever, and never saw or was in contact with them again.

"Oh, yes, I'd love to hear that story. I always wanted to know how you got to London all by yourself. Weren't you scared, Bubby?"

My grandmother ignored my question. Probably she never heard me speak, I reasoned. Once she had made up her mind to reveal something of her youth, Bubby seemed to leave the present. I was used to that pattern, so I smoothed out my blanket across my chest and laced my fingers together.

"Once Avram and I promised to meet at his cousins' house in London, on Whitechaple Road, it was, my village got smaller and smaller. And I saw that the houses were so old, and resting their heads on each other's shoulders because even they were so tired of the life there. There was no money, and even though months had gone by, no one fixed the damage of the fire, and the nearby part of the forest that was burned looked like a bunch of giant pointed black sticks pointing to heaven, like they dared to accuse God of something evil. It seemed like the whole district was dying before my eyes. I was waiting, just waiting for a letter from Avram to tell me he was ready, that I should come. Rivka knew I was waiting. She said when it came, she would read it for me."

Mary grunted at herself then, and I knew it was her embarrassment that she had never learned to read.

"I remember that I lived my days out with no purpose: It was like there was a veil across my eyes, and water clogging my ears. I didn't cook, or clean, or even sew. I didn't see my sister Dvorah, even though she was always trying to get my attention, and my mother stopped trying to forbid me to go to Avram because she saw I didn't even hear her. And once she saw that I was gone already in my heart, she began to mourn me. She didn't sit shiva, exactly, but she cried all the time, in silence, and she stayed in bed a lot, like she was sick. And even Dvorah couldn't cheer her up no matter how she tried. As the days went by, a thick shadow crept over the house. I didn't try to talk to my mother, because I didn't want to stay there anymore, so I think I must have been mourning her too. And I blamed her, too, if I'm honest, because she didn't see who my father was. If I looked in her direction, I would put my hand up alongside my eyes, so I couldn't see what was before me. My father was already a ghost for me for a long time, and even if he was there, I never saw him."

The story was not turning out to be like a fairy tale, where the prince rescues the princess from the ogre, I thought. It was unnerving to even hear her allude to what had happened in the river, or even mention her father. I could hear the television murmuring softly from the living room downstairs, and I nearly got out of bed to escape the coming cold of the winter of 1905. But my promise to my grandmother to keep all her secrets included hearing them, no matter how painful and frightening they were.

"Finally the summer was ending, and the air at night was beginning to make me hunch my shoulders into my shawl. Soon it would be Rosh Hashanah, and when God would write in his book, he would be writing about me in my new life in London with Avram. And then, Rivka," and here Mary's voice caught itself in a guttural moan, and she stopped talking. It was like a cudgel had come down silently, and crushed her voice. I sat up instantly and pushed the blanket away. I shifted my feet to the floor and began to stand up. Bubby had stopped talking in the middle of stories before, but not like this, in the middle of a sentence.

"Bubby! What's wrong, Bubby? Do you feel all right?" I had bolted out of bed, and was across the room, about to snap on the light switch. My grandmother, completely unaware of the movement in the room, resumed speaking.

"Then the worst thing happened." She was silent again, and my heart was pounding in my chest. I tore back to my bed, and slid swiftly under the blanket, waiting to hear what could have been worse than I had already heard. "Rivka got sick," she cried, and I could hear her sniffling quietly, as if her friend had fallen sick just that day instead of more than fifty years earlier. "It started with a belly ache. Mrs. Goldshtain thought it was from the cabbage soup. But it lasted for days, and it got worse and worse. I went there as soon as I heard. But who would have told me? I don't remember." Again she paused, and I heard more sniffling and sighing. "When I went into her house, I saw Rivka lying on her parents' bed. She usually shared with her sister, of course, but she was too sick. The whole house was darkened as if any ray of light would have killed her. The bedding surrounded her, and all I could see was her head. She was as pale as the sheets. Her eyes were sunken into their sockets, and glassy, and the rims were red like they were bleeding. Underneath there were black smudges like a Cossack had beaten her. She was moaning, but it was soft because she had no strength. I ran to her. 'What is it, Rivka? What is wrong?'"

I nearly answered the question because it had been posed so compellingly. Only at the last second did I remember that I was not part of story. I lay there silently.

"Rivka couldn't speak. Her mother was sitting on a three-legged stool by the bed, weeping quietly. Every so often, she would reach out to feel her daughter's forehead. 'She's burning, Mary, burning with fire,' Mrs. Goldshtain said to me. 'And the pain in her belly is like a beast. She can't walk, and she can't even take a sip of water.' She spoke to me like Rivka wasn't there to hear. In that moment, I knew Rivka would die, I just knew. I ran from the house; I ran to escape from the dying. I ran to the river where we used to swim and where," and here she stopped talking again.

I could picture my grandmother in her shawl, in a crumpled heap, sobbing by the edge of the river, filled with anger and hatred for the way life was. It must have been easy for her to leave that village.

"It took two weeks, almost, before she finally was released from her misery. I saw her only once during that time. I went to her house and when I saw her skin was yellow, I clenched my teeth. I bit down on my tongue and it started to bleed. In a second, my mouth was filled with blood. I looked one last time at Rivka and I shot out the door instantly and spat blood onto the dirt right outside Rivka's door."

She paused and seemed to be looking at the splash of blood spattered on the ground, and streaked up onto the bare wooden wall of the Goldshtain's house. Imagine if your best friend dies, almost right in front of your eyes, I thought. Any animosity I had felt for Patty evaporated instantly. And even the children on the block that my mother had instructed me to ignore gained a new warm glow as I flicked through their faces and considered their deaths. How could Bubby have stood such misery? A deep moaning sigh came from my grandmother's bed and she picked up the story.

"Then I knew there was nothing to wait for anymore. I packed a bag right after the funeral, a bag made of carpet, with two wooden handles. I took a shift and extra stockings, and only my needles and a thimble. Dvorah wanted to give me her good woolen skirt, but I wouldn't take it from her. Anyway, it would have been too small. Dvorah was crying as she watched me put a wedge of cheese wrapped in a cloth into the bag with a loaf of rye bread. She loved me, Dvorah, even though I always ignored her since she was born. I don't know why. I miss her, little Dvorah. I think she never left Mama."

Again there was stillness in my bedroom. So that's why Bubby's youngest sister had never come to America: she stayed to take care of their mother. And of course, that meant that Bubby never saw her again. But Bubby must wonder if she's still alive! Could she still be alive?

"My thick gray shawl that I got from my father's sister, Aunt Leah, I would wear for warmth. I begged Louis to take me to the train. But he said no, and he wouldn't look at me. 'But. Louis, you have to take me right away, because everyone knows that I have to go, I have to find Avram.' But his eyes met with my sister Tova's, and then she was suddenly interested in straightening the tablecloth, and he was suddenly interested in finding his book, and I darted around the table to find her face, and I pulled his sleeve, but they wouldn't talk to me. And then I began to scream, oy yi yi, I screamed and I screamed, with my hands on my face, like a demon was grabbing my throat and yanking the screams out of my mouth. 'What is it? What do you know? Is Avram dead?' I was frantic, pulling her, pushing him, stomping my feet, snatching out my hair. They wouldn't talk to me. I remember I threw myself on the floor and pounded it with my fists over and over. I think they thought I would go mad any moment, or maybe I was already mad, so finally I saw them nod at each other.

"'Mary, you can't go to him,' said Tova softly. I began to scream louder, and thrash around wildly. 'I'm going, I'm going,' I shrieked again and again. Tova knelt down to me and grabbed my hands. She held them together in her hands, and said, 'Shah, Mary, shah,' until finally I had no more strength to scream any more. I leaned into her, and buried my face in the gathers of her skirt. Louis began to talk. 'Mary, there was a letter. A man brought it weeks ago, but Mama said to hold it until Rivka got better. She knew you would want your friend to read it to you.' I listened to him without breathing. I knew if Avram didn't want me to come to him, I would have to walk into the river, and stay there until I was dead. I couldn't find a way to live in that house in that village any longer."

By this time, I too had nearly stopped breathing. I was crying softly, and no matter how I tried to hold on to the knowledge that I had that Mary would go to London, and she would meet and marry Avram, and she would have children with him, and eventually come to America and end up in that very bedroom with the oak beds and the pink wallpaper, telling me the story, I couldn't believe it. All the happy stories that my grandmother had told me when I was smaller were merely a prelude to the real tale of her life, which was continual and constant wretchedness.

"'But then Rivka died, and so I opened the letter.' Louis paused and my terror settled around me like an icy winter snowfall. I was moaning and weeping quietly. And then he continued. 'I'll tell you fast, Mary: Avram has another woman. Her name is Esther Bagoudis, and he says he is sorry, but he wants to marry her. He says you and he made a mistake after the fire, and after all, Esther is there in London, and you are far away, here in Ulla.'"

I had never heard the name of my grandmother's town until that moment. Bubby had always said she couldn't remember when I asked, or it wasn't worth mentioning, or it would be like a curse coming from her lips. But why did she say it now, with absolutely no hesitation? This story must be even more painful than the unutterably horrid one about her father in the river. But how could Avram love someone else? He had said he loved her, that she would come to him in London, that she was beautiful. So much for beauty, I thought. Every story I had ever heard about a beautiful princess who lives happily ever after in the end was absolutely a lie.

"'So, Mary, how can you go to London? There's no one for you to go to.' For my brother, the story was over. The ending had come, and it was bad. But it was over. He walked to the table, pulled open the drawer, and took out the letter that had been placed there until someone would have to tell me about it. He walked back to where I was lying in Tova's arms and dropped it into my lap like he didn't care anymore about my misery. 'Get up now, Mary. You have to make a life here. You are the best embroiderer in the village, and you could sell your work in the market. People will forget that you were forsaken, and someone will marry you some day. Some man, maybe a rich older widower, will want a beauty like you.' Tova must have felt my reaction: I flinched when he said I was forsaken. She was still murmuring to me like a loving sister that I never knew I had, but suddenly I stopped listening to her. Because a new feeling began to grow. It was first a humming feeling, then it was growling softly, and as the minutes passed, and Tova and I began get up to our feet, the feeling grew and swelled until it was bigger than my chest. Soon it would burst out of me, and inflate the whole house until it would split apart into a million pieces. Before I was even straightened up, the feeling was a howl, a shrieking howl with evil fiends holding it up and blowing and whistling through it.

"'I will never make a life here, you little beast,' I screamed at him. He backed up until he was against the door. He reached behind him and felt for the latch. His mouth had fallen open and his lip was trembling. He found the handle, backed out quickly, and then he turned and ran. Then I twisted around to face Tova. 'You can stop feeling sorry for me, my sister, because this is not going to happen to me. No one is going to "forsake" me, as our learned and proper brother put it. There's one thing I have learned, even if I can't read, or write, or be a slave in this house, and that is that I am beautiful. Even he just said it. My eyes are beautiful, my mouth is beautiful, my hair is beautiful, my shape is beautiful, my every move is beautiful.' Tova was holding her face, and her mouth was shaped into a perfect round circle. She was looking to run from me too. But I raised my voice, so everyone could hear me, every man or wife or child in the neighborhood. Mama was surely going to be shamed, but I didn't care. 'I will find my way out of this village, and out of this region, and I will find my way to London. And then I will search every house on Whitechaple Road, wherever that is, until I find Avram the man who promised to marry me and take me away from this life when we were standing on that hill with a fire burning and roaring right behind him. And I will marry him. And do you want to know why, Tova, and everyone who is listening to me scream with self-satisfied pleasure? Because I am beautiful, and I will not be forsaken or forgotten and I will not be denied.'"

I could hear my grandmother panting from the exertion of her angry outburst, and my mouth was as wide open as my grandmother's sister's had been. The old woman who was usually quiet, agreeable, shy, and too frail and vulnerable to even speak loudly, had become a sturdy, proud and determined individual. I had believed from the time that "The Ugly Duckling" had been read to me that a person's outward appearance wasn't important, that it was what was inside that counted. But here was my grandmother who had learned just the opposite, that looks are the only thing that mattered. And that belief had such a stranglehold on her mind that it enabled her, no, it forced her to confront her circumstances and act in a way that would have been unheard of, and even scandalous at the time. My grandmother's rapid and raspy breathing was beginning to return to normal, and her rage was dissipating. I suspected that my grandmother was still awash in her youth and wouldn't hear me, but my confused reaction leaked out anyway. "Wow, Bubby, I can hardly believe how brave you were. But I think you should have gone to London and told him you wouldn't have him even if he changed his mind about Esther Bagoudis." Much to my astonishment, my grandmother had heard me after all.

"You're right, my darling Sarah." Her voice was even and logical. "You have never been smarter. And now, I think we should go to sleep. Maybe soon I'll tell you about my first sea voyage. Would you be interested?"

"Interested? I'm ready-spaghetti!" And we both laughed at the expression that we had invented together when my grandmother was teaching me how to make tomato sauce the way Mrs. Russo, her neighbor from a summer in Rockaway Beach had taught her. And then the laughter gently subsided, and as the furies of the story of the letter fell away, we drifted into our separate dreams.

When I think back on that story, I am astonished at how quickly we recovered from our separate understandings of the events. My grandmother forgot the sting of her abandonment and was eager to concentrate on her determination to go to London and somehow save her own life. I was still stuck back in the scene of her best friend's death. And yet, when my grandmother shifted the focus to the next chapter, the adventure of traveling to London, we both shut the book on one sorrow and looked forward with some sort of optimism to what was coming next. It was like we lacked the ability to sustain an unhappy memory. I suppose it's the key to life: the ability to unhook the past from the present, like the coupling on a train car that's being shunted away, and look forward.

Ten

There was a bigger than usual buzz of conversation the next Sunday when the family gathered around the kitchen table. The sisters interrupted each other, each voice growing louder than the one it had stepped on.

"I would never wear black to a bar mitzvah," pronounced Aunt Esther haughtily. "You want people to think you're mourning a happy event? What's the matter with you?"

"You wouldn't know an up-to-date style if it was dropped on your head," replied Aunt Jean dismissively. She dipped her hands into her huge black leather purse and began searching through one small container after another. "Solly, where did I put that swatch?" She was not really asking him for information; she was just holding everyone's attention. He knew it, so he didn't even try to answer, and the rest of them knew it too, and they never even shifted their gazes to him. "Ah, here it is. Look at this, Esther. Have you ever seen a richer satin? And see the beading? Bugle beads will be along the entire edge, sparkling and shimmering with every move I make. What do you know about gowns, anyway?" She shook the square of fabric in her sister's face, and smugly folded it back into the treasure chest that was her handbag. Her face glowed, as she seemed to picture herself whirling around a dance floor with someone. But who, I wondered from my perch just beyond the kitchen door? She wouldn't have looked so dreamy and transported if it was Uncle Solly twirling her in her mind's eye. A story that my mother had told me flickered into my head as I watched my aunt zipping her purse. After Uncle Solly had been wounded at the Battle of the Bulge, he was sent to an army hospital to recuperate for months. He was finally able to call his young wife who was supposedly waiting for him back home in the Bronx. But when his call came, instead of the tearful and grateful voice he expected to hear, he got a whiny woman who had been to a party the previous night. "Jean, it's me, Solly! I finally got to use the phone! How are you?" My mother recounted the phone call in her derisive voice.

"Oh, Solly, I'm not feeling so good today. I think I maybe had too much to drink last night at a club I went to with my friends."

"Can you believe my sister?" said my mother, as incredulous as if the insult to her war hero brother-in-law had just occurred. "The man is in a hospital, lucky to be alive, a medal winning soldier wearing a cast that holds his arm out to here," continued my mother with outrage in her voice, her arm held away from her body perpendicular to her chest, "and his wife is complaining to him about her scotch induced headache from a party, a party she went to while he was. . . . The woman was selfish then, and she's selfish now."

But the discussion around the kitchen table swirled on. "I'm wearing the dress I wore for Philly's bar mitzvah," Aunt Rose mumbled, almost under her breath, from her post at the sink. She couldn't seem to decide if she would be permitted to join the conversation. Before she could be told that her opinion was of no interest, she bent down to pick up a crumb from the floor. If anyone happened to glance toward the voice, she'd have disappeared, safe from reprobation.

The event that had excited the sisters was cousin Daniel's bar mitzvah, which was to take place a month later. The invitations had arrived, and the one that had come to my family was propped importantly on the desk in the hallway. It was the most glamorous thing that had ever come through the mail slot, I thought. There was the outside envelope lined with glimmering gold paper, with their name and address written in sweeps and curlicues even fancier that my mother's swirly handwriting. But inside that was a second envelope, this one with only our names, and inside that was the actual invitation, covered with a protective sheet of tissue paper. The words stood up from the card, and I ran my fingers over them thinking that even blind people might be able to read them. There was a gold picture of a torah that gleamed and caught the light, and the wording was formal, "...request the pleasure of your company," and curiously the numbers were written out in word form. Unbelievably, even the children were invited. My brother David would need a suit, and my mother would have to take me shopping for a formal dress, the first one I had ever had. This would be almost as exciting as a wedding, I thought, but I didn't plan to talk about it at school the way girls talked about the weddings they were invited to, because I was afraid no one would have heard of bar mitzvahs, or if they had, maybe no one would understand about this huge formal affair. Better to just keep it to myself.

The sisters' husbands were quiet as usual when their wives argued with each other. Once, I remembered, Uncle Milt had ventured into one of these disputes. They were looking at a photograph of the four of them sitting around a table, all dressed up, and they were trying to remember which restaurant they had gone to when they celebrated VJ Day. Uncle Milt looked at the picture and said with great authority, "That's the Parkway Restaurant downtown. I remember it was upstairs, with big windows," and all the women forgot their disagreement, banded together instantly and turned on him. His face turned fiery red in response to their attack. Why did he even care, since he wasn't even there? They nearly drew blood, even though their weapons were words. Not one of the husbands ever hazarded into that treacherous territory again.

The only other silent person at the table was the hostess of the coming affair, Aunt Marly. She sat nervously at the end of the bunk seat, dressed in a pair of shocking pink silk pants and a matching jacket. Her red hair, just like Lucille Ball's, I suddenly registered, was swept into a French knot, not a wisp out of place. She smoked one cigarette after another, the lipstick-stained butts accumulating in a big ceramic ashtray. Her eyes shifted from one sister-in-law to the next as each loudly added her opinion. No one but Aunt Marly listened to anyone, I could tell, because no response followed the previous remark with any logic. But Aunt Marly, who might indeed have some thought to add, said nothing. It seemed like she was afraid of them, I thought, or afraid of something. Uncle Mayshe was next to his wife who was sitting there in her haze of smoke. Occasionally he slid looks at her, as if he was making sure she would continue to behave herself.

"Okay, Marly, get up. I'm going. Get Daniel in here," Uncle Mayshe erupted suddenly. The discussion stopped as he nearly pushed his wife to the floor in his haste to slide out of his seat.

"Where are you running to, Mayshe? Maybe Marly wants to tell us about her dress?" said Aunt Esther. But her tone was sarcastic. I could see that Aunt Esther knew Marly didn't want to share anything with her husband's sisters, and she also knew they already thought her dress would suit the tramp they thought she was, even though they hadn't seen it or heard it described. Marly stubbed out her cigarette, and left the kitchen to find her son.

I couldn't decide if Marly looked relieved to be leaving, or maybe just pleased to have something to do: locate Daniel and get him out the door. I swung back and forth between my excitement at the anticipated shopping excursion for the dress and my discomfort about the mysterious Aunt Marly. I wandered away from the kitchen door, and the new discussion my aunts had taken up about why Mayshe had left so abruptly faded into a quiet distant rumble.

The month long approach to the bar mitzvah crawled along slowly. My mother and I went to Saks Fifth Avenue and found the most perfect dress for me. It was red, "the only color an extra fancy party dress should be," pronounced my mother with a loving smile as she considered my image reflected dozens of times in the three-way mirror. The saleslady, attired primly in a neat navy blue dress, nodded her head in agreement. The dress was made of a stiff ribbed silk fabric and it had a full skirt that stood away from my waist as if I had just twirled around even though I was standing still. But the best part was the top: the dress had inch wide straps above its fitted bodice. No more Peter Pan collars with necklines up to my chin. This was really a grown up style. I could hardly believe my mother thought it was appropriate. "I think I need heels for this dress," I ventured.

"We'll see," my mother responded. That meant it wouldn't happen, I knew. My mother was avoiding a fight in Saks Fifth Avenue's dressing room.

"You'll find something perfect in the shoe department on one," the saleslady said. "I saw a pair of black velvet shoes there just yesterday."

"No," my mother replied. "I think we'll get a pair dyed to match." I nearly swooned with happiness. If bar mitzvahs were this wonderful, I began thinking of other boy cousins I had that might be coming up to age thirteen. But there were only girls besides my brother whose thirteenth birthday would be ages away. My other male cousins were all older than thirteen already. Why had there been no gala balls for them, I wondered. Maybe most people didn't have these lavish affairs. Maybe Uncle Mayshe was the richest man in New York. Or maybe everyone else in the family was poor. I had no one I would ask and no way to know the answers. Whether my family was typical or different from other families was simply unavailable information. I never asked because I feared the answer would make me more uncomfortable than not knowing.

We stopped at Chandler's Shoe Store and ordered silk shoes with heels that were no higher than my school shoes, but tapered to seem like they were. The toes narrowed to a point, and there was a sparkly button on the strap. "And we'll get our hair done together, Sarah, before the party. How would that be?" We were walking through the parking lot to the car,

"Can we take Bubby to the beauty parlor with us? She would want to get her hair done, don't you think?"

My mother paused as she unlocked her door. She seemed to be picturing the ordeal of getting her paralyzed mother through the rigors of having her hair styled. "Okay, Sarah. We'll take Bubby with us. We'll have to wash her hair at home before we go, though. She could never stand to have her head lowered back into the sinks they have."

"And don't you think we should get her a new party dress? What about shoes, too? She doesn't have any fancy clothes."

"Aunt Ruthie is taking care of that, thank goodness. I am not her only child, Sarah, although you might think I was." The shimmering mood of the shopping trip snapped. We rode home in silence, and only when my father met us at the door and asked what we had bought did I remember what a beautiful dress I had, and how exciting Daniel's bar mitzvah would be.

It was like getting ready for Cinderella's ball, I thought as the three "girls" of the family, as my father called us, left for our day of beauty. And when we came home, hair lacquered to immovable stiffness, he pronounced us, "as gorgeous as three Marilyn Monroes." We all dressed: the men, my father and brother, knotting ties together; and the women, my mother, my grandmother and me, zipping each other's party dresses and spraying on perfume. My grandmother was even more quiet than usual. She kept looking around nervously, as if she were waiting for someone to come in with bad news. I almost asked her what was wrong, but I didn't want my mother to accuse me of looking on the dark side of any situation again, so I concentrated on the impending ball. The drive seemed endless, but finally we pulled up to the hall and a valet opened the doors for us. After we had assembled under the canopy and smoothed the wrinkles out of our dresses and lapels, the valet drove the car away.

The party room was filled with Uncle Mayshe and Aunt Marly's guests, including my mother's family. Everyone was dressed in shine and sparkle. The sisters stood together assessing the other guests, leaning their heads toward each other and speaking out of the sides of their mouths. I didn't know anyone but the familiar crowd from the Sunday gatherings, but it seemed like the room was filled with hundreds of beautiful guests. Could Uncle Mayshe and Aunt Marly know all these people? I felt as though my aunts and uncles only knew each other. Strangers and friends were in the same category: outsiders. My own parents were friendly with some of our neighbors, but my mother made it clear over and over, "Don't speak to other people about family. You can't really trust them. Only your family is forever." Then the music quieted, and the bandleader asked the guests to find their tables. I had my place card that I had picked up from the flower-garlanded table near the entrance. I was seated with all the kids, away from my parents. I chose a seat as the trumpets began a heralding cascade of notes. "And now, your hosts," announced the bandleader, and the doors flew open and in strode Uncle Mayshe, Aunt Marly and Daniel. They were all smiling, and the music swelled as everyone applauded. This was unbelievable, I thought. It really was like Cinderella's ball, or someone's ball, anyway. Uncle Mayshe and Daniel had on tuxedos with shiny satin lapels and patent leather shoes, and Aunt Marly was wearing a floaty yellow silk dress that sparkled with thousands of diamonds. I searched the room for my parent's table, and saw all my aunts bunched together with their heads slanted towards each other. Their hands were not clapping like everyone else's, but were up next to their mouths, whispering secrets like elementary school girls on the playground at recess. And they did not look like they were enjoying the party. They were clearly judging what was wrong, in their estimations. What was wrong with the room, the band, the food? I could see they were adding things up, and they'd have topics for weeks. Bubby was seated at the head table with Uncle Mayshe and Aunt Marly. I couldn't really see her from my seat, so I stood up every few minutes to check on her. She looked frozen in place, like she had been turned into a mannequin in a store window. I tried to think what was frightening her, but it was useless.

The party went on despite the sisters' nearly silent dissatisfactions. Daniel lit candles on his cake as various people were called up to help him. All Uncle Mayshe's siblings with their spouses had their turns. Each was greeted with applause. Aunt

Marly's brother was called too, but the applause was smaller. After all, I noticed, if a whole table full of people seems to sit on their hands, the sound will be smaller. Before long, a singer was introduced, and although I had never heard of him, there was a wave of impressed murmurs from the guests. It was Bobby Short, and he accompanied himself on the longest piano I had ever seen. How come Uncle Mayshe knew someone who was obviously famous, and a black man as well? The only black people my family knew of were house cleaners who came occasionally to help with seasonal cleaning projects. As my gaze drifted around the huge ballroom, I realized that there were other black people besides the entertainer on the stage. And after his performance, he went to sit with them. They were all dressed in rich gorgeous satin dresses, or had flashy flowing silk pocket-handkerchiefs. The women had feathers or diamond tiaras on their heads. These people must have been other famous entertainers, or famous for something that I couldn't even imagine. They didn't look like anyone I had ever seen. And Aunt Marly was spending a lot of time at their table, I noticed. What could that mean?

Then there was dancing, including a rousing hora, the circle dance that lured everyone but my mother's family to the dance floor. In spite of the negative moments from my aunts, I thought the entire event was glamorous, and the best thing I had ever attended. Until it was almost time to end.

It was after midnight, the latest that I had ever been allowed to stay up, and some of the children were beginning to get cranky and tired. My brother David had been running around the room wildly for hours, and he was sound asleep on the floor under his chair. My parents were on their way over, my father holding a plate piled high with samples of every dessert that had been wheeled in on long sweets-laden tables. There was even a fountain flowing chocolate sauce, and my father had held his plate under the stream and guided a river of chocolate over everything. "We're about to leave, Sarah. Say goodbye to your cousins. Joe, put down that plate and get David off the floor, would you please?" My mother's voice was uncharacteristically harsh to her husband. I knew she rarely spoke to him the way her sisters spoke to their husbands. The sisters always teased her about it, too. "Oh, you, you're different," they had each commented to her. And it was always a way of dismissing her. My mother must be exhausted too, I thought.

But just then, I became aware of some kind of scuffle over near Bobby Short's table. And the music slurred quickly into silence. Chairs were scraping back, and all eyes turned toward the noise coming from across the room. David awoke suddenly, and began to cry loudly in his confusion of where he was and what was happening. Some of the men began pushing towards the scuffle, and the crowd parted to let them through. It was through the open space that I caught a glimpse of what was going on. Uncle Mayshe was standing over Aunt Marly, holding her wrist with his fist, slapping her with the other hand back and forth, to the left, then to the right. She was sprawled on the floor, her dress splashed all around her like a raging torrent of yellow silk, her legs thrashing at impossible angles as she peddled them to try to escape the blows that kept falling on her from every direction. She was screaming, loud piercing howls, and Uncle Mayshe was screaming, too, one curdling curse after another. I stopped breathing as I heard my uncle's voice calling his wife a whore, a lesbian, and a bunch of other acid-dripping words that I didn't know, while she screeched and yelped incomprehensible replies.

My father put his plate of dessert down, scooped David up into one arm and my mother grabbed my arm. My father put his other hand on his wife's shoulder and guided her quickly towards the door. I was being pulled along in one direction, but my face was turned grimly and resolutely to the spectacle across the room. Some clumps of people rushed toward the fight, while others swept themselves away. The din continued as I was yanked steadily out of the room. Just as I was pulled safely into the lobby, I caught one final glance back to the terrifying scene, and I glimpsed an almost ephemeral picture of my cousin Daniel crouched into the corner farthest from the panorama of his ruined celebration, hiding his eyes with his hands, his mouth open in a big gaping circle, his tongue trembling, just like in a cartoon, but not comical in any way.

"But what about Bubby? Where is Bubby?" I cried with fright as we pushed through the glass doors on to the sidewalk. "We have to get Bubby!"

"I'll go," said my father. "Give this ticket to the valet," he said to my mother, "and wait in the car. Lock the doors." As he turned to go back into the hall, my mother seemed about to protest, but one look at my pale face and trembling lip seemed to stop her. She handed the ticket to the outstretched hand of the uniformed young man, and gathered her two children near her. "What trash," she mumbled to herself. "That Marly is the scum of the earth, and she has pulled my brother down to her level."

I reviewed the scene I had just witnessed. Wasn't it Uncle Mayshe who was being the bad guy? Wasn't it Aunt Marly who was sprawled across the floor trying to protect herself from the raining blows? Wasn't he the one who was yelling at her all those horrible names? So why was my mother accusing Aunt Marly of being trash and scum? Why wasn't she feeling sorry for poor Aunt Marly? And Daniel, I thought, what about Daniel? Questions sloshed around my head, but they didn't pour out of my mouth. There were no answers to be had, I knew. And as my father walked through the door guiding a stone-faced Mary to the waiting car, I also knew the entire incident would be blanketed with hushed silence and buried. My father guided her gently into the back seat next to David, who had fallen asleep again. "You okay, Ma?" he asked.

"I'm never okay, Joe. This is just another night," she replied. I heard a loud grunt of disdain from my mother. My father climbed into the driver's seat and looked across at his wife, silently warning her not to admonish her mother. It would be another example of pretending you didn't notice something right in front of you, something that made loud noises, had an evil stench, and kept reaching out arms in your direction. I would never ask my mother or anyone why Uncle Mayshe was so angry with his wife, or what happened after my family had left, or if anyone helped Daniel. Uncle Mayshe and Aunt Marly would be back for a Sunday visit before long, I knew, and I would look them over surreptitiously from my living room doorway perch, but no one would betray any hint of explanation. Aunt Marly would be dressed up in some fancy outfit, her hair would be stiffly arranged, Uncle Mayshe would peel off a bunch of twenty dollar bills from a bulging wad he kept in his pocket, and announce to anyone who was nearby, "Hey, get me some Chinks, whaddaya say? I want to eat Chinks." And life would go on as usual.

Decades later Uncle Mayshe and Aunt Marly would die ignominious deaths, penniless and cursing each other to their last breaths. They hated each other, I suppose, and each had clear memories of their own and the other's indiscretions. But they somehow thrived on each other, too, like a pair of inseparable parasites. What enabled my uncle to behave like some kind of demented monster? How did he learn that kind of cruelty?   What kind of poison flowed in his veins, and how did it get there?   From where

I stand now, I think I have some answers.

## Eleven

"Bubby, could you tell me about how you got to London? I was looking on a map in school today, and I think Belarus is very far from England. How did you do it? Did your brothers take you?"

I remember that I used to contrive prompts for my grandmother so that she would be amenable to picking up the nighttime stories, especially if some daytime event had pushed her into a melancholy funk. It had been weeks since the fiasco at Daniel's bar mitzvah, and we were settling into our beds one night when I decided the hiatus had gone on long enough. My grandmother's silence during the day, the listless way she ate her meals, and the subdued nightly moans that came from her as she slept were clear signs that she was unreachable in her sorrow. Part of me wanted to ask her about what she thought about what had happened. But I didn't dare, thinking that somehow I would come to understand everything eventually, and that asking Bubby to talk about such a horrible event would be just piling up more misery on her. She never brought it up. Maybe to her, it wasn't part of our story structure, and there was no mechanism to analyze anything. But that evening, Bubby had seemed slightly perkier to me, asking me about my piano lessons, and questioning why I only played with one hand at a time. "Bubby, I'm just learning," I explained, happily aware that my grandmother might be returning to her old self. "I'll use both hands before you know it. I'm in a recital in the spring, you know, and you could come and hear me. I'll use both hands by then, I'll bet. You want to come?"

My grandmother agreed in her usual way. "If I'm still living, Sarah, I'll come." I wasn't even annoyed by my grandmother's maudlin expression. I knew I could make the nightly stories continue that night.

"How did you go? By horse cart? Maybe a stage coach?" I knew about stage coaches from the cowboy shows that David was addicted to. I realized they were not likely to have been in Belarus, but I thought Bubby might have laughed. She barely heard my question.

"I went because of a letter, Sarah," Bubby began. I knew very well about the letter, the one about Esther Bagoudis, and how Rivka had died right when the letter had come, and how angry the letter had made her. It was odd to think that Bubby had forgotten that she had told me about the letter.

"I know you know about the letter. But isn't it something that a woman who can't read a word could have the path of her life set out before her because of a letter that was addressed to her? I should have learned to read. I should have listened to Mrs. Goldshtain and learned with Rivka and the other girls. Some parents didn't let their daughters learn. But all my sisters learned. Why didn't I want to learn?" Here she paused. I knew the answer to the question. The silence while I waited for my grandmother to resume was as dead as the leafless trees of a winter landscape. We were both thinking the same thought, but it hovered silently in the room. "Him," Mary finally intoned. "Him. He ruined my life." My eyes filled instantly with tears, and they spilled over the rims of my eyes silently. Any mention of my grandmother's father brought that same immediate response. My thoughts skidded past my own loving and protective father and that made the tears flow faster. I wiped my face with the hem of my blanket, and the story continued.

"No one knows the real story, Sarah. All my children think they know how I left my parents' house, and Ulla, but they don't know the truth," began Mary, with a conspiratorial giggle. Ulla, I thought. She almost never referred to her hometown by its name. In an effort to forget the past, I had sometimes thought, she had really forgotten the name of the place. And no one knew the real truth? And now I would learn it? The tears that had sprung to my eyes so instantly at the mention of my great-grandfather now receded just as quickly. I always felt honored and fearful at the same time when my grandmother awarded me this way. Some of the secrets were like sweet fairy tales, or like peeks into the serene rural past, but others were terrifying. I was fully aware, even as a nine-year old, that they were all true, even those too horrifying to have involved real people, my own ancestors, because they were beginning to throw some light on the behavior of the crowd that bunched themselves into the yellow bunk seats in my mother's kitchen every Sunday. How different were the behaviors of those long dead people and the ones I saw every week, after all?

"Tell me the fake story first, Bubby, the one everyone knows." Rikki had indeed told my brother and me the tale of her mother's departure from home. It was a version that tried to explain how a child could leave her parents and her home, knowing full well that she would never see them again. The idea of permanent separation from their parents is harrowing to children, and even though the occasion of the telling us the story was when my parents were going away on a vacation to Puerto Rico, not leaving us forever in the care of the perfectly capable but unlikable Mrs. Farrington, we needed

reassurance that all would be well.

"That's what I want to tell first, Sarah, the lie." My grandmother's voice had slid

down to a growl of contempt. Thinking about her now, I realize that for her whole life,

she must have felt like she had a slender fish bone caught in her throat, one that didn't

block her breathing, but was a constant background irritation. She couldn't quite

swallow the deceit that made her presentable to her children and neighbors, and she

couldn't cough it out. Her sisters and brothers knew what had really happened, I realized

back then, and my grandmother must always be on guard when they visited, for fear they

would let it slip and expose the hornet's nest of misery that she had turned her back on.

My mind was wandering down this path of sudden understanding that my grandmother

had pointed to, but the story was continuing, so I abandoned it for the moment, but

promised myself I would go back and explore there later.

"So Rivka was gone, and the letter had come, and I was getting ready to go to

London to find Avram. Many people from my village had gone already to America, or

England because everyone knew the life there was collapsing like a squash that was

forgotten and rotting in the field. But no one in my family had gone yet, because they

were too frightened to leave what they knew, even though a decayed smell was hanging

all around their lives. But they knew I was going. After I had announced it at the top of

my lungs to the whole neighborhood, they knew very well. I don't know why the houses

didn't crumple into the earth from my screams, they were practically dissolving before

our eyes anyway."

The chuckling that came from my grandmother at the thought of the houses slipping off their rickety foundations surprised and delighted me. I was amazed at my grandmother's astounding ability to put her misery away into a compartment. She left the moment of terrible anguish as easily as my father changed the radio stations in the car when commercials came on.

"So, the story goes, they bought me a going-away present. In fact, there were two presents. My mother had been sewing a coat, a woolen coat, made of deep red. She meant to give it to Dvorah, who never had anything new in her life. My mother knew that Dvorah was the child who would never leave her, and she wanted to give her something that hadn't been worn by everyone else in the family first. And Dvorah was so sweet." The pause that followed was threatening to derail the story. The sister that she had ignored all the years that they lived just inches away from each other in a two room hut had become the source of constant guilt in her old age. But then she continued.

"The coat had a short cape attached that fell just to my wrists. The waist curved in and fit me just so, I think she made it a little big for Dvorah to grow into, and near the edge of the cape and down the placket and even at the hem at the bottom, there was embroidery. The threads were silk, so rich, in black and purple, and there was even a silvery French knot along a green leafy vine. You never saw anything so gorgeous. The whole edge was bound in a velvet ribbon. It was like it had been made for a nobleman's wife. Who knows how my mother found these materials? It must have cost the whole purse she was saving for Passover clothes."

I was lost in picturing the scene. I saw the fabulous coat. I could see my grandmother receiving it from her mother's hands, all the family looking on lovingly.

They were all kissing her, and wishing her a safe trip, and pressing other tokens into her hands, a handkerchief, a small pair of brass candlesticks that had been saved for her dowry, and a bunch of flowers.

"The other gift was a big carpet bag. It had wooden handles and two straps with metal buckles that closed across the top. I could carry bread and cheese with me for my journey, and I had a place for my few possessions. On the last day, I went to the cemetery to tell Rivka that I was going, and I asked her to look after me. I knew she would. I never said goodbye to her mother. I never said goodbye to anyone. But I looked around the house one last time. It was dark inside; the windows were small and made of oiled paper that never let in enough light and too much cold. We walked together, the story goes, the whole family even including my father who hung back, nervous that I would do something to him, the fool, and crossed the fields toward Beshankovichi where the train stopped once every day. There was a rickety wooden siding built there, in the middle of the field where the tracks ran. The roof was meant to keep the rain off the people waiting, but it blew in through the open sides. Another failure for the people who scraped up a life there. We waited by the side of the tracks, standing and then sitting because the train was late, or we were early. My mother had food for us, hard-boiled eggs and challah because we were pretending to celebrate something happy. But no one was really happy, because I was shaming them. Who ever heard of a young woman going to meet a man she wasn't married to? No neighbors came with us, just my mother and father and my sisters and one brother, Louis. Everyone cried when they heard the train coughing from the distance and then saw the smoke from the locomotive. My mother cried for sadness, I think, my father from guilt, my sisters because their mother was crying and my brother for the embarrassment of the whole situation. I cried too, but I was happy to be going. I knew I'd never see my mother again. But somehow that part of it kept itself away from me. I had plenty of time to realize that later." In my darkened room, both grandmother and granddaughter stared through their minds' eyes at the scene that had been sketched. But the glowing depiction was a lie, and both of them knew it. My grandmother paused for a few minutes. I thought for a second that she would let the story rest there, at least for that night. It was a lovely, bittersweet tale, and it was lovely to bask in the glow it created. But that's not how it unfolded that night. The truth followed.

"This is what all my children think. But what really happened is different, my darling Sarah. Are you ready to hear?"

"Is it awful, Bubby?"

"There was a coat, first of all. And it looked just as I described it to you and everyone else. And my mother was making it for Dvorah, just like I said. She used to work on it at night by the light of her oil lamp after Dvorah went to sleep. It was going to be a surprise for her and she never saw Mama working on it. I knew it was finished because all the extra thread had been wound onto spools and put into the chest by the door. I can see it now, the coat, folded between layers of a bleached flour sack. And there was no place to hide anything in that house. House? No, it was a dark hut with a tin roof. And tin was better than many had. Most people had thatch, which was rotten and crawling with bugs and nests of mice. My father's aunt paid for the tin roof for some reason that I don't know."

Her voice stopped, as she seemed to examine the house she grew up in and was about to escape from. While I waited for my grandmother to remember where she was and continue the story, I tried to see what she was seeing. I could barely sketch in my mind the scene she was describing, because it meant I had to erase the scene of the loving saddened family that had been standard family lore. I had to be ready for a new version of that beautiful young woman's departure. And then the voice began again.

"The coat was in a big carpet bag that was kept on a high shelf above my mother's bed, that same bag that was in the other story, the one that everyone thinks really happened. The shelf had pegs under and that's where her black Sabbath dress with the white lace collar was hanging, and her heavy shawl that she kept for the winter cold that poked its fingers into our bones. I didn't know what else was in that carpet bag. I thought it had the linens and the feather pillow that my mother brought to her marriage. She never used any of it, not that I saw. No need for anything beautiful, I guess, in that life. But the coat: as soon as it was finished, I simply waited for the moment that my mother would leave the house, which I knew would happen on Thursday when she'd go to the market. Dvorah always went with her to carry the bundles. I watched them walk out the door and make their way along the muddy rutted road. My mother had on a gray shawl that she draped around her head, over her shoulders, and crossed in front of her. I watched her tuck the ends into the waistband of her skirts and the apron that was tied in the back. She called to Dvorah who was skipping ahead of her, always happy, Dvorah. Dvorah waited, looking back until my mother reached her. I saw my mother's back and Dvorah's smiling face as they held hands and began to make their way to the market square. I was standing by the door of the house and then I took one step towards them and I whispered, 'Goodbye Mama, goodbye little Dvorah.' And then I turned back to the house, went inside, climbed up on my mother's bed and reached for the carpet bad. I dumped it out on the bed, but some of the things tumbled to the floor. I was in a big rush so I ignored it. I pulled the coat, the beautiful coat for Dvorah, out of its white sack and held it up before me. It was so rich, the embroidery and the velvet ribbon edge, it made me tremble because of what I was planning. That coat was the finest thing that had ever been in that house. I opened the buttons and slid my arms into the sleeves. It felt like music was playing.

"I took the bag and filled it with bread, cheese, my needle case and my Sabbath clothes. And then I walked right to the tzedakke box where my mother kept money to give to the rabbi when he came around to collect for charity. Every house had a box like that. I opened the lid and took every coin that was in there. And then I opened the chest by the door and wrapped my fingers around the leather purse that had all the money that my father had saved from what his aunt gave him. It was money they were going to use to send my brothers to America. The czar's army would be coming for all the young men soon, there had been an announcement, and they would never come home. But I was planning to never come home either, and I was sure my need came first."

Outside my window, a dog began barking fiercely, as if a prowler were intruding on his territory. "Maybe there's a squirrel trying to get into the garbage pail outside, Bubby," I tried to explain the barking. But my grandmother didn't react to the dog or the explanation. By this time, her usually frail and hesitant voice had taken on a sinister tone, as if she were frightened by her memory and needed to justify it and explain it to herself at the same time. I forgot the dog, and began to think. She stole the family's money? I was used to shocking stories from my grandmother, but this was something different. No wonder she never told the real story to her children! And she took Dvorah's coat? That explained her mournful tone ever time she talked about the sister she never saw again. She probably never pictured her unless she was shivering in the Belarusian winter, with no coat to warm her. I was trembling in sympathy with my great aunt's loss. Did Bubby think when she took it that Dvorah might die of the cold that very next winter, I thought with horror? No, she could only do what she did if she convinced herself that Dvorah would be fine. But she never really knew, did she?

"I put the coat back in the bag and buried the money in my boot. I walked out the door for the last time and turned up the path that led out of the village to the north along the river, to Beshankovichi, where the train would stop the next day. I never once looked back. If I had to cross an open field or meadow, I ran. When I came to the river, I could hide in the bushes that grew by the riverbank, and I didn't care when I stumbled over the willow tree roots over and over. I was afraid that they'd come looking for me, and I was also afraid that they wouldn't come looking for me. Do you understand, Sarah?" But I was trying to digest the facts of the story, and I wouldn't begin to make sense of the motives for a while. And I had long ago learned that the explanations of the various ethical dilemmas that my relatives presented were generally unavailable.

"And then it was night, so I could hide better from people. I opened the buckles on the bag and took out Dvorah's coat that she would never see. I put it on, and it was so beautiful, but this time, I couldn't hear the music playing anymore. I closed the buttons and I kept my focus carefully on my plan. The cape swirled from the shoulders to my wrists, and the velvet edge almost glowed in the dark. I heard howling from nearby, and

I was afraid of wolves, because everyone always warned about wolves coming in the night to eat anyone who was unwise enough to be out. But nothing came to eat me alive, and no one came to bring me home. I think they didn't know yet about the money. Who could imagine that I would steal? There were other night noises, too, beside the wolves, from animals that I didn't know. Some sounded like the wailing souls of dead infants trying to escape their birth pains, or maybe drunken peasants looking for women to rape. I could barely understand their language, but I kept trying to listen for words among the night noises. There was only howling. I never slept for a minute that night, and the whole time I crept closer and closer to the crossing where that train would come and deliver me to my future. I had to go to London somehow, you know, and find Avram. I had to get him away from Esther Bagoudis and make him honor his promise. I had not the slightest doubt that when he saw me again, he'd forget her in an instant and march me right to the nearest rabbi and marry me. I knew I could get what I wanted. But what I didn't know was that getting what I wanted would not really get me what I wanted."

There was silence as the grandmother and her granddaughter thought that bit of wisdom over. And then from the grandmother followed a sigh full of all the pain that her life had brought her.

"Did you have to wait long for the train, Bubby?" I asked, trying to extract some kind of happy ending to this chapter of my grandmother's story.

"No, my Sarah, not long. It came almost with the dawn, and I was the only one waiting on the siding for it. I saw a dairyman with his cow go by. The cow had a bell around her neck, and I heard them coming before I saw them. But they went by me without even a nod. And no one else came to stand with me. Then I heard a train whistle, and soon the big black locomotive rumbled into view and slowly stopped, right in front of me. I remember the carriage: it had wooden sides, with beautiful carvings that had once been polished, I think, but then they were crusted with mud that faded into dusty streaks. When the man lowered the steps, I picked up my big bag and began to climb into the train. He looked me over fast, and I saw in his face that he understood, somehow, my whole story. I knew I had to use him for my ends, so I looked back at him, shyly like, through my eyelashes. 'Can you help me, sir,' I said to him. But he didn't understand me, my Yiddish. I was afraid to try his language. I didn't know enough, just some words that would work in the market, or related to embroidery. Nothing useful for a trip to London.

"It didn't matter though. He understood what I meant without understanding my words. He stared at me hard as he lifted my bag out of my hands and into the train. The stare was clear: for a fee, he could help. I had no papers, no permission to leave, and somehow he must have known it. I walked past him into the car, my boots clicking along the wooden floor. I planted myself into a seat, swirling my radiant coat after me. By the time he reached me with my bag, the train was lurching forward and I had dug a few coins out of my boot for him. I handed the money over, and he nodded. We had a contract then, you see. I knew he would take care of me on my journey. But it wasn't only the money, I knew. When you are beautiful, Sarah, when your face is even and your skin is clear, and when your eyes are wide and your lashes surround them like a fringe of silk, and when your curves are shaped just so to promise things, and your curls escape from under your hat or scarf, and bounce down your back with every step you take, then the world can be an easier place. I knew even then that being near a beautiful person is like coming into a house from a winter storm and standing next to the stove. The warmth from the grate spills over you and into you, and you feel lucky to be standing there. I knew that when I got on the train, I was a surprise for that man, that he must have felt like he had come upon a flowering bush in a clearing in the woods. But, Sarah, nothing is for nothing. That I was to learn soon enough."

How could Bubby be so shallow and vain, I marveled. It was impossible to understand how she made decisions.

"I looked at the landscape as it began to fly by my window, flat and brown. I saw the deep forest far away by the horizon, and I imagined my village, beginning to come to life, with the people crawling out of their huts like bugs or rats, to search for the day's living. But I turned away, and began to consider what I had to do next. I didn't even notice how amazing it was to be riding on a train, faster than anyone in my family had ever gone. The truth was, I wasn't like anyone in my family, so why compare my life to theirs? The train was almost empty then; who would be traveling before the morning prayers were finished? So I closed my eyes and tried to rest. The trainman would take care of me. I was quite sure."

The bedroom was silent for a while. I heard my grandmother's breathing slow, and I knew she had fallen asleep. The story was over for that night. I heard a sharp quiet drumming sound against my window, so I sat up to investigate. The temperature had slid lower, and sleety rain was slanting against the glass. Imagine Bubby out in the cold winter, traveling on a train across the country toward London. But London was across the water, and first she had to get to the edge of the land. But what edge would that be? What country and what city was she going to come to? Did she even know where to go?

I tried to see my grandmother in her sister's beautiful coat with her dark curls pinned up under her hat, which I imagined to be dark red, like Passover wine. Some of the unruly coils of hair would have been escaping their confines and tumbling down her back and wisps of it would have been framing her face. Her boot heel would be drumming the floor with nervous anticipation of the journey ahead. She would have leaned her head onto the window and pretended to be going to sleep, but her tapping foot would have betrayed her.

It was amazing: the young Bubby didn't seem sad or frightened to be leaving her family and striking off on a long and dangerous flight to a man who didn't know she was coming, and had made it clear that he didn't want her anyway. She was completely sure that her plan, as sketchy as it was, would result in success. I imagined that my grandmother was picturing the warm reception she would find in London, the joyous wedding that would follow, and the "happily ever after," as I would have put it then, that would be inevitable. And all because she was so beautiful? I visualized my grandmother sitting up, turning toward the glass and finding her reflection there. I saw her lifting her hand to her unruly hair and rearranging it with a casual push at a comb that had slipped. What was going through her mind as the locomotive exhaled black puffs of smoke into the morning air? Did she think that God had made her this way for a purpose? Did He want people to look at her and feel a pleasurable constriction in their chests, or a warm flow of blood to their faces? Did she love herself for it, or did it seem like a burden to her? Probably it wasn't a burden yet, I considered, but there were hints that it would turn out to be a responsibility that would weigh her down. That's probably what she meant by, "Nothing is for nothing," and "I would learn soon enough." I pulled the blankets up tightly under my chin and tried to think of something pleasant, like a trip to see "The Nutcracker Suite" that my mother was planning for the family in a few weeks. It was to be just the four of us, my parents, my brother and me. Bubby was going to stay with Aunt Ruthie for a few days, and we would pick her up after the ballet. Before long, I was asleep.

Twelve

My mother was screaming into the phone when I opened the door and burst into the warm kitchen. I had walked home from school through the drifts of snow that had accumulated all day. "Sarah just walked in, Ruthie. No, Ruthie. Absolutely not! I'll have to call you later, Ruthie. And you better change your plans, I'm warning you, Ruthie, because my day is not going to be altered one bit!"

I dropped my schoolbag by the door and began to unwind my scarf. "It snowed its head off, Ma, and my socks are wet because snow fell into my galoshes, and I'm freezing. My lips are blue! Look!" My voice was filled with delight, but the instant I read the mood of the kitchen, my face fell and my mood deflated like a popped balloon. I remember that my stomach dropped when I saw my mother's face, which was knotted into a grimace, and her nostrils were flaring. She looked like a horse that was racing madly for the finish line, not the usual mother I found after school. I interrupted myself when I realized my mother had not heard any of it. "What's wrong, Ma? What's the matter about Aunt Ruthie?" Even as I asked the question, I knew what it was about, because it was what it was always about: Bubby.

"Nothing, Sarah. Nothing is wrong, that I promise. Everything is just fine, just fine." She emphasized these words with slow deliberateness and her face resumed its normal proportions. "Put your schoolbag away, and stop dripping water on my floor, Sarah. Put your wet boots on the towel I put on the floor in back of the door. When they're dry, you can put them away in the sliding pond." My mother turned back to what she had been doing before the phone call, which was rinsing the salt off a large piece of meat that was set on a white porcelain board that was tilted into the sink. I could see my mother was gritting her teeth and flaring her nostrils again as she thought about her sister Ruthie. I sat sideways on the edge of the bunk seat, laughing to myself about the phrase, the sliding pond, that had become the family name for the boot box that was built into the bottom turn of the staircase, near the front door. Trying to remember how that name had come about, I bent over to open the buckles of my red galoshes, and used the toe of one boot to pry off the heel of the other. I bent my shod foot across my other knee and pulled off the remaining boot with clenched eyes and clenched teeth. I lined up my boots as my mother had instructed and peeled off my wet knee socks. I began walking toward the door to the hall, intent on hanging up the socks in the bathroom before my mother could issue new instructions that were obvious before she said them. I had already resolved to make myself invisible until whatever had angered my mother in her phone call had retreated from her mind.

I lined up my wet socks on the towel bar, ran upstairs and scooped a dry pair out of my top drawer. My grandmother was lying on her bed, not yet awake from a nap. I sat on the edge of my own bed to slide my feet into the pink anklets I had chosen, and watched my grandmother sleep. Her mouth was gaping, open wider on one side than the other, and her hair looked like a white storm scattered around the pillow over her head. I could hear her involuntary little moans, as she must have been working her way through some painful memory in her dream. And then suddenly, with a startled jerk, she was awake.

"Did I wake you up, Bubby? Why are you up here during the day? Do you feel okay? It snowed! Did you see?" My excitement about the snow bubbled to the surface once again.

"No, my Sarah, you didn't wake me," Mary said, denying the obvious fact. "Anyway, it's about time I got out of bed today. I wasn't feeling so hot this morning, but now, I'm ready for the day. Please, Sarah, could you give me some juice?"

I crossed the room to my grandmother's bedside, and handed her the small glass of juice that my mother must have left there earlier.

"What does, 'Not so hot' mean? Did you have pains again?" I was never sure that my grandmother's illnesses were really physical. She didn't have a disease that anyone told me about, and she didn't get progressively worse or better. So maybe it was pain in her mind, built up over her whole life. I always searched my wits for the right combination of words that, once pronounced to my grandmother, would instantly erase the scars that seemed to be oozing and bleeding in her memory. But not only could I think of nothing appropriate, I could never summon the nerve to say I wished I could fix my grandmother's pain. So I often found myself right next to Mary, even looking directly into her eyes, unable to reach across what was clearly there, but always unspoken. I realize now she must have been suffering from depression. Her body was bent and twisted, but her mind worked fine then. And her memories must have been so lethal that she was under their dark spell all the time.

"It doesn't matter, my Sarah, because I'm fine now. Snow? You never saw snow like I had when I was your age."

The possibility of talking about my grandmother's childhood, right out loud in the light of day, was such a shock to me that my plan to tell her about my socks getting wet simply dissolved from my brain. There was an instantaneous pause before I grabbed the opportunity.

"Was Ulla near a big city, Bubby?"

"Not big like New York, Sarah, my darling beauty. It was near Vitibsk. Do you learn about Vitibsk in school?"

"No! I never heard of it. We're learning about Long Island, here, where we live. Did you ever go to Vit-whats-ski?" I felt a bit dizzy from the possibility of this door to my grandmother's past cracking open and trying to tread carefully so she didn't slam it shut. "Did you ever go there?"

"Yes, I went there. I went more than once."

"How far was it from your village, Bubby?" This was so exciting. I was sure that no one in my family knew anything about this. It was like a normal conversation, different from the mood of the nighttime tales. I wondered if it had to be kept secret. "How far was it?"

"I don't remember." She paused, thinking. "Two days," she said triumphantly, as if a veil had been swept back for a clear glimpse.

"Two days? You walked for two days?"

This confused my grandmother. She had to focus again on a trip she had made over fifty years earlier. "No, Sarah, we didn't walk to Vitibsk." She was beginning to withdraw, I sensed.

"Did you go in a horse cart? Maybe a train? I can't tell how far away two days is if I don't know how you traveled." My frustration was about to overwhelm my caution. I took a calming breath and tried a new direction. "If I get out a map of Russia," I said as I reached for the children's atlas my mother had given me, "would you show me where you lived?" I opened the big book and flipped past all the American states that formed the first half, and turned as quickly as I could make sense of the maps, to Russia, before my grandmother could refuse. I remember that Bubby laughed nervously, seemingly unwilling or perhaps unable to make sense of a map. Anything involving reading and books terrified her. She held her right palm to the side of her face as I sat down next to her, on the edge of the bed. I moved the map into my grandmother's lap, and both of us looked down at it, uncomprehendingly. "Which part did you live in, Bubby? Where is Vitsky? It's a very big country, you know, where you came from." I was mispronouncing the city on purpose, hoping that my grandmother would find that amusing enough to stay involved in the topic and not so intimidated that she would shut down.

"I don't remember," Bubby said, clearly embarrassed. "Maybe here?' she said, pointing to a blue amorphous shape, obviously water. I laughed, thinking my grandmother was making a joke, teasing me, totally innocent of the depth of my grandmother's ignorance.

"That's a sea, Bubby! Stop kidding! Really. Show me where you took the train when you left for England. But how could a train go to England? There's water in the way." My enthusiasm was not as infectious as I hoped it would be. Maybe I was trying to squeeze too many questions into one little conversation. My grandmother was beginning to slide her legs around, and I had to stand up or be bumped to the floor. "Are you getting up, Bubby?"

"Yes, my Sarah, I'll go now to the bathroom. Help me with my shoes." Her voice had retreated into its more common plaint, and I knew the map search and the likelihood of any other information was over before it had begun. I dropped the atlas on the foot of the bed. I opened the laces of the black orthopedic shoes, unbent their broken backs, and lined them up for my grandmother's hobbled feet. "Don't worry, Bubby," I assured my grandmother as she struggled with the first shoe. "We can study the atlas later. Maybe I can ask Uncle Morty on Sunday. He must know where Ulla is."

"Nobody knows, Sarah. Just forget about it. It doesn't matter to anyone." Her feet were crammed into her shoes, the backs bent out of place again, and she was leaning forward off the edge of the bed, struggling into her unsteady upright position. "Don't bother Uncle Morty, Sarah. He doesn't know." She shuffled out of the bedroom, leaving me about to protest that I wouldn't be bothering him. But then I realized that this was another subject that my grandmother found agonizing, like almost everything from her past, and she coped by ignoring it. So I picked up the atlas and put it back into the empty slot in the little bookcase next to my bed. I ticked through the people I could question about my grandmother's decision to keep this simple question, where Ulla was, buried. Mother? Father? Aunts? Uncles? No one.

I sat down on the top step and bumped down the whole flight on my backside. The pleasure I used to get from this antic was gone. I knew I was too old, but I figured I'd give it a try. As I turned the corner into the kitchen, I realized that my mother was on the phone again.

"So she tells me, if you can believe it, that Mama can't come for the few days I ask, the one time a year I want to take my children to one event, she tells me it's out. I've been talking about this for months, Jean, months. I bought tickets for us." There was a pause and I could her Aunt Jean's voice but not make out any words. "No, Jean. That's not true. She told me weeks ago, remember when we were talking about Marly?"

Another pause as I sidled into the yellow bunk seat, trying to be invisible. "I don't want to rehash Marly, Jean. That's over, and good luck to the both of them. Poor Danny. But Jean, I'm telling you so you can call Ruthie up and give her a piece of your mind. You can take my side for once, Jean, it won't kill you!" My mother banged the phone down, but continued talking as if she were still connected to her sister Jean.

By this time, the meat that she had been rinsing salt off was tucked into a yellow enamel pot, blanketed by sliced onions and potato wedges, and simmering on the stove. The water was running in the sink over the white porcelain board, and my mother had turned her attention to scrubbing the residue of the meat with a vengeance that it did not require. "I don't care if she stays by herself. We're going to that ballet!"

"What ballet? Who'll stay alone?" I knew the answers to these questions, but I wanted to alert my mother that I was there so I wouldn't hear something I knew my mother would not want to explain. This dance was old and familiar to both of us. I recited my mother's response inside my head as it was spoken.

"Never mind."

"Why is Bubby still upstairs, Ma? Is she sick?"

"Well, she said she had pain when she got up this morning. I gave her one of her pills, and she fell asleep right away. Maybe she was just tired. Did you speak to her?"

"Yes. I showed her a map of Russia to try to get her to show me where she comes from." I was venturing near a shadowy subject. I was daring myself to open it, hoping that my mother would momentarily forget that she didn't want to discuss it, ever. But Rikki was vigilant.

"She would never be able to make sense of any map, Sarah. Anyway, that's all past history. Just forget it. Do you want a snack?"

In my imagination, a door slammed shut. Why was my grandmother's story so secret? One Sunday, all my aunts and uncles somehow had gotten on the subject, and I had heard for the only time, the story of Mary going to the train station dressed in her beautiful coat with the embroidery on the edge of the matching cape, and how everyone in her family had cried at the sad farewell as beautiful Mary set off to England to marry her handsome Avram. It never came up again. It was almost as if they knew that version of the story was a lie, but they preferred that rosy false scene to the ugly truth. No point in dwelling on it too much, though. It would not hold up under frequent scrutiny.

"Okay. Can I have hot chocolate and cinnamon toast?"

My mother balanced the porcelain board in the dish rack, dried her hands on her apron, and said, "Coming right up, Miss Sarah. Guess what! Did I tell you we are going to see "The Nutcracker Suite" next Sunday? Daddy, David, you and I are going to the city together. Does that sound good?"

I had overheard the organizing of these plans, but I wanted my mother to have the pleasure of surprising me. "The ballet! Really! Can I wear my velvet dress? Does Bubby know? Can she come, too?" This last question tumbled out by mistake. I knew that was impossible, and I hadn't really meant to ask it aloud.

"No, Sarah, she can't. She's either going to Aunt Ruthie's for the weekend, or maybe she'll stay here by herself. I think that will be fine, the more I think about it." My mother poured milk into a small white saucepan and turned to the cabinet to search for the cocoa tin. Her back facing me said, the discussion is closed; don't ask again.

I sat down at the table and studied the pattern on the tablecloth with my index finger. Bubby stay alone? What if she had an attack? I didn't know what exactly having an attack meant. An attack of what? But that was the phrase that was used, and it seemed to involve extreme pain, somewhere. But where, exactly? Her heart? Her stomach? Some other place? There was charged silence in the kitchen as my mother stood stirring the milk, and I sat tracing the flowers on the tablecloth. She poured the steaming cocoa into a cup and carried it to the table.

"Cinnamon toast, you said?"

"I changed my mind," I said softly. "I'll just have this for now. Okay?"

There was no reply, because my mother had slipped back into her angry mood, and I knew she was too guarded to trust that she could keep the venom back.

"Okay," I repeated.

My mother looked at me for a moment and seemed to focus her thoughts. Then replied. "Whatever you like, Sarah. Let me know if you change your mind back." And with that, she left the kitchen and I heard her footsteps going up the stairs, probably to check on her mother. I watched my hot cocoa cool, took a few small sips so my mother's efforts wouldn't have been wasted, and then walked to the sink and poured out the rest.

Thirteen

When I got into bed that night, my grandmother was wide-awake in her bed. The morning nap had ruined her usual bedtime sleepiness. I was still preoccupied with my fears about who would stay with Bubby on Sunday when the rest of the family went to see the ballet, and my fingers were smoothing the blanket absently, without my even knowing it.

"Should I finish about my trip on the train, Sarah?" Bubby's voice was full of energy. Did she even know about the argument that was raging between her two daughters?

I instantly tucked my hands inside the blanket, their worrying movements forgotten. "Yes! What did the train look like, Bubby?"

"What did it look like? It was a train. How do trains look?" She did not like to be distracted from the narrative thread she had in mind. "Didn't I tell you already once? It was big and black, with wood panels on the side that had red and gold painted trim, and words written in curly letters. There was a big chimney on the locomotive, and giant clouds of black smoke, blacker than Morty's cigar, much blacker, were coming out of it as the train came closer, like the smokestack was belching from a terrible stomach ache, maybe from spoiled meat. Then, the train wheels screeched like an old peasant selling turnips in the market on Thursday. I covered my ears to block out the noise. Then the smoke slowed down like the train's belly was starting to feel better, and it stopped at the little platform where I was waiting." She seemed, on second thought, to enjoy composing that description.

"What did the inside look like?" I was taking advantage of my grandmother's tone of voice, which seemed to welcome more questions about the train.

"Sarah, did you forget everything? I told you this, didn't I? I remember that the floor was made of wood. My boots hammered on the floor demanding attention, like I was an important person, as I walked along the aisle. I was looking for a seat, and I was also looking for someone to sit near who would be a safe companion for me. Many were making their way out of Russia then, you know that, right? But few were girls alone. At first, my train was almost empty. That's why I bribed the trainman. Remember I told you? And maybe that was better than another young girl." Her story paused then. But her voice wasn't tired, so I waited for it to continue.

"I think I took a little nap, but anyway, I kept my eyes closed for a while. The train stopped once in a while, and I could hear footsteps come near, and then go past. Some of the steps were heavy and shuffling, like a man would make if he were exhausted from his life. There were enough like that to explain the worn out wood down the center of the car. But some were light and frightened, almost like a bird trying to get out of the way of something. One time, I remember, I heard a noise like a herd, a big bubbling family, with children's excited voices, and a mother trying to shush them and a father who coughed like he had tuberculosis. When I peeked through my eyelashes, the trainman was always posed casually, nearby. He didn't let anyone sit near me. But after many hours, my hunger nagged me out of my drowsiness, so I sat straight. I could see we were pulling into a town, and I saw the trainman was coming right over to me. He touched the brim of his cap, very polite, and told me I could get off for a few minutes to find something to eat. I can still see him, making movements with his hand going to his mouth, like he was an actor in a play with no words, signaling to me that there would be food at this stop. I remember I pointed to the big carpetbag I had with me, to ask him if I could leave it if I got off the train for a few minutes. He pointed up and back to his own eyes and the bag. I knew I could trust him."

I listened from my bed, covers pulled up tight to my chin, and tried to picture myself in the role of my grandmother. Leave my home? Leave my mother and father? Never see David again? I understood that she had come to hate her father, but her mother? Maybe the problem was she already felt alone in her family. Her father hurt her, her mother didn't fix it, her sisters resented her, and her brothers were too involved with God to care about their sister and her worldly problems. Maybe stealing money and clothing and then making my way through the night to a railroad siding and bribing a man in a uniform who spoke a different language and belonged to the culture I had been taught to fear was not so impossible to believe. And here was Bubby, spinning out this tale with such authority in her voice, that I knew it was true.

"The wheels were screeching, like Aunt Jean when she's yelling at her children," my grandmother began again. I remember I giggled at the idea of my aunt sounding like the sound of metal squealing against metal, and I considered a rejoinder, but the story rolled on.

"I tried to look out the window to see where we were, what it looked like, but the windows were streaked with dirt, so I just stood up and straightened my hat. I saw right away that all the heads had turned to look at me. It was like I was the ruler of the car, and anything I told the passengers to do, they would bow to me and run to do it. But I ignored them; they were sad and broken peasants, and I was not one of them." She stopped for a moment, as if she were surveying her subjects. I heard her sniff, as if she had sensed some unpleasant odor. "I walked right down the middle of the car, clicking my boots very loud on purpose, so they'd know I was someone going someplace important, doing something important. They watched me, I could see from the corner of my eye. But I never looked at them directly. I think maybe they were examining Dvorah's coat, my coat, and wondering who could I be wearing such a rich coat, with silk embroidery on the edge. And then I stepped down to the platform. There were crowds of people here, all of them busy with their bags and baskets, and their children, all on their way out of their old lives, like me. There were women with black scarves around their heads, some selling bread, and some with flaky pastries filled with potato or maybe meat, even. A man was offering hot tea from a big samovar, and a few passengers were standing near him, sipping from tin cups. And the noise, Sarah, the noise of people crying out their goods, like a big market, bigger than the one in Ulla every Thursday, much bigger; it was dangerous, I thought, and exciting at the same time. And the train was right there, breathing its noises slowly, like resting after a big race, waiting next to this bazaar, which wasn't really a bazaar, you understand, just like one. And the train, it kept on breathing slowly, like a horse resting up for the next part of the journey. I saw men in uniforms like my trainman who were passing bags and trunks up the steps of the train cars, and the bags would disappear inside, pulled in by other men I couldn't see. The building there, the station building, Sarah, it was as grand as a palace."

I couldn't understand why my peasant grandmother with practically no experience outside her tiny village wasn't terrified of the scene she saw when she stepped out of the train. But she wasn't. As she described the setting, it was clear to me that my grandmother could see the scene she was describing, as if she were standing next to a big smoking train at a train station somewhere in Eastern Europe right at that moment. I heard the excitement in her voice, like she was in the middle of her quest to find Avram in London and start their lives together, and go on to live happily ever after. It was as if all of her future, the life she had already lived, was still the shiny unopened package it must have been back at that moment. It struck me as unspeakably sad and I began to cry quietly because I knew the future that my grandmother seemed to be blind to. I wished I could stop the story and freeze it forever right there, with the rosy anticipation of a golden future still in place. But then I realized, I wouldn't be there in my pink bedroom right then, listening. I wouldn't exist, and neither would my mother, or her family, or anything. And now, I have an even more harrowing realization, which is that life seems to require some ugly misery to propel it forward. Why would we move on with our lives if we couldn't have a sense that something better awaited us? Everything happens for a reason? The clichés fall into line.

"That station, Sarah, had the biggest building in the world, I thought at the time. It was taller, much taller, than the tallest trees in the forest where I went with my father, and it was red brick, with rows and rows of windows, and columns holding up a grand roof, and doors going in and doors going out. It was unbelievable, Sarah, just unbelievable." I tried to think of where this station could have been. But I had no inkling of what Eastern Europe looked liked in the very beginning of the twentieth century, which is when I figured this journey was taking place, and my grandmother was so immersed in the scene she must have been looking at in her head, there was no possibility of interrupting her to ask. I also knew that she probably didn't know where she was then, and never had.

"And then, in the middle of the yelling, and the children running in circles around their parents, and then crying as they were yanked back to those terrified adults, and did I tell you I even saw soldiers with uniforms and caps? Oh, Sarah, in the middle of the hegdish, I saw another girl, alone in the crowd, like me, traveling alone. But she was carrying a book, so not exactly like me." The last bit was in a slightly different voice. I knew what the word hegdish meant because Aunt Esther used it to describe any room that wasn't neat enough to suit her exacting standards. For a split second, I remembered when Aunt Esther had lifted the plate her husband was eating from to brush away the breadcrumbs that had accumulated as he ate, saying, "You're making a hegdish of my kitchen!" But my grandmother was rushing on, and the image of Aunt Esther evaporated.

"'Hello, Miss,' I said to her. She was bouncing, like, going from one foot to the other, very nervous. She was slight, like my sister, Tova, and she had a scarf with fringes along the edges that covered all her hair, very proper, and she was wearing glasses, spectacles, like a little professor she looked. And I could see her eyes through the glasses, big like saucers darting up and back, all around. She was frightened I could see, not sure what she should be doing. 'Are you traveling alone?' I asked her. I was laughing to myself because I was going to make use of this girl. We could make a good pair, because I had guts and brass, but she had a book, and do you know what that meant, Sarah? That meant she could read, and that reading would get me to London, I was sure of it."

She was triumphant, sure of herself, uninterested in her new companion's destination, and easily able to justify using her just as she had justified using her mother's savings. There was a side of Bubby, I realized then with a chill of an unpleasant discovery, like finding scattering bugs under a lifted log in the back yard that was selfish and cruel. I filed that understanding with the piece of my grandmother that valued appearance over all other assets. And then I tried not to keep looking at those facts.

The story seemed to have hit a pause. I was sure my grandmother had not fallen asleep, because I could hear her breathing interspersed with some soft groaning. "Are you feeling bad, Bubby?" I asked, beginning to push back the covers and sit up.

"No, Sarah, I'm fine. But I'm sad now."

"But why? This is a good part of the story. You even found a friend to go with."

"A friend, yes. But that's the sad part. I found someone to be my friend and help me, even though she didn't know me or anything about my past, and she never asked, so I didn't have to lie, which was good. And we did travel together, all the way to London, because she was going to her aunt there, her mother's sister, and that was good. And she knew how to go, she had it all written out in a letter from the aunt, where to take the train, where to change to a different train, how to go to Bremen, that was where we had to go to get the boat to London, who to look for in Bremen, an aid society that would be there, and they were there. Everything. I could tell you everything. I remember the whole trip, Sarah, I'll tell you everything. Sarah! Suddenly now, I remember the name of the river where I swam with Rivka, where my father. . . . Sarah, it was the Zapadnaya Dzvina!"

The Russian words slid off her tongue as if she spoke the language fluently every day of her life. She seemed to be waiting for me to comment on the name of the river, but just as I began to say what a beautiful name that was, my grandmother raced on as if she had nearly forgotten that I was there. "But one thing is gone, Sarah, one very important thing I can't remember." Now she was crying, moaning louder and louder. Any louder, and my mother would have exploded into my room demanding to know what was the matter, accusing her mother of being sick or me of some other infraction.

"Shh, Bubby, shh! Just tell me what it is you don't remember, and maybe I can help you." I never liked the scenes when my mother burst in, upset about something. It never sounded like she was upset, but rather that she was angry.

"No, Sarah, you can't help me. No one can help me. That girl who helped me, she even had food with her that she shared, that sweet young lady, the only person who ever saved me and took care of me, but God help me, the problem is that I can't remember her name. Her name, Sarah, her name is lost. I only remember how she helped me, took care of me, really, because without her, I would have never found London, never found Avram, never had children and in the end, Sarah, even you wouldn't be here. And I don't remember her name." She stopped speaking, and just whimpered softly.

I considered the implications of my grandmother's lament. The idea of never existing came back. It was a little scary, but probably an exaggeration, I thought, hopefully. Getting to London couldn't have been that mysterious, even if you couldn't read. After all, Bubby set out to do it herself in the first place. I knew it all meant more, but I wasn't sure what.

Now I understand more clearly. To my grandmother, the regret she felt because of her illiteracy was all tied up with the failures of her life, the abuse from her father, the indifference of her mother to what her father had done to her, the disdain of her siblings and their anger and resentment of her refusal to accept her lot in life, the constant squabbling of her children, and maybe even the mysterious loss of her son. I can see the threads all knotted up together in that one failure: to her, it was all because she couldn't read. The more I turn it over and over, the more I dissect the fragments and scraps of the story that I was told, the more I think my grandmother was wrong. The threads could be pulled apart a different way, and I think that the original knot, the one that held the whole tangled skein together, was not about deciphering letters and words. That, I think, came second. The real problem was how someone had taught my grandmother, and maybe it was her own abusive, misguided father, that her beauty mattered more than anything. The false values that she held right up to her death, after more than seventy years of evidence that beauty was a quality that had failed her, that was the real problem.

But I couldn't deny that every fairytale heroine was beautiful, and they all lived happily ever after, according to the stories. And I know that Aunt Jean had been the prettiest aunt, and she had more friends than all the other aunts put together. And look at all the movie stars: they were rich and famous, all because they were beautiful. Even in school, I remember that when my teacher had told the class that every child in the class was beautiful, everyone had laughed at how ridiculous the teacher was. No one thought everyone was beautiful, not really. And who had been the most popular? Gail Gordon, of course, who had also been the prettiest girl in the school.

The whole world had it wrong then, and it still does.

This problem had been too complicated for me, then. After listening to the tale of the now nameless friend, I was exhausted. I knew I had to think about my conclusion more. I turned over in my bed, pulled the blanket closer around me, and waited for sleep

to release me from my thoughts.

Fourteen

The Sunday of the trip to the ballet was unlike the usual Sundays of my childhood. None of my aunts or uncles, and none of their children would be coming to visit. There would be no pot roast aromas wafting out of the oven, no potato pancakes frying in oniony oil, and the cookie cabinet would be fully stocked at the end of the day, even though it was Sunday. But unlike the other rare Sundays without relatives, this one could not be explained by the absence of Mary.

During the summer, my grandmother usually stayed with Aunt Ruthie and her family in their bungalow rental in Rockaway, and so on those Sundays, the family gathered at the seaside for their weekly visit. And on rare occasion, Bubby visited one of her other children in their cramped apartments, so everyone would squeeze themselves together in another kitchen. But this rainy, cold November Sunday was one of those occasions. This was the day that Rikki had decided that her half-paralyzed mother could be left on her own while the family drove to the city for a presentation of the Nutcracker Suite. As it turned out, my understanding of the family outing was not quite accurate, and ordinarily, finding out at the last second that some major fact had been kept from me would upset me enough to make me anxious. What did it mean? Why wasn't I told? Did it mean there was an even bigger, more dangerous secret? But this time, I was so fretful about leaving my grandmother with only Mac the dog to keep her company, that when Rikki casually mentioned the change in plans, I barely registered a quiver.

"Daddy's coming along with us for the ride to the city, Sarah, but he's not going to the ballet." Rikki spoke over her shoulder as we were getting into the car. I had been waving tentatively to my grandmother, who was standing just inside the door to the kitchen. My brother and father were walking down the path towards the car. I shifted my focus from her grandmother's gesturing hand, which was signaling me to go and have a good time, to my father. I saw that he wasn't wearing a shirt and tie, standard for city visits, but an open neck knit shirt.

"But why? I thought this was for the whole family," I was momentarily distracted from her grandmother. "Then why can't he stay here with Bubby?" I was dangerously close to whining, something my mother had no tolerance for.

"Sarah," said Rikki barely masking her exasperation at her daughter's constant worrying. "We're all going to the city, just as we planned. But Daddy is going to visit a friend of his while we are at the ballet. Do you want to know who the friend is?" The last bit, the question, was said with a jaunty smile, as if she were trying to change the mood, or just distract her daughter.

I looked back to the kitchen door as my father and brother opened their car doors. I barely heard my mother speak to me. My grandmother was gone, and the door inside the storm door was closing.

"Sarah? Do you?"

My attention snapped back to my mother. The two car doors slammed in quick succession. My father started the engine, tooted the horn twice, and put the car in reverse.

"Do I what?" I tried to concentrate.

"Do you want to know who Daddy's friend is?" Joe laughed, and began to make exaggerated monkey noises. David laughed uproariously, even though the noises weren't that funny.

"Okay. I do. Who is the friend?" Joe and Rikki looked at each other and laughed while I gazed back and forth between the two of them. I found my parents' mood a little contagious, and I smiled, too. "Who, who, who? I'm asking, but you keep laughing."

"You sound like an owl, Sarah," said my father. "Whooooo, whooooo, whooooo," he teased me, and then the car was filled with silly gales of laughter as we turned the corner and made our way toward the highway that would bring us to our day in the city.

"No, really, who is the friend?" I asked when we were all composed again.

"Daddy is going to the zoo in Central Park, Sarah. He wants to visit a certain ape that lives there." Rikki dissolved into giggles again. I thought the idea of paying a call on an ape was as funny as my mother seemed to think it was. I smiled as I pictured my father and a big hairy ape on opposite sides of a cage wall having a conversation.

"When the ballet is over, he'll meet us right outside the theater. We'll all go home together."

Somehow, David didn't start complaining that he wanted to go to the zoo with his father, instead of the ballet. The car was filled with silence, but it wasn't an angry or resentful silence. But I was troubled by the plan in spite of also seeing the humor in it. I didn't see why my father was coming at all, and why he couldn't stay home and work on one of his projects and keep an eye on my grandmother. I knew they loved each other, and I knew it couldn't be that he had refused that duty. I couldn't imagine the discussion that had led to this plan. I remembered that my mother had said that there were four tickets for the ballet. Just as I was about to re-open the discussion and ask what happened to the fourth ticket, an explosive burst of lightning flashed across the sky and seconds later, a huge crack of thunder broke the silence. It was so loud and insistent, that everyone actually involuntarily ducked their heads for a second.

"What was that?" Rikki asked, leaning forward to scan the sky. "I never heard such loud thunder in my life!"

David examined the sky outside his window, but seemed more awed than frightened. I felt tears well up and splash over onto my cheeks. Without really understanding what I was crying about, and not wanting my mother to know I was crying, I turned toward my window and let the tears spill silently. I surreptitiously used the corner of my coat collar to try to absorb some of the liquid, but it was made of velvet, and it just smeared the wetness around. I wiped my face with the back of my hand, and tried to take a deep breath that would calm me.

"I didn't even realized the sky had darkened," remarked Joe. "We were laughing so much about that ape, the storm just snuck up on us." The rain had begun to pelt the car, and Joe slowed the car, as the visibility was growing obscure. We drove on, but our speed was down to a crawl.

"Will we make it to the ballet?" I asked.

"There she goes," said Rikki, her annoyance at me nearly instantaneous. "If there's something to worry about, we can count on Sarah. Of course we'll make it to the ballet. Haven't you ever seen a rainstorm before? Maybe you can worry about the bugs drowning, Sarah, or the dogs getting wet in their masters' backyards."

Rikki was irritated, and only trying to make me see there was nothing to be alarmed about, but her last comment had the opposite effect. I could now picture Mac in the yard, attached to the long chain in his dog run, trembling, with cascades of water pouring off his back, and down his legs. I imagined him out there in this sudden storm, howling with fear and discomfort, wanting someone to come outside and unclip his lead and take him into the warm, dry house and give him a dog biscuit to comfort him. But no one could come, because all his possible saviors were encased in this car, barreling slowly away from him, unable to hear him or help him.

"Oh!" I gasped involuntarily. "Mac is outside. Who will bring him in? He must be soaked."

"Don't give it a thought, Sarah," said Joe calmly. "Mac will not mind being wet in the least. He's an outside dog, Sarah. He doesn't care about a little rain storm." I sniffled a few times, but felt calmer after my father's reassurance. I knew he was right about Mac. He would probably howl at the thunder to show it he was boss, and hunker down under a bush to wait out the storm.

After the initial exuberance of the storm, the weather settled into a steady cold downpour, punctuated with an occasional patter of sheets of sleet. Joe picked up speed and before long he stopped in front of a theater, and his ballet-bound family darted out of the car and across the puddle-strewn sidewalk. I glanced back over my shoulder just as I got to the door to the lobby that my mother was holding open for me. I saw my father pilot the car into a stream of taxis and buses. I hoped he was right about the dog.

As it turned out, the ballet was magical. The audience was made up of groups of children chaperoned by an adult or two, and everyone was dressed up in party clothes. All the girls wore plaid taffeta dresses with satin sashes, I noticed, similar to the one I wore. Some of the boys had on ties and navy blue blazers, but some were dressed like David, in neat argyle patterned sweaters and corduroy pants. The mothers were in suits that nipped in at their waists, and the fathers looked like they were going to go to their offices right after the performance, even though it was a Sunday. I felt uncomfortable that my father was spending time with an ape while all these other fathers seemed to be enjoying the ballet. But my uneasiness evaporated when the music and dancing began, and the story of the little girl and her dream absorbed my complete attention. When the Christmas tree began to grow, right on the stage in front of them, and it began snowing what I would have sworn was real snow, David actually stood up in front of his seat, rapt with wonder. Rikki could not persuade him to sit again, but no one seemed to mind. And then, in a flash, the curtain came down, the lights in the theater came up, and it was over.

Before the mood began to fade, while the pictures and sounds were still rich in my mind, my brother, my mother and I were installed back in the car with my father, and we were on our way home.

"My friend, the ape, sends his regards," said Joe. And the magical spell of the ballet was broken. I realized, with a sickening feeling in my stomach, that it was still raining, that Bubby was still alone, that the dog was still outside, and that we were far away in the city, and wouldn't be home for at least another hour. Every light we stopped at took an eternity to turn green. There was endless traffic lined up to get into the tunnel. Horns sounded in a dissonant concerto. Finally I couldn't bear it any longer.

"Isn't there another way to go?"

"Yes, there is," answered Rikki instantly. "But we picked this traffic jam for your entertainment. Do you like it?"

I heard Joe say, "Shh," to his wife, and I stared out the window as the cars took turns merging into ever fewer lanes until they blended into the two rows that disappeared into the tunnel. I watched the white lights flash by as we made our way under the river. I wondered if we were in a tube that floated through the middle of the water, and fretted that it might spring a leak while we were driving through to the other side. Or, maybe worse, if the tunnel bored under the river bed, through tons of mud and rocks that could shift and tear a hole in the walls, and sheets of murky mud and river water would begin to engulf the car. My mother was right about me: I worried about the hidden dangers lurking everywhere. But my mother never asked me about the source of my anxieties. She was angry but not motivated to understand it or help me overcome it.

But then we suddenly reached the light and air and the toll on the other side. And before long, we were retracing our morning route in reverse. When we passed beyond the stone gate that marked the beginning of Nassau County, I knew we'd be home before long. It was still pouring that cold nasty rain down, but now I felt like my mother had been right all along. We'd be back in our house, telling Bubby stories about the ballet, and the ape, and the tree growing, and we'd be eating warmed up mushroom and barley soup, and all would be back in its usual place. I felt silly to have worried about everything so much, and I resolved to have a more light-hearted attitude in the future. The world was full of jokes and ballets and children in party clothes. I would be enjoying things more, from now on. And Rikki would be calmer, too, I thought, if I could stop giving her things to feel angry about.

Joe steered the car into the driveway, and slowed to a stop. "Home again, home again, jiggety jog," Rikki recited. She always said this at the end of one of their trips, and usually David and I joined in for the "jiggety jog" part. We knew every nursery rhyme by heart, and even though we were too old to find most of them entertaining any more, this one always happily punctuated our returns. I got out of the car, and puddle hopped my way to the kitchen door.

But something was wrong. The door was open, and the house felt as cold as the outside. Instantaneously, the magic of the ballet evaporated. "Bubby! Where are you?" I called nervously. "Bubby!" I screamed louder as I ran through the downstairs and bounded up the stairs, knowing that my grandmother wouldn't have tried to go up herself. I burst into my bedroom, but of course, both beds were empty. She was not in the house.

By this time, my parents had realized that Mary was not in the house. I heard my mother say to no one, "Did Mayshe come for her? Why didn't he tell me he was coming?"

But Joe had run through the breezeway that separated the kitchen door from the garage. As he got to the back yard, he called back to his wife, "Rikki! She's here! Get some blankets ready!" I could hear his voice filtering into the house from the back yard, and I ran to the window in my parent's room that overlooked the dog run. I tore the drape aside and tried to see through the rain-smeared window. But I could see only a smudge of color on the muddy ground. It was the gray of my grandmother's coat, and I could make out the outline of Mac standing right over the fallen old woman. I automatically tried to wipe the window clear, but of course the rain was on the outside. I reached up to the sash and tried to push the window open, but it was stuck.

"Oh, my God. Mac killed Bubby." I stood paralyzed at the window, and saw my father's figure bend down over the gray smear. I was shocked by what I was seeing, and tried again to lift the window to see more clearly. The action outside was confused and unclear, like an Impressionist painting examined at very close range, but moving around. Nothing was distinguishable, just blobs of moving and still color.

A David smear moved unevenly across the scene, I knew his red jacket, and it leaned toward the brown smear of Mac. He must have unclipped Mac's lead, because the brown smudge began to jump around the backyard landscape. Then a smear of navy blue, like Rikki's coat, entered from the left, and darted erratically across the panorama, sometimes one blotch of color moving ahead, and sometimes another, holding a tangle of colors like the quilted blanket that I was supposed to have carried upstairs before we left, but I had forgotten to do. I continued to watch the splotched drama unfold outside the window. My father took the quilt from my mother, bent down and spread it quickly across the gray smudge on the ground. Then, with one effort, he hefted the whole bundle together into his arms, stood up, and made his way jerkily across the yard and out of the scene. The rest of the blobs of uneven color followed him, leaving me staring at the wet, empty yard.

A noisy commotion entered the kitchen door, and I could hear my mother distinctly above the other voices. "This is on Ruthie's head. This is on Esther's head. This is on Jean's selfish head. I couldn't have one day, not one day. Sarah! Where are you? Get down here!" And then her voice changed, as she spoke to someone else. "Yes, I need an ambulance for my mother." I knew it was her phone voice. "She fell and was outside in the rain for I don't know how long. No, we just this second found her, I don't know what her temperature is. Just can you get over here?" And then she gave the address.

I snapped to my senses. Mac had not killed my grandmother. I dashed down the stairs and ran to the couch where my father had laid Mary, and was bending over her rubbing her good hand between his two hands. "Ma! Ma! Can you hear me? What were you doing outside in this weather? Oh, there you are Sarah. Go get more blankets, will you do that?" He spoke quietly to me.

"I'll get the one from my bed. It's very warm." I ran up the stairs, ripped the blanket off my bed and was back down in the living room before I could even form new thoughts. I heard my grandmother's voice, very faint, as I approached with the blanket.

"I went out to get Mac, poor dog. He was wet, Joe, and howling. It was a pity on him. I just went carefully to him. I put on my coat, Joe, so you shouldn't worry. But he was so excited to see me, the dog, that he was jumping around. I'm sorry to cause so much problems here. I lost my balance, you know, while I was bending down to open the leash."

"How long were you laying there, Ma? How long?" Joe asked her gently.

"Not long, Joe, just a little while. I'm sorry I'm causing such a problem. I'm fine now. Please, I'll just rest here."

"Ma, you're soaked through. Rikki called an ambulance. She's waiting in the front with David for it. They'll be here in a minute. Don't worry, Ma. You'll be fine."

"Please, Joe. No ambulance. I don't want to go to a hospital and get killed there. Please, tell Rikki to send them away."

I stood listening, too terrified to speak. My father realized suddenly that I was there, and he took the blanket from me and tucked it tightly around his mother-in-law. "I should have stayed with you." But this apology was more to himself than to anyone listening. "She'll be fine, Sarah. Just stay out of the way."

I heard the siren before I understood what it was. Then there was a bustle of men with equipment, like oxygen tanks, and an IV pole, and a stretcher. And while I clung to the wall, scarcely breathing, my grandmother was lifted onto the stretcher and carried out the front door. The blanket from my bed was left in a crumpled pile on the floor, and the sound of the siren began again, and then grew quickly fainter until it disappeared. I peeled myself away from the wall, and walked over to the blanket. I picked it up and buried my face in it, not crying, and barely breathing.

"Sarah, your mother rode in the ambulance with Bubby. We'll stay here and later one of your aunts will bring her home." I nodded to my father, and then the sound of his footsteps retreated. Then I heard him call from the stairs, "Sarah, she'll be fine. You go to bed now. She'll be fine. Tomorrow is school." And then I heard his footsteps going up the stairs. I stood in the living room clutching my blanket. Nothing was fine, I thought. Everything was wrong. I felt like the new resolve I had felt in the car to look at the world in a more carefree way was wrong. If I worried, that would be like an insurance policy. I would be ready for all the unseen dangers. If anything turned out happily, it would be a bonus, like a surprise party that you really didn't know about.

Fifteen

"I'm very lucky, Sarah, you know, very healthy," my grandmother seemed to be bragging. And she had only just come home from the hospital. The absurdity of her comment struck me like Milton Berle wearing a dress on TV: it just made no sense. Here was a half-paralyzed lady, so ancient that she had grown up without electricity, without cars, without anything that I recognized as ordinary, a lady whose life story was filled with misery and misfortune. This is lucky? I sat quietly by my grandmother's bedside, waiting for an explanation.

"Look, Sarah, I'm here in my bed, in your room, warm and comfortable again. You see? I told your mother I didn't need the hospital. A little rain, that's all. So what?"

"Bubby, it wasn't a little rain. And you fell, remember? You could have broken a bone. And you had fever, remember? You had to go to the hospital. Remember all the tests they did? Now you're fine, yes, but last week you weren't fine at all. And you scared me to death! No more going out to rescue dogs, okay? Mac doesn't mind being wet; I'm sure of it. He was probably howling at a bird or a squirrel. Or maybe he heard the mailman. You know he doesn't like the mailman. Remember that time my mother's new license came in the mail, through the mail slot? And Mac grabbed it as it came in and chewed it to pieces. He sure showed that mailman, didn't he?" My grandmother and I laughed at the memory. I remembered that Rikki had not thought it was the least bit funny at the time, especially when she had had to spend an entire afternoon at the Motor Vehicle Bureau trying to get her new license replaced.

"Do you want to drink some juice, Bubby? I could get you some fresh juice. This glass smells sour." I had lifted the glass from the night table to my nose.

"No, Sarah, I don't want to drink orange juice in the middle of the day. I'm only in bed because your mother is nervous that I'll get fever again, and I don't want to make her crazy. But if you like, I could tell you about my first boat ride. Does that sound good?"

I couldn't believe that I was about to hear one of my grandmother's stories in broad daylight. Up to that point, it was only the cover of night that enabled Bubby to speak. I had thought that if my grandmother could actually see me, look at my face as she unfolded the tale, her voice would be as paralyzed as her left hand. But now she actually seemed cheerful about beginning a new chapter right in the middle of the afternoon.

Since her return from the hospital, Bubby had been in unusually good spirits and very full of life. I recognized it as part of my grandmother's pattern: every time she had to see a doctor, even for an ordinary check up, she became skittish and brooding. But then, right after she was pronounced healthy and free of the cancerous tumors she was sure would be coming to claim her momentarily, her demeanor soared and she had a burst of energy that seemed to subtract years from her age. She dreaded doctors and blood tests, but as soon as the news was good, she delighted in having cheated death again, and practically flirted with the doctors and nurses. It was like the nervousness before was a magic charm of some kind. And when the spell worked, it was like an elixir. And the quick recovery after her fall in the yard was having the same effect as a clean health report. Maybe I was more like her than I had ever realized. Maybe I learned how to negotiate the world from her, and maybe she saw that in me and it began to explain why I was the grandchild that was being let in on all her secrets.

"Of course I would! Do you want me to go over to my bed while you tell?" I was in the process of standing up from the edge of my grandmother's bed.

"No, stay right here, Sarah." My grandmother had grabbed the sleeve of my sweater, and yanked me back to my perch. She left her hand on my arm and the connection between them felt sturdy and safe.

"So you remember that I took a train, right?" I knew there was no need to answer. I nodded, in case my grandmother needed confirmation in this new daylight setting. But almost immediately, I could see that she was slipping back in time, looking at the small light fixture on the ceiling of our bedroom, but seeing herself as a young woman in a train station in Eastern Europe. It seemed like a veil of hypnosis had dropped over my grandmother; her face relaxed, erasing some of the deep lines that were gouged in her forehead and around her mouth, and an involuntary sigh of relief escaped from her lips. The grip on my arm stayed firm, however.

"That young woman, that lovely girl I met, we went back into the train, and I led her to my seat. We sat together for the rest of the trip; we changed trains together in Warsaw, following the instructions she had on her paper. We even leaned on each other's shoulders and slept when we got tired. I remember it was a long trip, and the train stopped many times and picked up more people just like us, looking to get out. Everyone was scared, I remember, with children crying, and some men trying to pray in the morning and the evening. People kept looking in their little money pouches, counting and recounting their money, trying to hide what they were doing because if you didn't have certain papers, like a passport or something, you had to bribe the guards. Everyone had to do it; it was a secret that everyone knew, so I don't know what they were trying to hide. Once, even I started to cry. 'What, Mary, what is it?' she asked me. I wouldn't tell

her, but the truth was, I was crying for myself, because I didn't have Rivka anymore, and

I was afraid I didn't have Avram waiting for me. I would never tell that, not to anyone,

and right away I thought maybe my fears were wrong. As soon as he saw me there in

London, he would run from that Esther Bagoudis, the one in the letter, run back to me

like a fire was burning behind him. I dried my eyes, and I never cried another tear about

Avram, never again in my life." I could see the young Mary sit up straight and square her

shoulders as the train carried her west toward England.

"And then we came to the German border. Everyone got off the train, I mean all

of us, the Jews, and the men and women went to separate little buildings. There, we

could bathe, and we saw doctors, and they fumigated us! I wasn't so scared then because

I felt myself getting closer and closer to London. I washed off all the filth of my past

while my friend held my coat and my skirt and shirtwaist and my boots. And then I held

hers while she bathed. But we were afraid to speak to each other out loud, because we

didn't know if our language would be the thing that sent us back. So we signaled to each

other, and it was hard to understand everything, and before long, we were laughing, it

was such a comical scene!" Mary's eyes danced as she remembered the laughter that

must have broken the tension of that moment.

"Our train went to Bremen, I remember because we had a neighbor called

Bremen, a leather worker he was, he tanned the leather. He looked like leather himself.

So in Bremen, we had to go to the seaside for a boat. But it wasn't far, I think." She

squinted at the ceiling, trying to conjure up a clear picture of her travels, but she shook

her head in frustration. "I don't remember how we got to the boat." She narrowed her eyes again and strained to see into the past. But that piece of the story was gone. I almost interrupted her to tell her it didn't matter, to just go on. I opened my mouth and almost uttered a sound, but caught myself. I didn't want to distract my grandmother and maybe break the spell. Luckily, my grandmother's voice continued.

"But I remember the boat. It was a small steamer, and it sailed four times a week. My friend knew. I remember we came just in time, and we paid money, the man said, 'Fifteen shillings, Miss,' I can see him standing by the boat. I didn't know what he meant, but it was the first time I heard English, so I kept repeating it to myself, 'Fifteen shillings, Miss,' like a prayer. And I still know it: 'Fifteen shillings, Miss,' he said." She paused, thinking over the significance. "It was a prayer, just like a blessing. And the boat took almost a whole day and night to cross the water. I never closed my eyes for a second, because as soon as I saw the land, I knew my new life would begin. The boat rolled around in the water, I remember, and some people got sick. Who knew from sea voyages where we came from? But I wasn't sick. I was almost floating in the air!"

The afternoon was passing, and I was afraid that my mother would be calling up the stairs at any moment to announce that she was bringing Bubby's dinner up on a tray. Just as Bubby was about to step off the boat onto English soil, that interruption would be a disaster. I crossed my fingers on both hands to stave off that intrusion.

"You had to be lucky when the boat docked, too. I saw a woman rejected by a man in a uniform, I think he was a doctor, because we were lined up, and he was examining each person's eyes, pulling down the lids, looking for something there. And she started to weep, and she even dropped down on her knees right there in front of him, begging. But, no, a man in a uniform came and pulled her up to her feet, and dragged her from the line and she was sent straight back to the shtetl where she started. I don't know

what her family did. Maybe the children went on with the husband without her. It was

awful to watch, but it had nothing to do with me. I turned my head away. I was lucky,

like I told you. And my friend and I had addresses with us, where we were going, which

you needed. I was going to 24 Whitechapel Road." Her voice, when she spoke the

address, became almost childlike, like the recitation that a first grader gives on the first

day of school.

"Then the night passed, and just when it became light enough to see, we sailed

right up the Thames River, and then we saw a big bridge right in front of us, bigger than

anything I ever saw, even bigger than that train station I told you about. I thought, now

I'm going to die, after coming so far, because I thought the ship would crash into the

bridge for sure. But no, we didn't crash. The bridge began to open right in the middle. It

was like a miracle, because just in time, the bridge got out of the way of the boat. And

then the boat turned toward the edge of the river, and we stopped at a dock. Again we

lined up, like cows coming in from the pasture, and we were put ashore right near the

bridge that opened, it was called, Sarah, I remember, Tower Bridge, just by the Tower of

London. Oh, it was so grand. It was really a new century. I thought I was dreaming,

back on the train and dreaming. But it was real. I could see warehouses, made of yellow

bricks, and big cranes, like giant storks, with necks that reached up to the sky, all around

the landing area, lifting bundles of this and that onto some boats, and off of others. Men

in tight fitting caps that covered their heads like yarmulkes, but bigger, were pushing big

wagons piled high with goods, everyone going someplace important. And the noise! I

held my hands to my ears! But I was afraid to put down my carpetbag, so I held it tight and tried to ignore the roar and tumult going on all around me. It was like a swirl of noise, like a whirlwind summoned by a dybbuk.

"There were certain women there, right where we got off the boat, trying to herd all the newcomers together, like a sheepdog gathers his flock. They swept us together, and suddenly I realized they were speaking Yiddish to us! Oh, the relief! People spoke my language in England. I never knew! What a wonderful country this would be! There were organizations of women, all with sashes that had lettering on them, and my friend read them to me: 'The Jewish Association for the Protection of Girls and Women,' 'The Board of Guardians for the Relief of the Jewish Poor,' 'The Hebrew Ladies Protective Society.' I remember them all, Sarah. And all were shouting to us that they would take care of us until we found our way, keep us from 'white slavers.' But then my friend saw her aunt, and in a second, she hugged me, and ran into her aunt's arms and out of my life forever. I don't know how that aunt knew what day to come. I just stood alone for a moment. And then I straightened my hat, pulled my coat down neatly in the front, and walked straight off the docks, keeping my head up, gripping my bag, wearing my beautiful coat, right into London. All the streets were paved with stones, and I could just walk along to find Avram. And I'm lucky, I keep telling you, because I spoke that address, 24 Whitechapel Road, to every person I passed, and each one pointed me closer and closer. No one would make me a slave; who would dare? My boots clicked right along the cobblestones proudly, and I think I must have looked like I was surrounded by a vapor of protection. Maybe angels were carrying me along. But I think I was alone. I was alone with my beauty. I told you I was beautiful, Sarah, didn't I tell you that before? It was safe and I knew it, because people are afraid of beauty; they think it has power, and so it does. I walked right to the door of 24 Whitechapel Road, and I got there when the streets were bustling with women carrying string bags of vegetables, with small children tagging along after them, holding on to the folds of their mothers' skirts, and men carrying trays and bundles on their shoulders. I held my bag, looked up at the building, a house with a polished stone step in front of it and rows of windows looking down at the street, and then I knocked."

"Sarah, where are you? Are you up there?" Rikki's voice broke the spell. My grandmother released her grip of my arm, and blinked her eyes a few times, as if she were waking up from a nap. Her forehead knitted itself into a frown, and she ran her tongue around her dry lips.

"Can you give me the juice, Sarah?" she asked. "I'm very dry."

"Sarah!" my mother's voice was more insistent. "Is Bubby awake? Please tell her I'm bringing her tray up in five minutes. Help her go to the bathroom, please." And then her footsteps retreated to the kitchen.

"I think the juice is sour, Bubby. How about some water instead?"

"I don't care. Sour is fine."

"Let me help you go to the bathroom. Your dinner will be up in a minute."

"It's dinner already? What happened to the afternoon, Sarah? Was I asleep?"

I found it a little disturbing that my grandmother didn't seem to remember that she had been speaking to her, telling me a story, for the past, how long? An hour, maybe? How come she didn't know? But then I realized: it was part of our barely spoken conspiracy. I got to listen to the stories that would tell the truth about my grandmother's past, and both of us went on pretending that it wasn't happening. Bubby knew very well where the afternoon had gone. But together, we would pretend it had slipped away unnoticed. No reason to ask any questions, or offer any explanations.

"Yes, Sarah, please help me to the bathroom. Where are my shoes?"

I leaned over, reached for the black orthopedic oxfords and straightened up the flattened backs, even though I knew her grandmother's misshapen feet would collapse them over again as she pushed her toes inside. "Here you are, Bubby. And when you get back, I'll puff up the pillows so you can sit up to eat. I wonder what you're having?"

As she stood up, my grandmother fixed her gaze on me. "You see, Sarah, my beautiful, I'm telling you everything. You'll know, you'll understand, and for you, all will be well. And I'll be free of it all."

But wasn't she already free? I didn't understand her words, exactly, but I knew she was using her story to help me, somehow.

And so the conspiracy continued, a separate world spinning on inside our house, seemingly oblivious to the actual world that was also spinning along, right beside it.

Sixteen

The winter wore on, gathering puzzles and unsolved mysteries as it went. When Rosemary Mullens asked her, Miss Sullivan, my teacher, told the class she'd like a man for Christmas. She was smiling as she responded. Miss Sullivan was usually stern and serious, so this demeanor was unfathomable. I pictured a tall man with a narrow mustache wearing a gray suit and a wide tie that looked like the wallpaper in the front hall, trying without success to fold himself into a box that would go under Miss Sullivan's Christmas tree. He was holding the lid of the box in his right hand, a red bow flopping around helplessly, as he tried bending his knees this way and that. Each time he crouched down, he twisted his head and neck a new way, attempting to become compact enough to disappear into the box. He raised the lid above his head as if he could set it securely on top by pulling his hand in at the last second. His face contorted and grimaced with each new failure, and as I watched the scene I was imagining, I grew more and more distraught that Miss Sullivan's Christmas would never be granted to her.

I found it almost impossible to concentrate on the lesson that had begun, about Russia having shot a rocket up into space. "President Eisenhower is calling for more serious science instruction for all American children so that you can all grow up and beat the Russians in the race," Miss Sullivan was announcing. I watched her face carefully to judge the significance of her proclamation. She had a wide mouth and long teeth that often had a smudge of pink lipstick across them. But there was no smile this time, and that meant it was serious, maybe even grim. Was there to be an actual race, like at the annual gym demonstration? I was a fairly fast runner, I knew, but I was better at rope climbing. Could this help in some way? I could see the whole school marching into the gym, everyone whistling "Grand Old Flag," which I began to hum in my head. I really knew the race wouldn't be about running and climbing, but Miss Sullivan had gone on to talk about something called the International Geophysical Year, set to begin when we returned after the new year, and since it was impossible to know what that would be, I had slipped into thinking about actual physical events. When the word Russia penetrated my worries, my thoughts shifted to a new scene in which my class lined up at the classroom door and filed silently into the hallway, faced the wall, and waited for a bomb to hit us or a bell to ring signal that all was well, and we could traipse back into our room and resume our lessons. At the word rocket, the imaginary scene shifted, and I could see everyone crawling under their desks as Miss Sullivan quickly lowered the blinds so that we wouldn't be hit by flying glass.

Relief from the fearsome thoughts finally came when Mrs. Taylor, the music teacher, arrived to summon the chorus members to our rehearsal for the Christmas concert. I lined up with the other altos, behind the sopranos. I wished I could sing soprano; somehow I had come to understand that it was a higher accomplishment. I looked at the children who were left in their seats, and worried that they must have felt even worse than I, a lowly alto. They weren't singers at all. During regular music class, they were called "mouthers," and they weren't allowed to try out for chorus. And what did they do back in the classroom while the chorus rehearsed? I envisioned them putting their heads down on their desks, too morose to even talk to one another.

I walked silently down the hall, staying close to the wall, one finger of my right hand brushing lightly along the cool green tiles that mounted nearly to the ceiling. I watched the back of Barbara Helper's head right in front of me, with its fiery red curls breaking disobediently out of the wide barrette that was clipped crookedly at nape of her neck. If it were my barrette that had become crooked, I thought, I'd want to know, and I almost tapped Barbara on the shoulder to tell her to straighten it. But we weren't allowed to talk in the hall, especially on the way to chorus rehearsal, when we were supposed to be thinking about getting our voices ready to sing. So I shifted my gaze to the floor tiles, and concentrated on keeping the toes of my shoes inside the lines of the dark green and light green boxes. I began to run through the lyrics of the songs we were to sing, and that stirred a new uneasiness in my thoughts.

The plan was to perform before the parents on the evening right before the last day of school before vacation started. On the last day, there would be a party, with cupcakes and exchanges of Christmas cards and gifts for Miss Sullivan, so there would be no homework worries to interfere with the performance. The entire program consisted of Christmas music, from light-hearted numbers like "Deck the Halls," to serious selections, like an aria from "Amahl and the Night Visitors." The evening would end with a very solemn rendition of "Silent Night," first in German, and then in English. None of us understood German, but we had memorized the German lyrics one guttural syllable at a time.

Every moment of the preparations for the concert had made me feel like an alien from another planet. I didn't know any of the Christmas carols when we were first given the sheets of music, and I watched nervously as everyone around me seemed to be able to sing without looking at the printed words. I opened and closed my lips, and gave voice to the tunes, which I did recognize, but since I felt like I was the only one who had to read the words, I studiously did not look at my song sheets. I memorized them at home as quickly as I could, before anyone could notice my ignorance. That hurdle accomplished, I could turn my attention to an even worse discomfort: speaking German. I had learned about Germans from my aunts and uncles. Usually my mother's sisters and brothers confined their gossip and complaints almost exclusively to members of the family or to the people they encountered in their daily lives. No one ever had an honest butcher, for example. Every single butcher in New York was a goniff, the aunts groused as they sat around the kitchen table during their Sunday visits. "I hope he burns forever," Aunt Esther would spit. "I saw him with his thumb on the scale, right there in front of my eyes. He even left a bloody fingerprint! I wouldn't shop by him again if he begged me!"

And dentists also came in for criticism. They were only in their offices to inflict damage to the teeth of their patients, they griped. My relatives interrupted each other as each one told an even more harrowing tale of the iniquities of the dental profession. "Look at this," Uncle Mayshe demanded, banging his left hand on the table as he held back the side of his mouth with his right one and twisted his head around. Everyone craned to see into his gaping mouth, including me who leaned into the kitchen from my perch at the door. "That louse dentist left me with a hole in my jaw! I'm supposed to chew on these teeth?" he grumbled rhetorically. They all nodded knowingly, and were silent for a moment until the sound of a child crying as he banged down the stairs interrupted them and refocused them to a new crisis.

But wishing a fire on someone's head, or calling another a louse was understood to be just conversation. When they wanted to express wholehearted opprobrium, when they wanted to describe the depths of human depravity, when they wanted to define someone as so evil as to be unredeemable, even to God, the word they reached for was

Nazi. They spoke the word as a snarl, their eyes narrowed and their nostrils dilated as if they had smelled something horrible, like the cadaver of a rat that had been poisoned and left to rot in a cellar. And Nazis were Germans, I knew. "No one in my family would ever buy any German product," my mother often pronounced as a proud declaration. She repeated this every time they passed a Volkswagen on the road. "And Wagner," she always hastened to add as if music had been the topic of the conversation, "was Hitler's favorite composer, that Nazi." The lesson was learned. Germans were scary, evil, and waiting to rise up again and enslave us all, or worse.

Singing a Christian song in German was terrifying and made me feel like an unwelcome outsider. I couldn't understand the serene faces of everyone around me.

The line of students arrived at the auditorium and we began practicing how to mount the risers that had been set up for them, "Without sounding like a herd of elephants," smiled Mrs. Taylor, and then how to file off in an orderly way. I adored my music teacher, but wouldn't dare approach her about my discomfort. No one else seemed frightened of the music she had chosen, and the truth was that I had only vague anxiety and apprehension. I couldn't express my worries because they were too amorphous. What, indeed, was I afraid of? Being part of the program felt, somehow, like a betrayal. But a betrayal of whom? And what did I imagine the consequences of singing with the chorus would be? I had never been in a concert before, so I couldn't picture the scene of the coming evening's performance; I couldn't formulate how it would play out. There was no one to ask. There was no way to understand the dread. But somehow I knew that bringing it home, letting anyone there know anything about the recital or my feelings about it, would be asking for it to get worse.

The day of the dress rehearsal, a Wednesday, was a steely gray day. The sky was lower than the treetops, it seemed, and it looked like it might crush the earth and all the people and houses beneath it. I woke with ragtag remnants of a bad dream spiraling behind my still closed eyes. In the dream, I could see myself in the upstairs hall, just outside the bathroom door. I saw myself looking into the bathroom, and standing at the sink was a witch in a long black robe that had tattered edges along the sleeves and around the hem. She had no rounded flesh around her wrist or fingers, only bony protuberances with reddened skin stretched around them. Her eyes were red-rimmed, and her nose was a pointy collection of hairy warts. She was holding a toothbrush in her left hand and a tube of toothpaste in her right, and she was squeezing the tube with the utmost care. As I watched, and I replayed the scene for myself several times, seemingly mesmerized by terror of it, out of the tube came a perfectly formed sickly green worm that fitted itself perfectly on to the toothbrush. Then the witch, satisfied that the worm was securely balanced along the bristles, turned toward me, and beckoned to me with the hand holding the tube of toothpaste. The head of another worm was drooping from the tip of the tube, but the witch didn't seem to notice. I shrunk backwards, away from the door, but the witch gestured insistently, demanding that I approach her. I watched as my dream-self walked forward into the bathroom and opened my mouth, and I watched as the witch inserted the toothbrush with the sulfurous looking worm on it into my open mouth. And then it was too much: my eyes flew opened, and I sat up. I retched and I vomited all over my blanket. I began to cry, but was interrupted by more vomiting.

"Rikki, Rikki," my grandmother screamed. "Hurry up! Come in, Rikki!" She shrieked and moaned alternatively, and that, mixed with my retching and crying brought Rikki into the room in seconds.

"Oh, Sarah, oh you're sick. Don't cry, my Sarah. You're just sick. A little virus, it must be." Rikki rushed to my bed, and as she began to scoop the blanket away, she turned over her left shoulder toward her mother. "Stop carrying on, Mama. You're making it worse here! She just vomited; she didn't die."

That brought a new cry from Mary. "Die! Who said die?" The cacophony increased.

"Sha, Mama, nobody said die. Sarah has a virus. Or maybe she ate something."

The mere mention of eating sent another wave of nausea over me, who retched again, but brought up nothing else.

"Don't mention food!" I wailed.

"Okay, okay. But you can't go to school today, you know. And if you don't feel fine by this afternoon, we'll go to the doctor. Meantime, go lie in my bed. I'll have to change all this bedding. Take off your pajama top, meantime, and I'll give you a clean one." Rikki turned to my dresser, pulled open the top drawer and plucked out a new pair of pajamas. "Here, Sarah, you might as well change the whole thing." As she handed me the clean clothes, she swept her other hand across my forehead. "No fever, Sarah. You'll be fine for the concert."

But I wasn't fine for the concert. I was sick to my stomach all day, sleeping on and off between bouts of nausea, and could keep nothing down. I slept fitfully through the night, and had shreds of nightmares that made me moan and toss and throw off my blankets. Every time I became wakeful, I saw Rikki sitting at the foot of my bed, watching me with a furrowed brow.

"This is very strange," I heard my mother on the phone with one of her sisters the next day. "No fever at all. I never heard of throwing up and not being able to eat one bite with no fever." There was a pause as she listened. "No, nothing is wrong. What has she got to be upset about? And her concert is tonight." Another pause. "No, of course she's not going. I have to tell her when she wakes up. She's napping now. She was up the whole night throwing herself all over the bed."

I stopped listening. Not going. Not going. I felt my hunched shoulders relax, and I swallowed slowly as the knot in my throat evaporated. I sat up enough to turn my pillow over to the cool side, and I lowered myself slowly into its softness. Not going. I was not going to my concert. I hummed a bit of "Silent Night" to myself and found the calmness uninterrupted. I tried a few of the German words, this time aloud. Then I heard my mother.

"I'm going, Ruthie. I hear her talking to herself. Sarah?" I heard the phone being hung up, and my mother's footsteps coming towards my room.

"Sarah, I want to talk to you about the concert," she began. I smiled to myself for a second, just before my mother arrived at my bedside.

Seventeen

After telling me about her arrival on Whitechapel Road, my grandmother seemed to need time to consider what she would relate next, because the stories stopped for several months. I was beginning to think the little conspiracy we shared had vanished, that she no longer had the need or desire to explain her life to me, but I didn't dare to ask for a new chapter, for fear that bringing the whole enterprise into the clear light of day would squash whatever possibility there was for it to continue. Meanwhile, plans were underway among my aunts and uncles about the coming summer. It had always been their practice to rent small bungalows in Rockaway Beach and escape from the steaming city, and every spring, the discussion of what specific street to rent on had to take place, and it was always contentious.

Rockaway Beach and all its tiny bungalows lay along the Atlantic Ocean in the outer reaches of Queens, and was accessible by subway, miraculously, so it was the Riviera of the middle and lower classes until well into the middle of the century, when widespread air conditioning ended its appeal. There were thousands of tiny rickety bungalows, each with a front porch furnished with three wooden rocking chairs, arranged in narrow streets that lay perpendicular to the glorious white beach. Some of the streets were paved, and others were filled with sand, right up to the top of the curbs. Every year, the owners of the bungalows readied them for the rental season by painting them in various pastel shades of oil-based paint. The air at the beach was never dry, and the result was a beautiful array of softly colored structures with permanently tacky finishes. I used to sit on a pale pink, a light blue or mint green rocking chair, musing about whether it was the proliferation of rocking chairs that had given the community its name, or whether Rockaway had lent its name to the furniture. As I considered the question, I would absently dig a fingernail or push a thumbprint into the never dry paint. Somehow, I observed, it didn't come off on clothing, or all the children would have been walking around with pastel streaked shorts, and all the mothers with pastel streaked housecoats. Fathers who left early to take the elevated subway line to work and returned late wouldn't have had enough rocking chair time to ruin their pants. But in fact, no one was smudged, so, I concluded, although the paint could be moved around on the chairs, railings and window trims, it couldn't come off.

"If they ever want to make one of those bungalows disappear," I once remarked to her mother, "all they need to do is throw a bucket of turpentine over it." Rikki laughed, and repeated my joke over and over to her sisters until they rolled their eyes in boredom.

The ubiquitous sand was another feature of Rockaway. "After last year," Aunt Ruthie might open the discussion from her end perch on the yellow bunkseat, "I wouldn't go back to a sand street if Bobroff paid me. I swept an entire beach of sand out of that bungalow every week." All the aunts and uncles began debating the merits of sand versus paved, interrupting each other, the volume instantly rising to deafening. I stood at the door between the kitchen and the living room as usual, and my aunt's pronouncement brought a series of scenes instantly to mind.

First, I could see Mr. Bobroff, the owner of all of the bungalows on several streets, standing behind the counter in his candy store on Edgemere Avenue, which seemed permanently in the shadow of the elevated subway line. He was going through the motions of mixing an egg cream for my cousin Stacie and me to share, first a squirt of chocolate syrup, then a splash of milk, and finally a stream of carbonated water, all the while stirring noisily with a spoon. We two young customers were sitting on green leather stools that were trimmed by a wide band of grooved chrome, spinning slowly left and right, our sandals dangling high above the step that was meant to rest a customer's feet on.

Then, as Mr. Bobroff slid the egg cream and two striped straws across the counter, that scene dissolved and was replaced by a view of Aunt Ruthie in front of the little stove in the kitchen where a pan sent sizzling sounds into the room, holding a broom offhandedly to one side, as if she'd been interrupted from her sweeping chore, and a fork in the other hand, turning over a lamb chop that would be Stacie's lunch. Who would want to eat a hot lamb chop for lunch, I wondered at my memory, in the middle of the summer at the beach? Certainly not Stacie, I answered myself, who never ate more than a bite of anything at one meal, no matter what she was served.

Aunt Ruthie and her broom and lamb chop melted away and I saw myself pulling back the covers of a small cot that was in the front room of Aunt Ruthie's bungalow, and brushing out the grains of sand that somehow filtered their way down to the sheets. I was staying at the beach for a week, and that little cot was my bed. Also in the front room was a big round oak table covered with a floral patterned oilcloth tablecloth. That tablecloth had been wiped free of sand so many times, that sections of the design had been rubbed off. There were six unmatched oak chairs around the table, which pretty much filled the room. In the corner opposite my cot, up against two walls, was the double bed where Stacie's older brother Sheldon slept. He was a teenager when I stayed with them that summer, and he merely brushed the edges of my life. He came in late, when I was already asleep, and left early for his job down the boardwalk at the amusement park. The only evidence of his even being there was his unmade bed that Aunt Ruthie attacked each morning, and his wet bathing suit and loafers in the outdoor shower enclosure that separated one bungalow form the next.

Throughout my reveries, the sounds of "Jailhouse Rock," and "Wake Up, Little Susie" alternated, dimly heard, from a distant radio.

The cacophony of the discussion in the kitchen broke the spell of my memories. "Are you planning to join us this year, Jean? Or maybe you'll go to the mountains with your so-called friends?" taunted Aunt Esther. "I hear your friend Edie is taking a place near the Raleigh. We don't have entertainment." The last word was dripped out, a syllable at a time, and I watched Aunt Jean's face to see if she would pick up Aunt Esther's sarcastic bait.

"No, I'm going to the beach, if you must know. Solly would have to get the raise he'll never be getting for the mountains. And how did you hear about Edie? While you were having your hair bleached the color of the week?"

Aunt Esther barely looked at her sister, but her "humph" told me that the barb had pierced her.

They began arguing about when they would venture out to the beach community to look over the available rentals. "I want to go right away," announced Aunt Ruthie. "I'm not waiting for Bobroff to give away the best bungalows to strangers."

"Ruthie, it's March, freezing cold. Who is he giving to in March?" replied Uncle Mayshe. His tone told his sister what a brainless idiot he thought she was. I backed away from the door, more than slightly afraid of Uncle Mayshe since cousin Daniel's bar mitzvah. In fact, the room grew momentarily silent, as if everyone were waiting for him to explode into the kind of rage we had all witnessed. There had never been any discussion or explanation about that ugly incident, and of course, there had been no apology from him either. But that sudden break in the usual bantering was proof to me that the rug they swept the past into was not big enough to hold everything.

Now the topic shifted. The talk about when to make the trek to Rockaway to finalize their summer plans grew faster and louder, and abruptly, they began to slide out of the bunk seats and send children upstairs to gather their coats that were arrayed across Rikki and Joe's bed. "Who says it's too cold?" and "Melissa, we're leaving!" and "Rikki, turn off the stove, you'll come, too. Where are the kids?" They stubbed out cigarettes, circled into the living room to retrieve pocketbooks, and shouted at each other about who would ride in whose car. Rikki followed one or another around, still holding her spatula and wearing her calico apron. "But why should Mama have to go out in the cold? I'll stay here with her. Or maybe Joe doesn't want to go. . . ."

"Joe, darling," Aunt Jean mimicked her sister. The rest continued to gather their belongings, but everyone laughed at Aunt Jean's tease, because they all thought Rikki's loving relationship to her husband was ridiculous and they all made fun of it.

I joined the milling throng, hoping I could be included in this unexpected adventure. It was unlike me to want to go anywhere with them, but seeing what the beach looked like in the winter was compelling. I stole a glance at my grandmother and found her smiling at her children's spontaneity, so I knew it would be safe to leave her. It was so rare to see a positive reaction to them, that I felt like it was a secret permission slip from her for me to go. "Sarah," said Uncle Jack. "Get your coat; I'll take you with us, and I'll bring you back later." I looked questioningly at my mother, who paused as she considered, and finally nodded her assent.

"Fine, but then I'll stay here. How can everyone fit?" The groove between her eyebrows smoothed, and she was suddenly smiling at her family. I knew that Rikki thought of her family in positive ways even though she hardly ever had evidence that they were as she liked to think they were. This moment seemed to justify her unreasonable opinion, and I felt at once lighter than I could remember feeling, just looking at my mother's face. I ran to grab my coat off the hook inside the closet door, poked my arms into the sleeves and made for the door before my mother could change her mind. I joined the swirl of my aunts, uncles and cousins as they filed helter-skelter down the driveway and into their cars.

The back seat of Uncle Jack's car was filled with bouncing, screaming cousins, and I found myself caught up in the merriment. The gray scratchy horsehair upholstery was strange under my fingertips. The lap blanket that dangled onto my knees off a fat rope like you'd find in a movie theater line, but attached to the back of the front seat, seemed alien and foreign to me. It was the first time I had been in Uncle Jack's car, and I felt like I had to quickly learn the ways of this unknown land that my cousins all seemed to be a part of. It was exciting and frightening at once. I craned my neck to look out the window beside me, just to check that we were really pulling away from my house, and that I was in the car, and not standing back on the lawn and waving. There was my mother, pulling a sweater together with one hand, her apron dangling below it, and her other hand waving gaily to her departing family. There was a fleeting view of my grandmother at the front door, through the storm door window, but before I could feel regret for leaving her, the car sped away, and we were on our way to the beach. "The beach in the winter!" I marveled. Everyone made it a chorus, and in a flash, they were chanting together, "The beach in the winter, the beach in the winter!"

They parked their cars, Uncle Jack's Buick with the row of bird's nest openings on the front fender, Uncle Morty's blue Ford, shiny from its usual early morning wash down, and Uncle Mayshe's long black Cadillac with its wide shoulders and arrogant shrugging slopes, one behind the other on the street they had rented on the previous summer. Everyone tumbled out on to the sidewalk, and I could hear a rapid succession of slamming car doors as I peered around the somewhat unfamiliar territory. Rockaway looked as different in the winter as a place could look. It was true that the bungalows were all there with their hipped roofs and little attic windows lined up along the sidewalk. But the pastel colors were frayed and faded, and boards had been nailed across all the doors and windows. Most unnerving to me was that all the rocking chairs were missing. The street was completely empty, and where a long neat row of cars was normally parked in the summer, I saw small white peaks of sand that the wind had deposited in periodic pyramids. The intervals between the fire hydrants, something that was never apparent in the summer, were even and regular, and the normally empty space under the ramp that led up to the boardwalk at the beach end of the street was nearly filled with wet gray sand. The clotheslines that I remembered from the summer were not there peeking from between the bungalows, dipping down from the weight of laundered sheets and towels and pajamas, and stretched from the back windows of bungalows to a central pole behind them. All I could find was one forlorn pole raked to a precarious angle poking out of the sand in each windswept backyard.

The adults took no apparent notice of what havoc seemed to have been worked on their summer refuge, but the children had grown silent and ill at ease. Finally, Melissa, the youngest cousin, spoke for everyone. "Who stole everything? Call the police!" And she started to cry.

"What is she crying about? Melissa, what's the matter?" Aunt Marly dared to interfere with the child of one of sisters-in-law.

"Mind your business, Marly," Aunt Jean came instantly to her daughter's defense, although she had ignored the crying until the interloper had tried to help. "What is it, my Melissa? Who hurt you?"

"Somebody stole everything we need for Rockaway," she sniffled noisily. "Where are the windows? Are the people locked inside?" and she began to weep in earnest again.

I stood off to the side, unwilling to let anyone there know that I was just as uncomfortable as little Melissa. My aunts would make fun of me, I knew, because although I had never seen Rockaway in its hibernation mode, unlike little Melissa, I should be able to figure it out, and they would see that as enough reason to ignore my feelings. It was just that knowing what had happened didn't make it easier. So I clutched my coat around me, pulled my hat lower over my face, and waited for someone to make it all right.

And soon enough, the whole crowd of them was crammed into the Bobroff's living room. The children were drinking hot chocolate and eating sugar cookies, and the adults were taking turns signing leases. Everyone was chattering happily, having left off carping and complaining in the glow of finalizing their summer plans, and the children had become so at ease that they were beginning to chase each other around the furniture. I was still apprehensive, and although I could see that all was well, I couldn't shake my discomfort, and I couldn't understand why none of my cousins seemed to have any remnants of it, even Melissa.

And then we were back in the cars, and Uncle Jack was driving me home. By the time we passed the Italian Ices stand on Peninsula Boulevard, a usual pit stop on the way home from Rockaway, but closed for the winter, everyone was asleep except Uncle Jack and me. We drove along in silence for a while, and then Uncle Jack interrupted my thoughts. "Some family, huh, Sarah?" I didn't think he wanted me to answer. He was, after all, not an original in the family: Aunt Esther had married him long ago, before the war. He'd always been an outsider to Bubby's children, I knew, similar to Aunt Marly or Aunt Rose, but he was rarely a victim of their sneers or nastiness. Husbands, after all, were necessities for the sisters. Still, Aunt Esther better not wake up and hear him have an opinion of the family, I thought. There was more silence. And then he said, "I don't know if there ever was a family that had more cruelty and viciousness masquerading as love and devotion."

I nearly gasped. Uncle jack knew some pretty big words, I realized. And he had been doing some weighty thinking. The truth is that he rarely said anything, usually. He was known in the family for his intellectual thickness and nervous tics. I had once overheard Rikki talking on the phone to Aunt Ruthie about how he had two sisters who were very devoted to each other. But I had never heard of Aunt Esther and Uncle Jack going to visit them, or inviting them over. Uncle Jack was always saying, "I got a good parking space and I'm not giving it up," whenever one of his children wanted to be driven someplace. Could that be the reason he never went to see his sisters? Or was it just that he had grown up in a family that was different from the one he married into? Maybe he knew more about families than he ever let on. And could he see into my head, somehow? And what did he think of what I was thinking every Sunday from my spot by the door into the kitchen? I could barely breathe.

"Ah, well. What are you gonna do?" he sighed. "You can't fight them once you've joined them." Then he laughed at how he had created a little twist of the common expression. And then I heard him make a sound that, if he hadn't been a grown up man, I would have thought was a sob.

I sat very still in my backseat corner, hoping he might think I too had fallen asleep. But then I gathered my nerve and spoke. "Why are they like that, Uncle Jack? Why are there so many secrets?"

He was quiet. I couldn't tell if he was thinking what the answer might be, or he hadn't heard me, or he was pretending he hadn't heard me. But then he took his eyes off the road for a moment and looked at me in his mirror. "It comes from a long time ago, Sarah. Even before I met Aunt Esther. No one ever told me the reason, of course. Maybe they're so involved with themselves that they don't even see what they're like. When I first saw Esther it was at a dance, and she was young and pretty, with big blue eyes. I told her right away that she had the nicest eyes I had ever seen and that I wanted to marry her. She laughed at me, but I came up to their apartment the very next day to tell her parents. I don't know where Avram was, but Mary, Bubby, looked at me and said, and I'll never forget it, 'Esther is stupid, an idiot, and if you want her, you're an idiot too. Go together in good health, idiot boy. You can be sorry later.' Esther was standing right there and she heard her mother talk like that, and she didn't even flinch. The rest of them were around, too. They all heard, but no one acted like anything cruel had been said. Imagine, Sarah, growing up where mean was normal. It was like there was a curse on them. I have no idea why it was like that. But it always was." He turned his eyes back to the road and I knew the discussion was over. He had been snagged into the web of the family by a pair of beautiful blue eyes, and even though he could see it was a web, he couldn't figure out how it had been spun.

I resolved to tell no one what my supposedly stupid uncle had said. Before too long, I was climbing sleepily out of the car and walking up the concrete driveway that was lit by a yellow spill of light through the kitchen windows of my house.

### Eighteen

Sometimes my grandmother would launch right into he stories with no hesitation, and sometimes she seemed almost unable to speak about the past. If she thought sometimes that the stories were too painful for a child, why was she able to overcome those qualms at other times? I don't think she worried about my ability to process them. Once she had chosen me as the official listener, I felt like she was as honest as she could be. She didn't seem to care if she came across as selfish or cruel. The truth is she never accepted any responsibility for any of her actions except one: the decision she made to ignore Avram's rejection and go to London and get him to marry her. And if that decision was based on how she, as a beauty, had learned to negotiate the world, then that wasn't her fault either. But for the whole year that she told me the pieces of her life, I never stopped wondering exactly what I was supposed to learn from it. She always said it would free me from the curse of her life, but the more she told me, the more I couldn't understand why she never apologized to anyone who was damaged by the supposed curse.

"Bubby, did you know that everyone is going back to Beach 49th Street?" I opened a conversation with my grandmother several nights after the trip to the beach. "Did you know that Mr. and Mrs. Bobroff live there all the time, even in the winter? I never knew there was a school there, but there must be, because they have three children, did you know that, and they must go to school, don't you think?" I was crowding all my thoughts together in one gush of excitement in the hope that my grandmother would pick up on at least one of them, and thus a conversation would open, and the possibility of a bedtime story might come about. "And you should see Rockaway in the winter! All the windows are covered with boards, and I could see all the fire plugs at once, and I don't know where they put the rocking chairs." I paused and waited for my grandmother to respond. The silence was long enough to make me think that Mary had fallen asleep, and that there would be no new chapter. But then I heard a sigh from the other bed, and my grandmother began to speak.

"The East End of London, that was the name of Avram's neighborhood. He lived in a house with apartments in it, with his two cousins, Chaim and Faivel. They sold junk, old metal things, and they bought, too. They looked for iron, I remember, old iron. Who could imagine that a living could come from old iron? Later I think they got rich; they had a yard with junk somewhere nearby, and men worked for them then. But when I first came, they were always dirty. Their hands were black with dirt, I remember, and even when they came from the vapor baths, they still looked stained, their hands. They were always together, brothers they were, and they came from the baths with wet hair, and red, raw faces, but their hands, they could never make them clean the whole time we lived with them."

My grandmother seemed to have transported herself with no effort back to her life in London. She pulled up images that were randomly connected, but vivid and fresh. "I reached the door, you know, after I walked from the dock, and stood with my carpet bag and waited for Avram to come there and see me. And I looked up and down the street while I waited. Later, I knew, I would learn what was behind every doorway, every shop, I would know the people, I would know where to buy flour to make bread, and where to buy soap and matches and a new hat. But that day, I just looked." I tried to see what my grandmother was looking at. I knew nothing about London at the turn of the century, so I had to wait for the scene to be filled in.

"I could smell food cooking, onions frying somewhere. Across the street, I saw a shop with a bell over the door that rang every time someone opened the door. And when it was open, I could make out a crowd of women inside, and some would come out holding parcels, string bags, and some would go in to take the places of the ones that went out. Later I learned that was the place you bought potatoes and onions and barley and lima beans. The women were buying to make cholent." There she stopped talking and sniffed the air, as if trying to find the aroma of the weekly baked stew that I knew was prepared in every household.

"And then, after I waited by the door for a long time, the whole afternoon, suddenly, the street was full of men instead of women. Work was finished for the day, and they were all coming home at the same time. The street looked like the train station that I saw when I was traveling, like a train had just emptied out all its passengers. I heard feet shuffling along the stones, and doors opening and slamming closed, but no one spoke to anyone. Their faces looked at their shoes, I could see that they were exhausted, used up, and so many seemed sad. For a moment, I thought maybe I shouldn't have come; maybe life was too hard here, not like I thought it would be, maybe Avram would never appear and I would have to sleep in the street. For a moment, I missed my mother, and Dvorah, and even Tova, and I thought of Rivka, dead in the cemetery, and her mother who tried to teach me to read, who was back in Ulla, weeping over her dead child forever." Mary stopped, and I could hear her sniffling quietly. She must have been thinking of Uncle Sidney, I thought. I knew that one explanation of his absence had it that Bubby's youngest son was dead. But another story, I remembered, claimed that he was locked in a mental hospital somewhere. Both were awful. But then my grandmother took a deep breath, and seemed to prepare herself to go on.

"When the street was empty, and all the men had gone into their own doors, I looked desperately around one more time. No one came, and so I picked up my carpetbag, and began to plan what I would do next. And then, just like that, he came around the corner. Avram. And he was walking quickly, wearing a black coat, and a silky bowler, a hat, you know? And his boots, I saw right away, were shiny, polished, and he was carrying a cane. But not a cane like an old man needs, no. It was a cane like a stick, with a silver knob at the top, gleaming like I would see my face in it. I thought to myself, my Avram is rich! And then he saw me standing there." Both my grandmother and I sighed and I imagined that they were both looking at the scene of Avram and Mary meeting again after their separation. If were a movie, I thought, violins would be playing, swelling up dramatically, and then he would sweep her up into his arms and The End in fancy script would appear on the screen. I waited for my grandmother to form words that could convey the golden memory.

A tale quite different emerged.

"Suddenly, he saw me standing there, and I was looking at his face, his blue eyes, to see what they would tell me. He squinted at me, trying to make sure he was really seeing what he thought he was seeing. First, he said, 'Mayrke, it's you?' He always called me Mayrke. I remembered I was still holding my bag, in front of his house I was standing, and I was nodding my head, yes, Avram, yes, it's me all the way from Ulla. But then, his eyes got black, and he looked up, looked at the sky, and a terrible roar came from his throat, a sound like a screaming jet plane makes now, or maybe a wolf in the forest who is hungry for flesh, and the roar filled the street and pushed on the doors and windows, like it would push them back out of its way." My first vision of the reunion of my grandparents popped open and disappeared like a soap bubble, and I slid lower and clutched the edge of my blanket, trying to prepare myself for something terrifying.

"The roar turned into fire and smoke and wind; it felt like hell had opened its door to let me see for a second. The roar smelled like a dead animal, like fish that was rotting along the bank of the river. Horrible." She was describing the moment as she remembered it, I knew, but could a sound have an appearance, a smell? It was impossible, I was sure it was impossible. "Bubby," I tried to interrupt, but I knew my voice was too quiet, and my grandmother was too far away to even realize she was being addressed.

"I dropped my bag, I remember, and both of my hands I raised right away to close my ears, and I pinched my eyes shut. I think I began to scream too. And then my knees turned to jelly and I fell straight down, like I was melting. And Avram let go of his cane and one hand pushed his hat brim straight up off his forehead, and his hat slid to the back of his head, and right off it flew. The cane smashed to the stone sidewalk, and it bounced and banged before it rolled away into the gutter. Every time it hit the stones, the noise was like a hammer hitting my head, banging my teeth together. The hat, I watched it, it was caught by the wind and it turned over and over itself until it landed in a puddle left by a horse. Avram watched it too, and I saw one of his hands reach towards it, like he could extend his arm like rubber from his sleeve and catch it before it was ruined. 'My hat,' I remember he wailed, 'My hat.' And then the roar was gone, sucked out of the air into the sky, and the smell and the fire and the smoke, everything disappeared in one

blink. And then we looked at each other, my Avram and me, we just looked and waited."

I waited in the silence of my room, relieved that the scary movie scene seemed

over. This was all the proof I needed that I would never go to those monster movies that

my cousins and my brother loved. Never.

"And then Avram spoke again. You'll never believe, my Sarah, what he said to

me next." She knows I'm here, I realized. It was amazing to me every time it happened.

My grandmother was far away, in the throes of some poisonous memory, completely

engrossed in the scene and distant from the safe little room where the story unfolded

itself, and yet she could bounce right back to the present and talk normally to me. Could

other people's grandmothers do that? It would remain a mystery; asking anyone would

reveal the secret story sessions. But then my amazement was interrupted.

"Sarah, are you still awake?"

"Of course I'm awake, Bubby. This is the most important part of the story ever.

What did he say? What were his words to you?" I hoped the mood might swing around,

somehow, that his words might be an apology of some kind for his initial reaction. Or

maybe something gentle and loving.

"He said, I remember it like he just spoke to me now, he said, 'Now I'll need a

new hat.' A hat, he spoke of, after I came all that distance, like a miracle, and all he said

was, 'Now I'll need a new hat.'"

"So what did you say, Bubby?" I asked, still hoping that a fairy tale ending might

happen.

"What did I say? I said, 'So we'll go tomorrow and buy a new hat, of course.' What else could I say? Then I stood up and we watched the ruined hat blow away down the street. Then he stepped into the gutter and picked up his cane, and he took out a big white handkerchief from his pocket, and he carefully wiped the whole length of the cane, inspecting it for scratches and dents. He held it out to me to look at, so I moved towards him to examine it too. It was completely perfect. No damage at all. He tucked it under his arm, and we both smiled. Then he picked up my carpetbag and held out his arm to help me go into the house. 'I must call on someone later,' he said, and I knew who he meant: Esther Bagoudis, his new woman. He must tell her to go away from him, I thought to myself, but would he?" She stopped speaking, leaving the question unanswered.

I lay there, wondering. But he must have done it because here I was, the granddaughter of Mary and Avram. And it seemed like he was glad Bubby was there, even though it was a shock at first. So maybe Esther Bagoudis was really no problem. Maybe Bubby would explain that he just made it clear to her that his first love had come, and that he really loved her better, and maybe she just went and married someone else, and lived happily ever after too. I considered this possibility as I heard my grandmother's breathing grow slower and deeper, and I knew she had fallen asleep. Happily ever after was just for fairy tales, I knew. Almost no one in my family seemed to be living happily ever after, with a cascade of flowers and smiling birds and deer and other creatures dancing around after them, the way the Walt Disney Show had it every Sunday night on television.

But maybe what I saw among my aunts and uncles was what happily ever after meant for real people, not cartoon people like Sleeping Beauty or Snow White. This was a dilemma that was too complicated for a tired girl, I decided. I tried to concentrate on the happy parts of the story, like how my grandparents had gone arm in arm into the apartment house. I smoothed the hem of my blanket, turned on to my side, and went to sleep.

## Nineteen

Now that the worst of winter seemed over, Rikki sent me off to school every morning with the same cheerful farewell, "Look for the first robin of spring today! Once you see that, spring will be here and it'll be time to put the cotton slipcovers on the sofa and take down the heavy drapes." She made these chores sound like fun, and although I knew that the word chores implied unwelcome obligations, it was clear that to my mother, household activities were the very definition of fun. She didn't object to cleaning her house, and she went about with grave determination dusting and vacuuming every day, even if everything looked perfectly clean to me before my mother got the cleaning equipment out of its basement closet. She even worked alongside Maggie, a cleaning woman who was sometimes employed to help with heavy cleaning.

But mostly, I knew that my mother liked to cook, and every day at 4:00, when she tilted open the storage bin from the bottom front of the refrigerator to extract some potatoes and onions, her face took on a glow of pleasure. She'd line up the potatoes on the wooden counter, reach behind the kitchen door for the apron that hung on a hook there, and take out the knives, peelers, pots, pans and bowls that she'd need for her dinner preparations. Dinner would be served at 7:00 every night when my father came home, and it seemed to me that three hours was almost infinity of time to cook the dinner that we would eat in fifteen minutes. But Rikki would be singing and stirring and tasting, and clearly enjoying herself. In later years, when Rikki went to work as a secretary at the Jewish Center, the only complaint she ever voiced had to do with missing her 4:00 o'clock appointment with her kitchen.

So I looked for the first robin dutifully. But to me, the real signs of spring had to do with my father's weekend activities. As soon as he shifted his focus from inside projects, like building a linen closet in the upstairs bathroom, or covering an old cabinet with wallpaper left over from my bedroom to provide some extra storage for me, to outside projects, spring had officially arrived. After months of cold and snow and ice and wind, the yard needed lots of attention. Instead of heading down the basement steps on an April Saturday morning, Joe would reach deep into the back of the hall closet for his old canvas field jacket, and head for the back yard. "Anyone want to come along for the spring inspection?" he'd call over his shoulders.

Without waiting for an answer, he'd be halfway down the breezeway, probably making a mental note of the condition of the climbing rose vines as he passed them. They'd get their first fertilizer feeding before the day was over, but by the time I could grab my heavy sweater off its hook and follow him, he'd already be checking the storm windows that he'd soon remove from the back porch windows and store in bins in the rear of the garage. I loved the little thumbtacks that had once been pushed into every storm window frame and windowsill. There were raised numbers on them, a matching pair of corresponding ones for each window, and in the fall, I'd helped my father find the right window for each of the heavy wooden frames he'd pulled from the garage. "Here's 23, Dad," I remembered calling to him from the corner of the porch as he came around the side of the garage holding the window sideways, one arm up on the top and one arm down underneath. "Okay, Sar, I've got 23 right here," he'd replied.

And now it was spring, I thought, and as I looked for the number 23 thumbtack on the bottom of the corner window, I thought about how much better it felt when I wasn't busy worrying and fretting about things. I loved being with my father, and I think it was partly because he was the anchor that prevented me from floating into the choppy water that was my mother's side of the family. Perhaps my grandmother saw him that way too, and just being in his house may have created the motivation to tell me her story. Maybe she thought she could be part of his anchor. My search for number 23 was rewarded; it was there, just as I had remembered. My father had gone on, however, because this was just the inspection, not the time to actually take off the windows.

"I need to get my saw from the basement, Sar," he told me. "One of the maples lost a limb and I have to even it and paint the wound, or we'll have sap bleeding out of that tree any day now." Trees can bleed? Was there blood in trees? No, I thought, not blood. He said sap. But in the few seconds before I'd reviewed my father's words, I saw a picture in my mind of every tree in the backyard with bloody bandages wrapped around their branches, grimacing wooden faces hidden partly by their leaves, and my father running disjointedly from maple tree to apple tree to peach tree, blotting oozing bleeding sores as he went. I shuddered and turned to follow him inside. He could fix anything, even bleeding trees.

By the time I got inside the kitchen, my father was already down the basement stairs. My mother was mixing something in a big crockery bowl, some kind of lunch salad, like maybe tuna or egg. I shrugged off my sweater, pushed it along the bunkseat and climbed up to get a look into the bowl. My perch on the end of the bunkseat gave me a clear view of the wooden counter which backed up to it and which was the central point of kitchen preparations. "Inspection over already, Sarah?" Rikki asked as she pushed the bowl to one side and set about chopping celery. "Go wash your hands if you're staying inside."

"I'm going out in a second, but Daddy had to get a saw to fix a tree branch that got ripped and is bleeding." The image of the wounded trees lit up and went dark in an instant. "And then he's going to paint it. What color do you paint a tree?"

"Not regular paint, Sarah. He's probably looking for the can of tar. That's going to take a while because it hasn't been used in, I don't know, maybe three years. It's really buried in the back by now."

"Tar? Like on the street? Would the trees really want tar on their arms? They're not roads, you know." I could now see the trees moving their branches around to protect themselves from my approaching father who was brandishing a can of steaming paving material like I'd seen used when my road had been given a renewed strip of shiny hot tar down the crack in the middle of the street.

"Sarah, for goodness sake, they're trees, not people. They have no opinions or feelings! And it's probably not that kind of tar anyway. It's pitch, or I don't know, tree stuff." I knew that Rikki's sputtering was her usual frustration at my overdone sensitivity. "You make everything into a person with a terrible fate, Sarah. What makes you think a tree has feelings?" At this point, she was chopping celery as if it had offended her. And then the phone rang, so she wiped her hands on the sides of her apron and turned to answer it. Her hello was annoyed enough to cause the caller to question her.

"No, Ruthie, I'm making lunch. You didn't interrupt anything. Sarah has been outside chatting with the trees." She listened and then laughed at Ruthie's remark.

I felt like my mother and aunt were ganging up on me, even though I hadn't heard Aunt Ruthie's words. I climbed off the bunkseat and began wondering what to do next. My father must have gotten involved in something in his workshop, because I could hear the quiet drone of an electric saw wafting up through the heating vent. And my mother was lighting a cigarette, a clear sign that she was settling in for a long chat with her sister. Bubby was sitting on the back porch, still enclosed by storm windows and protected from the chilly April weather. My brother David was out playing somewhere, as usual. I didn't feel like going out to the porch; there was a clear view of the back yard and the trees. No need to bring that scene into fresh focus, I thought. I wandered along the hallway slowly, trailing my hand along the pattern of green Asian ladies and many tiered pagodas in the distance. I began climbing up the stairs, taking them two feet at a time on each step, pretending that my legs had been sewn together because of some newly discovered dread disease.

"Stop crashing around, Sarah!" my mother yelled from the kitchen. "I'm on the phone and I'd like to hear!"

I pronounced myself instantly cured of the leg disease. I walked up the rest of the way on my heels, just to see if it was possible. I went to my room and opened the wooden box I had gotten two summers before when my family went on vacation to Lake George. There were some treasures kept there, like the shell Aunt Esther had brought me from Florida, and a few barrettes and buttons. I sat on my bed, dumped out the contents of the box, and began to rearrange them.

After a while, I heard the phone being hung up downstairs, and a kitchen drawer being open and then closed. And then I heard my mother shriek.

"Joe! Joe! Come up quick!"

I stood up quickly, shifting all the treasures off the bed and onto the floor. I paused for a moment, trying to decide if I should bend and pick them all up, or fly down the stairs to my mother. Leaving a mess on the floor would probably have consequences. But my mother's cries were continuing. Leave the stuff, I decided, but with my foot, I gathered everything together before I ran out of the room.

"Mommy! What's the matter? What happened?" I reached the top of the steps, and pictured myself leaning out and flying through the air down the stairwell and landing neatly upright at the bottom. I actually grabbed the newel post with my right hand, and bent forward to test the possibility. It was immediately clear that it wouldn't work, so I clattered down and tore around the corner into the kitchen. Rikki was poised over the sink trying to wrap a dishtowel around her left hand, which was pulsing blood into her right hand, the sink and the towel.

"Don't look, Sarah. I'm fine. Call your father, please."

I looked at my mother's face, which had gone from its usual color to the whitish shade of her cigarette ash. My gaze shifted down to my mother's hand, but at the sight of the blood I jerked my eyes away. I looked for something else to concentrate on, and I lighted on the wooden counter. There was a basket with several bagels nestled into a napkin, each one cut open ready to be made into a tuna sandwich or simply buttered, which for a second, I decided was the way I would eat mine. Then I remembered my mother whose hand was bleeding into the sink. "Sarah, please, I said I need Daddy up here. Stop standing there just gaping. And don't look at me. I'm fine." I stared for another second, and Rikki screamed over her head, "Joe! Can you please come up here!"

When my mother stopped calling to take a breath, I realized that the sound of the electric saw in the basement was still whining distantly. And I flew to the top of the basement stairs and yanked open the door. The volume of the saw seemed to have been cranked up to the highest setting. So I didn't even try to shout above it. I leapt down to the bottom in three steps.

"Dad! Dad! Mommy's bleeding in the sink! Come quick!"

My father kept working and said without shifting his gaze, "I can't hear you, Sarah. I'm sawing something. I'll be done in a minute."

"No! Come up now! She's bleeding!"

The sawing continued, and my father focused intently on the board under his saw, guiding it expertly under the screaming blade. I knew he had no idea what I was saying, and I was afraid if I distracted him, he'd cut off his hand, or at least a finger, and then I'd have two parents bleeding. I looked nervously at the stairs, and knew that my mother could hear the saw as it continued to buzz without a care for her need. I knew that my mother's telling me not to look meant that she was protecting me from something horrific. And in my imagination, the sink was now completely full of my mother's blood, covering all the dishes that had been waiting to be washed, and there was none left inside her to hold her up. By now, she was probably on the floor, crumpled in front of the sink, still trying to wind the kitchen towel around the cut, but for no reason now, her blood having poured itself into the sink. I wanted him to stop sawing and fix my mother. His very presence usually calmed me, but that magic wasn't working now.

Finally, the saw stopped. The sudden silence shocked me momentarily. Then I found my voice. "Mommy is bleeding in the kitchen. I think her blood is all in the sink, now. She needs you to go up there."

Joe's, "What!" came as he raced up the stairs. I was left standing in my father's workshop, looking at what he had been doing, which was cutting equal size boards and stacking them against the wall. I remembered that he was planning a new ceiling for the porch. I formed an image of my father holding boards against the old ceiling and hammering straight up, a nail gripped in his teeth ready to be the next one. And then his voice intruded. "Sarah! I'm calling you, Sarah! Come up here!"

I tore up the stairs, two at a time. "What should I do?" My mother's hand was neatly wrapped in a new dishtowel, and her jacket was spread across her shoulders. I glanced quickly into the sink, steeling myself for a pool of blood with dishes poking up through it. The dishes were there, but the liquid was mostly clear, with just a few streaky smears of pinkish red.

"Bubby fell asleep on the porch, Sarah. She didn't hear all the commotion." Joe's voice was calm, regular, and not panicky at all. How could he be so calm when his wife's blood had all come out? But where was it? I looked at my mother. She looked as serene as the statue of Buddha I had seen in my Social Studies book in school. She looked like she had a pleasant secret. "So you have to stay here for when she wakes up," my father continued. "David is at Jimmy's house, so he'll be fine there. Do you think you'll be all right? I'm going to take Mommy to the Emergency Room. I think she may need a stitch or two in her hand." Now he was smiling. What could possibly be making him smile? "Maybe I'll cut open the bagels with my band saw from now on, right Rikki?"

And with that, he held open the kitchen door, and Rikki walked through it, under his arm. "Don't frighten Bubby when she gets up, okay, Sarah?" said my mother over her shoulder. I followed them to the door, held the outer door open and leaned out. I watched my father open the car door, watched my mother get in and slide over to the middle, and watched him go around to the driver's side. He got in and started the car in one fluid motion, and in a second, he had backed the car off the driveway and was piloting his wife up the street. His right arm, I noticed, was draped over my mother's shoulder, like the picture of a date I had seen in my cousin's *Seventeen* magazine.

I closed the door and sat down in Aunt Ruthie's regular spot on the end of the bunk seat. Tomorrow they'd all be there, as usual. And my mother would have a bandage on her hand. There would be lots of noise as she told the story of the hand. But now the house was so quiet, I could hear the wall clock ticking from the hallway. I heard the furnace in the basement igniting as heat turned on. Then I heard my grandmother's voice calling faintly from the porch. "Rikki! It's chilly out here. Do you have my sweater near you?"

Maybe it wasn't quite ready to be spring yet. After all, I hadn't seen the first robin yet. I stood up to bring my grandmother the pink sweater that was hanging from the back of her chair at the head of the table. I tried out a few explanations in my head of where my parents had gone as I walked toward the porch. Would Bubby say her daughter's accident had somehow been part of the curse? Would she tell me not to worry, that for me everything would be fine?   Maybe that would launch her into a new chapter of the story.  "Bubby, I'm coming.  Wait till I tell you what just happened."

Twenty

That night, everyone went to sleep early. All the excitement of Rikki getting

stitches in the palm of her hand and the flurry of phone calls that resulted had worn us

out. The explanation was the same for each call, but Rikki's comments on being ignored

as she nearly bled to death upset me, even though I could tell from my mother's tone that

it was all meant to be funny. Every time the phone rang, I knew it would be another

sister or brother and my mother would repeat her performance. The image of my

mother's blood filling the sink while the sound of the saw droned on in the distance

looped repeatedly through my mind until I couldn't stand it anymore. When my

grandmother announced that she was going up to bed, although it was only 7:30, I

decided to go up, too.

"I'll go up with Bubby," I volunteered. "You can't really help her anyway, Ma,

with your bandage. And I'm tired."

"But don't you want to watch TV, Sarah?" asked my father.

"No, I'm going to sit with Bubby while she goes to sleep."

"That's very good of you, Sarah. Thank you for helping me," said Rikki.

My parents were next to each other on the sofa, a bunch of pillows cradling

Rikki's hand. They looked at each other while they took turns speaking to me, but I

didn't think they were paying the least attention to what they were saying. It was like

their voices were on automatic pilot. I caught up to my grandmother who had reached

the bottom of the stairway, and followed slowly behind her as she began to negotiate the

stairs, always leading with her right foot, her good hand braced against the wall.

"We'll have plenty of time for me to tell you about how I got rid of Esther Bagoudis," said my grandmother, offhandedly.

I stopped and grabbed the banister with my left hand. I gasped at the shock of my grandmother's mentioning my grandfather's girlfriend's name, right on the stairs, in easy hearing distance from the living room, where my parents were talking to each other in quiet voices. It was stunning to even talk about the stories, let alone say that name out loud. I knew that my mother would recognize the name because Aunt Ruthie sometimes used it when she wanted to compare someone she was talking about to a person of extremely low stature. "She's an Esther Bagoudis in my book," she might pronounce. Everyone in the family knew who she was, but no one actually talked about her in normal tones, as if she had been a real woman, with a personality, and relatives, and a tragic tale. They seemed to think of her as a character in a comic book, or a radio soap opera from the distant past, like Stella Dallas. Now, here was Bubby, walking up the stairs and offering me information about dealing with Esther Bagoudis, a real person.

"Shhh, Bubby. We don't want them to know you're telling me your story, do we?" I tried to warn my grandmother about my parents' proximity.

"Don't worry, Sarah my darling. Soon the story and everything will be finished." Her voice had a kind of dark, ominous tone, full of implied meaning.

"What do you mean, Bubby?" I asked as I guided my grandmother up the last few steps. "How can the story be almost over, when you only just got to London?"

Mary straightened up, took a deep breath, and aimed herself toward the bathroom. "I'll be in the bathroom for a minute, Sarah. Don't worry about the end of the story. I'll tell you the end before the end." She began to shuffle away from me, who was left at the top of the stairs with my forehead creased in confusion.

"You'll tell me the end before the end? That doesn't make any sense, Bubby. How do you tell the end of the story before you tell the end of the story?"

The bathroom door closed and I stood trying to understand my grandmother's cryptic words. She often confused the language, I decided, and this must be an instance of that. I walked into my room and opened the dresser to take out my pajamas and my grandmother's nightgown. I had just enough time to pick up the treasures that had fallen off my bed that afternoon when my mother had called for my help. That seemed days or even weeks ago, I thought, as I put the shell back into the wooden box. I heard my grandmother's paralyzed foot dragging along the hallway floor, so I quickly turned down the blankets of both beds and puffed up my grandmother's pillow.

"Here, Bubby, sit down and I'll help you with your nightgown. Did you take your medicine?"

"Don't worry, I keep telling you. Everything is done and will be done, Sarah." She's talking so mysteriously, I thought to myself. She was setting an uncomfortable tone, and I was beginning to feel nervous about the story to come. What did she mean by "getting rid of Esther Bagoudis," anyway? Maybe this was going to be one of those tales that left me with nightmares chasing me around my sleep.

"Here, Bubby, lie back, and I'll scoop your feet under the covers." I was trying for a tone of normalcy, in an effort to guide my grandmother back to her normal way of speaking.

"I'm lying, I'm lying, Sarah." Did she mean she was reclining, which she seemed to be doing, or did she mean the truth was a forgotten commodity? I couldn't read her at all. I pulled up my grandmother's blanket, snapped off the ceiling light, and began changing into my pajamas.

"I don't want you to be upset when I die, Sarah."

My hands began to shake instantly, and I buttoned the front of my pajama top wrong. I had to undo the whole row of buttons and start over. "Please, Bubby, stop talking about that. It makes me very sad."

"There's nothing to be sad about. You'll know everything, and I'll be done. It's very important for you to know everything, to learn everything. And then, what will I have to live for?"

"This is a terrible discussion! And you're hurting my feelings, because I don't want you to leave me."

"Okay, Sarah, never mind. Get into your bed, and I'll tell you what happened the night I found Avram." I squinted through the dim light that the hall fixture was casting into the bedroom, studying my grandmother, trying to understand which of her comments was the true one. But Mary was settling back and looking up at the ceiling, as if she were trying to conjure up the scene that she was about to pick up. I could see that my grandmother was more focused on the past than on her uneasy granddaughter, so I got into my bed and propped myself up against the headboard to listen.

"The building where Avram lived with his cousins was the biggest building I was ever in. Not as big as that train station, but this was a house, a big apartment house. Maybe it was nice once, when it was built, but even I could see that those days were long over. I remember that place like I was there yesterday, Sarah. The cousins lived in three rooms, big for two men. And I remember that they paid three shillings for rent, and every week a man came to collect. Once, Mrs. Salomon next door, we used the same toilet, right in the hall, she didn't have the rent, and Shimon, that was the collector's name, Shimon, he banged on the door, screaming, 'Three shillings or you'll be on the street by tomorrow, Salomon, tomorrow morning!' Shimon didn't know that Salomon wasn't there anymore. He had deserted his family, but he couldn't help it. He had no work he could do. I think he tried working in every trade, peddler, buttonhole maker, butcher, shoemaker, even a corpse-watcher he was. But he loved the Talmud more, he wanted only to study, and so he never lasted in any business. And sure enough, the next morning, Shimon's men came and emptied out the whole flat into the street. Mrs. Salomon and the four children, I remember they sat there on the bundles, waiting for what to do next. I don't know what happened to them."

My grandmother paused, seeming to watch the scene she was remembering. I too could see the forlorn family huddled together on their belongings, three barefoot children in ragged clothing and their haggard mother holding a whimpering baby, right in the middle of the sidewalk with a throng of people sweeping toward them, parting like a stream around boulders, and passing them by. But what did all this have to do with Esther Bagoudis? My grandmother's memories were crowding each other out, and the thread of the narrative was lost somewhere, it seemed. But then she took a deep breath, and seemed to blow that memory away as she exhaled. The tale resumed.

" So Avram and me, we walked into his cousin's home for the first time. I stopped by the door, and Avram went to speak quietly to Chaim. Faivel sat by a table, a plate of food was in front of him, and he just looked at me. I knew he was admiring my coat, so I stood up straighter and I smoothed out the front so he could study the embroidery better. He never smiled or said a word to me. I think I was too beautiful, and I scared him." I could hear the smile in my grandmother's last words, but they were followed by a sound of disdain. "Tsk, tsk. I don't think Faivel spoke ten words to me the whole time I lived there. He was a cold fish who had no business to judge me." I feared that my grandmother would be derailed by the anger she still felt for her husband's cousin, and anger that had festered for half a century. But it seemed that she was so accustomed to that anger that she was able to box it up again in an instant, and the story was picked up.

"Chaim glanced at me a few times as Avram spoke in whispers to him. I looked around, and I saw an oilcloth floor, so dirty that the grime hid the pattern on it. And I saw also a large dresser for dishes and glasses and pots, maybe, but the shelves above it were almost empty, and the few pieces I saw had chips and missing handles. While Avram spoke, the room grew darker and darker, until finally, Faivel stood up, and went to light the gas mantle that was hanging from the ceiling. Then I could see the stove, black polished iron it was, with a fire behind a grate, and a copper coalscuttle next to it on the floor. The stove, for some reason, they kept clean. Maybe they never used it? Later, I found out there were cook shops around Whitechapel, so maybe they took in food from outside.

"Then Chaim turned away from Avram and spoke to me. 'If you're living here, you'll work. So there's the Sunlight,' he said and pointed to a big bar of yellow soap, 'and you can go tomorrow and get washing soda and Reckett's blue dye, and start on the washing.' Avram stood quietly. Chaim was naming things I never heard of, but I would learn, oh yes. I would learn to scrub on a wooden washing board, and wring until my hands were knotted with cramps, and hang the clothes from a rope across the room, and heat the irons on the stove to take out the wrinkles, and scrub the floor with a stiff brush on my hands and knees until the colors appeared again, and go every day for food to cook, and keep it in the wooden frame with the wire mesh that hung from the window outside, and keep the Passover dishes in the small dresser, and hang up the fly paper, and burn the sulphur candles to kill the bed bugs, and boil the sheets when there was finally enough money to buy them, and take in bundles of cloth from E. Moses and Son to make mantles for women, embroidered with silk threads, no one could do it better, they said. Yes, I learned it all."

This tirade had exhausted my grandmother, I knew, and I sat up and looked over to her bed to see if she had worn herself out. But I could see the rage on my grandmother's face, could see her lips pursed around her toothless gums, and her good hand pulling rhythmically on her right cheek. She wasn't worn out; on the contrary, she had uncorked a gush of adrenaline, and was just getting warmed up. I lay back against my headboard, wondering what all this had to do with Esther Bagoudis.

"After Chaim spoke to me, Avram, who was listening with one hand on his chin, spoke. 'Mayrke,' he said to me, and I looked at him, expecting him to tell me it would not be my job to clean his cousin's house. 'Mayrke, I must go out for a while. There is something I must do. You'll stay here with my cousins and unpack your carpetbag, and tomorrow we'll go together to buy a new hat for me.' He never mentioned a word about how Chaim spoke to me! I should have seen then. But I didn't.

'Out?' I said to him. 'Where out in the middle of the night?'

'It's not the middle of the night, Mary, and it's not your business to question where I am going. You'll unpack, and soon I'll be back'

"And then he nodded to his cousins, stepped around me, opened the door and left. I looked from one unsmiling face to the other, and then Chaim pointed with his chin to one of the other doorways. So I picked up my bag and marched past the two of them through that doorway and into a bedroom. It was cold in there, and it wasn't even winter yet. Almost the whole room was filled with the bed, and along the wall were some hooks to hang things. I hung my coat on one hook and then I opened my bag, hung my other shirtwaist and my shift on another one of the hooks, and sat down on the bed to make a plan. I knew, Sarah, where Avram had gone. He went to Esther Bagoudis. But I didn't know why. Maybe he went to tell her that Mary, the most beautiful girl in the world had come to him, and he would rather be with her beauty than with anyone else. But maybe he went to tell her that something terrible had happened, that someone from the old country was chasing after him, and they two, him and Esther, would have to run away that night, maybe to Manchester in the north where some Jews had gone, like Wolf Blumenfeld, who made wooden barrels, he took his family there, to get married. How could I know which was the truth? Oh, how I wished for Rivka that night, if only she hadn't died and left me with no one to talk to."

I considered the two possibilities as my grandmother mourned quietly for her long lost friend. There were some despairing moans that wafted across the space between their beds, and I nearly got up to comfort her. But I didn't want to break the spell that always settled around the story telling, so I waited hopefully. I'm here, I thought to myself, so Avram must have gone to tell Esther that he didn't really love her. Poor Esther! What ever became of her after she was jilted, I wondered? It wasn't her fault that Avram obviously didn't tell her the truth when they met. But maybe the version of the truth that I thought I understood because of my family's disdain for the mysterious Esther Bagoudis wasn't the truth that really happened. There could be only one truth, I knew, but what if you were standing at a different angle when you observed events, or when you heard about them or retold them? Maybe Esther Bagoudis married someone else, and there was a girl who lived a life that was parallel to mine, and she knew a different truth. I was deeply involved in trying to piece together an answer to the question of truth when my grandmother began speaking again, and so I determined to come back to it another time.

"And then suddenly I knew what to do. My mother would have died if she knew the plan, but my mother would never know. She was there, in Ulla, and I was here in London, and I knew we would never see each other again. And she had maybe already sat shiva for me after the way I left with the money and Dvorah's coat. Sarah, don't hate me after I tell you what I did."

"Hate you, Bubby! I could never –" I started to reply, but my grandmother wasn't really interested in an answer.

"My plan was to take off all my clothes, and lie down in the bed there in that cold room, and wait for Avram to come back. And when he came into the room, he would see me there, and he would come to me because he would have no choice, he would move without will. I would wait for him with my hair unpinned, and my arms would be open and my legs would be open." I gasped. The picture my grandmother presented meant bad things, and even though I wasn't quite sure exactly what those things were, I knew enough about them to catch my breath and wait for the rest of the story. I pulled the blankets tight around my throat, and tried not to hear what I was hearing. But Mary's voice went on, sounding sly and menacing and somehow proud.

"And he would give me a baby and it would be that night, I knew it would be that night, and then no matter what plan he made with Esther Bagoudis, he would have a new plan with me. If Avram left me for Esther Bagoudis, nothing in the world would be as it was. The air would grow black, the birds would weep, the fruit would die on the trees and fall into stinking mounds of rot, the trains would steam off their tracks and pile into smoking heaps of bent and crushed metal and wood, and flies would swarm in great buzzing masses. Haystacks would catch fire, and rivers would swell over their banks and flood the towns and fields. No one would fall in love and then the first-born in each house would sicken and die."

The words were Biblical. Suddenly, outside the window of my bedroom, there was a sound of squealing tires, and I heard the crack and thud of two cars meeting each other with powerful force. A dog yelped in pain and a cat shrieked an angry response. And then I heard sirens wailing. It was too much to think that it was a coincidence. My grandmother's words and the implications of what she had said were so ugly that the world, which must have been passively listening outside the window, had to react.

"Do you mean you tricked him, Bubby?" I spoke with a tone that was so incredulous that I could barely be heard. Of course, no one heard me anyway. The fairytale love story dissolved and was sucked away in a roar that rivaled my mother's vacuum. Didn't Bubby love him? Didn't she make her way all the way from Ulla to

London because of love? And didn't he marry her because she was as beautiful as a princess who glowed with goodness and inner light? And didn't they create a family of seven children because they were so in love that they wanted to bring more and more love into the world? Everything that I had understood was shattered into shards like a drinking glass that slides out of wet hands and explodes into a million sparkling razors. And just as all my old ideas were swept away, new ones rushed in to take their places. My family, the boisterous bubbling crowd that grouped itself together every Sunday but acted towards each other in ways that were often inexplicably nasty and spoke to each other daily but often with scathing venom, that family arose not from some romantic adoring attraction. No, those men and women surfaced and evolved into their poisonous mutual attraction from a calculated lie. And the liar was my loving and beloved grandmother. She was the one responsible for all the unhappiness in the family that spread into wider and wider circles each week. She was the one who was in the middle of their tangled up jealousies, suspicions and despair. But the worst of it was that I realized there was something terribly wrong inside my grandmother's head. She was a person who was the victim of a man, her father who had hurt her because he had no control over his evil impulses, and she then used herself on another man who she thought would have no control over his own impulses. The whole thing was too impossible.

Silence was coming form my grandmother's bed. "Are you there, Bubby?' I didn't know if I meant to question whether my grandmother was all right, or if the grandmother that I had known up to that point was the person in the other bed.

"I'm here, Sarah. But I think I need to go to sleep now. You go see how your mother's hand is feeling. We'll talk again tomorrow, okay?"

I slid out of my bed and went into the hall. But I knew I couldn't go downstairs and see my parents. My new knowledge was rambling all around my brain, and I didn't think it was safely tucked away enough to allow for a normal conversation. I turned into the bathroom where I sat down on the edge of the bathtub and tried to read the label on the bottle of shampoo. As I read, I quietly pictured the latest version of the Breck girl that had appeared on a page in the *Seventeen* that Stacie had left on the night table of the extra bedroom. And as I did those two things, silent tears poured over my eyelids and down my cheeks. After a while, I blew my nose into a length of toilet paper, and went back to bed.

## Twenty-One

The news about my mother's accident was exciting to my family for only a few days. Bigger news was brewing for them in their crowded apartments in the Bronx. The details, they promised in a flurry of phone calls, would be forthcoming on Sunday. I saw some kind of resignation on my mother's face as she spoke to first one sister and then another. A blue sling held her bandaged hand close to her chest as if she were hugging herself with one arm. She couldn't pilot the noisy vacuum cleaner around, and so Joe did it when he came home from the city.

"What would be so terrible if you skipped vacuuming for a few days, Rikki?" he inquired with a smile playing around his mouth. He steered the vacuum cleaner around the black and white checked armchairs in the living room. He was still wearing the suit he had worn to work, the jacket hanging from the back of Mary's chair and his tie tucked inside his shirt just below the tie bar. He had to shout his question over his shoulder to be heard over the roar of the motor. Rikki was following him with her forehead furrowed with worry lines, pointing to corners and under tables, making sure that not a square inch was missed. She ignored his question, rightly recognizing it as affectionate teasing. I was following behind him because although tools and machines were second nature to him, seeing the vacuum cleaner in his hand made me uncomfortable. The world was askew if my father was cleaning the living room.

I stepped after him as if he might hand off the vacuum cleaner to me like a baton in a relay race. But when he backed up and drew the vacuum cleaner after him, he ran right into me, stepping on my feet.

"Sarah! What are you doing following me like a shadow? Did I hurt you?"

"No, I'm okay," I replied, reaching down to rub my ankle.

"What's going on around here?" He turned off the vacuum cleaner and pulled the handle upright. The room was instantly quiet, and I relaxed my shoulders, which had been drawn up to my ears in the din. "You're mopey, Rikki, Sarah is attached to my leg, and where is David? He disappeared outside the second he finished his dinner. And where have you put Bubby, Sarah? I think she went to the bathroom and fell in!"

I giggled even though any image of Bubby's being hurt usually frightened me. "I think she's maybe sitting on a folding chair in front of the house. I told her it would get dark very soon, but she said spring is here, and the world is new again. David got her coat for her before he left. I think he's playing Ring-a-levio down the block. They started two days ago, so maybe the game is almost finished by now."

Rikki was momentarily alert. "Ring-a-levio on a school night? I don't understand how he thinks it's fine to go out without doing any homework. Joe, you'll have to talk to him." I looked at my mother, waiting for her to relax her face so the two lines between her eyebrows would disappear.

"Should I vacuum or talk to David?" he said, smiling. It seemed to me that he was unconcerned about both tasks. Only my mother saw them as serious enough to knit her brows together.

Rikki remembered her husband's question, and responded as if there had been no intervening discussion. "Nothing is going on around here. And we'll hear about it on Sunday." She seemed unaware that she had contradicted herself. Joe wrapped the cord up and down, looping it around the two brackets on the vacuum cleaner handle. He watched his wife as she sat down on the piano bench, her arm clutched tightly to her chest. The fingers that protruded from the end of the bulky bandage were splotchy

brown, stained with some solution that the doctor had poured on her palm before he

stitched it closed. My eye was drawn repeatedly to the brownness of my mother's

fingers. And even though the procedure had been explained to me, I couldn't help but

think that the doctor must have removed her whole hand and sewn on someone else's,

someone with brown skin.

"What will we hear about on Sunday, Rikki? Which of your sisters told you

which story this week? I thought I smelled the phone lines burning all the way in the

city." My gaze darted for a split second from my mother to the hallway where the phone

was sitting serenely on the desk. It was a joke, I told myself. The phone lines weren't

burning.

"It's not important. Never mind." She looked at the carpet, and bent over to

retrieve a small piece of lint that her husband had missed.

"Rikki. What is going on, I asked you?" The smile was out of his voice. He

beckoned to me with his chin to roll the vacuum cleaner away to its place on the top

landing of the basement stairs. I began to push it away, but listened as I went. All I got

from my mother's half of the phone conversations was that some big changes were about

to happen. Each time my mother hung up the phone, she sat where she was and dusted

the surface where the phone rested, or the phone itself, over and over, all the time

cradling her wounded hand carefully.

"All I know is that Jean started something, some complaints about the Bronx, that

she's never going into her butcher's store again, and the vegetables in the green grocer's

are rotten, and something about lettuce leaves on the floor. She was threatening to slip and break her leg, if that would make Solly happy. But then she wouldn't tell me anything else. But then I spoke to Ruthie, and she said Jean is right about the Bronx, which is the first time I've heard Ruthie agree with Jean about anything. But then Stacie came in screaming so she hung up right away, and she's not answering her phone. And Esther, well, do I need to tell you about Esther? All I can get from her is humphing." Just as she paused to collect her thoughts, Joe imitated Esther's humph. It was the perfect blend of disdain, disgruntledness and displeasure. Suddenly both of my parents were laughing. I closed the basement door and came into the living room. They were now sitting next to each other on the piano bench, and my father kept repeating Esther's humph, each time exaggerating it further. They laughed together uproariously, like two silly third graders, I thought. But at least the lines on my mother's brow had disappeared.

"So I guess we'll find out on Sunday, just as they promised," said Joe, the laughter finally dissipating. Rikki was wiping away tears of laughter that had trickled out of her eyes.

"I guess," she agreed. And for the moment, the house felt normal again.

It rained that Sunday, a cold, early spring rain, and that forced all the cousins to find activities inside. They were all crammed into the basement, and they had created a huge tent city there using all Rikki's extra blankets and summer slipcovers that had been stored along the walls in wooden bins. They had used the laundry lines that were strung across the room, first pulling down all the drying laundry in their frenzy to get something to hold up the blankets. I tried to tell them that Rikki would be angry. "We have to ask first! The laundry is getting all smushed! Please, we have to ask first!" But my cousins were too excited to hear my protests, and probably didn't even notice when I backed away and retreated up the stairs. If I couldn't stop them, I wasn't going to be involved. My mother liked her house to be orderly, and creating what Bubby would call a hegdish in the basement would not be greeted with enthusiasm. I walked up the stairs, my cousins' screams fading as I drifted through the door at the top of the stairway and closed it behind me. I wandered into the living room and took up my post by the door leading into the kitchen.

"I'm taking an apartment in the building across from the school. My girls can just roll out of bed into their classes," Aunt Jean was announcing.

"You'll be in the middle of the screaming kids in the playground, Jean. This appeals to you?" Aunt Esther scoffed at her sister's ignorance. "I'm taking two blocks down. My kids will walk two blocks and like it just fine." She turned her attention to retrieving a cigarette from her purse, and for her, the subject was no longer of any interest.

"It figures you don't care if they get wet going to school, Esther," put in Aunt Ruthie. "But when did Jean start caring about her children's convenience? You've become suddenly a devoted mother, Jean?"

"As a matter of fact, bitchiest sisters in America, I already visited the new school, P.S. 206, and I put my name in to run for president of the P.T.A. And when I left the building, walking down Queens Boulevard, every person I passed was looking at me with green jealousy eyes." Aunt Ruthie and Aunt Esther glanced at their youngest sister who sat with her arms crossed with a self-satisfied smirk on her face. I considered whether someone could willfully change her personality. Aunt Jean was probably getting involved with her children's new school just to make herself look good, I decided.

Everyone was clustered around the table, even Aunt Rose Aronsky, looking down at some plans that were spread out from one end to the other. Mary sat in her straight chair at the head of the table, silent and seemingly ignored, and her children leaned over her, almost shoving her out of their way, as they examined whatever it was that was on the table. It looked to me like they thought she was in the way, and something about the way she sat, maybe her posture, the tilt of her head, made me think she thought she was in the way, too, and was just serenely waiting to die. I shoved that thought aside, and I inched into the kitchen to try to get a peek, but the wall of aunts and uncles in front of me made it impossible. Aunt Jean went on with her pronouncements.

"I don't know why I stayed in the Bronx this long. What, am I waiting to get killed there? And the hills? Who can walk up those hills forever? I can't wait for the buildings to open. They told me and Solly by next month, we'll be in, right Solly? And I'm not taking one stick of furniture with me. I'm buying all new." As they all murmured agreement, I was amazed at my aunt's words. She never acknowledged that she was in a partnership with Uncle Solly on anything. Uncle Solly looked adoringly at his wife, probably overjoyed at having been recognized at all. Apparently, Uncle Mayshe noticed too. He listened to her speech, and replied, "Azoi?" which I knew meant, "So?" But the tone didn't indicate warm interest, like he wanted her to go on with this very fascinating topic. It was, rather, sarcasm. He was always waiting to look down on one of his relatives.

"Did you tell Eli the peddler that his shtupping days are over, Jean?" That brought on an eruption of jeers and angry remarks all around. I didn't know the Yiddish word he had used, but his tone was unmistakable. He was accusing his youngest sister of something improper, or immoral, or maybe even illegal. But he ignored the disdain of his siblings. "Or maybe he'll follow you to Queens, Jean? Are you worth his time?" That brought on a new spate of reprovals aimed at him, which he also ignored. "Come on, Marly, I'm leaving. Get Daniel up here. I don't need to look at apartment plans all day."

So, I thought to myself, they're all moving to Queens. Uncle Mayshe and Aunt Marly already lived in Queens, having moved to a house about a year earlier. And Uncle Morty and Aunt Rose had left the Bronx, too, but I couldn't remember when that had happened. Now their sisters were following, moving with their families into a new complex that was almost ready for occupancy. I listened carefully to the conversation, trying to determine the implications. Everyone seemed excited about this new chapter in their lives, and so I relaxed into the glow their conversations were creating. The carping among them toned itself down after Uncle Mayshe left, and they began speaking excitedly about paint colors, and new kitchens, and how close the subway was. Even Rikki, usually silent while her sisters and brothers carried on in their regular way, had things to add to the discussion. "You'll be so close, now. I can bring Mama for a visit even during the week," she ventured. Interestingly, I thought, they ignored her. There stood my mother, her arm in a sling, and no one paid her any attention. For a second, I considered inserting myself into the bubble of noise in the kitchen, to defend my mother. But I knew the aunts and uncles would make fun of me, and probably of my mother, too, so I remained quiet. My grandmother glanced back over her shoulder, somehow sensing my presence, and flashed me a look of understanding. In one fleeting instant, my anger was becalmed. Mary turned back before I could return a look of thanks. But her having reaffirmed our special partnership made me glow with importance.

I faded back into the living room, and scrolled through my memories of visits to the various apartments in the Bronx that I knew. I thought of the linoleum with nursery rhyme motif on the floor in Aunt Jean's kids' room. The words of the poems were printed whimsically beside the pictures, but I remembered that before I knew how to read, I would look at the charming pictures of a cow jumping over a smiling moon, and a boy leaping improbably high over a candle in a shiny brass candlestick, and a fat king sitting on a tiny upholstered stool counting piles of money while a flock of blackbirds flew out of a pie perched on a table just over his left shoulder, and recite each one with flawless precision. My older cousin Veronica, Aunt Esther's snobby daughter, had been awestruck, I remembered. "You can read, Sarah? You're, what, six? Five? How do you know how to read?" Veronica questioned me with a combination of admiration and disdain. I knew I wasn't reading, exactly. Rikki had read and recited nursery rhymes to me and my brother so many times that I knew them all by heart. But I let Veronica think what she wanted, calculating that telling her the truth would bring more teasing than I'd know what to do with.

That memory of Aunt Jean's house dissolved, and I thought of the out-of-bounds living room in Aunt Esther's apartment, where a tell-tale foot print on the carpet would result in a fast slap across the offender's face. The family didn't gather at Aunt Esther's house often because Bubby never stayed there, and they always went where she was. I imagined that Aunt Esther's meticulous housekeeping was another reason that family gatherings there were nearly unknown. I remembered that I was once eating a piece of Aunt Esther's homemade cake at her kitchen table, and Aunt Esther had lifted the plate before I had finished to wipe the table of crumbs that had fallen around it. "Do you want me to get cockroaches? Stop making crumbs!"

I also recalled the one time they were all there, and the aunts and uncles had been allowed to sit in the living room, but the children had not been. I pictured myself lined up with several of my cousins along the scalloped edge of the carpet between the hallway and the living room, watching our lucky parents sitting around on the forbidden furniture. We kids leaned into the room, risking reprimand but enjoying our daring, I remembered, but we were quickly shooed back the bedroom where we were allowed to play. "And no food in the bedroom!" Aunt Esther's voice followed them. "I'm not getting cockroaches for the likes of you!" I didn't feel exactly unwelcome there, just deeply inside Aunt Esther's atmosphere, which was different than the one I was used to. Even its negativity took on a certain warm nostalgia in memory, now that they were leaving that apartment.

I imagined myself filing out with my cousins, and then I saw myself in Aunt Ruthie's small apartment, with its more crowded but more welcoming living room. There was the dark green velvet sofa with the rich green fringe along the bottom edge. Hanging above it was a dark painting of a dashing soldier from olden times brandishing a gleaming sword and riding a heroic horse whose forelegs were reared high in the air. I remembered trying to figure out the story the painting was depicting, but I never got beyond the words of a song my mother used to sing that began, "In days of old, when knights were bold." The words after that were too antique for me to understand, and the painting was too dark, anyway. My memory trailed down the narrow hall to the bedrooms, which were so small that the beds and dressers completely filled them, leaving no room to play.

I snapped back to the present, feeling regret that I'd never see those things again, and I couldn't understand how my aunts could be so unconcerned about the loss of the familiar their families might feel. I wandered out to the porch and watched the rain pelt the backyard. It looked like the sky was crying too, I thought. I wondered if the cousins even knew what was in store for them. They were all downstairs playing in tents made of blankets. Maybe their impending moves to Queens had inspired their game, I thought. They were constructing blanket houses down there, after all. I didn't understand how they could be so carefree in the face of the upheaval just ahead. New houses, new schools, new friends, new paint colors, new furniture. I thought the whole prospect was terrifying. But none of my cousins had even mentioned it. They must be experts at burying feelings, I decided. But truly, wasn't I good at the same skill? I used my ability to hide feelings in a different way, and it surfaced in the form of worry. They were either better at it, or maybe it came out in some different way. I never heard anyone except my mother speak to any of them without criticizing or deriding them   No wonder they had hard shells. Now that I'm looking back, I see that those hard shells never softened, and the resulting adults are isolated from the other people because of them. They can't allow any warmth to penetrate in or out, and they have no idea that trusting people makes the world better, easier, and more comfortable.

I sat on the glider, pushed up and back with my feet that just barely reached the floor when I sat back against the cushions, and watched the rain.

Twenty-Two

That night, after my aunts and uncles had folded up their new apartment plans,
emptied the usual stockpile of snacks into lunch bags and departed for the Bronx for
perhaps the last time, my grandmother and I mounted the stairs together. My parents
were tidying the kitchen and murmuring quietly together, maybe about the implications
of the impending moves. I was still uneasy about the revelations of the most recent
chapter in my grandmother's tale, but that didn't cancel my need to know what happened
next. Maybe, I held out hope, it all worked out differently than it seemed it would.
Maybe, I thought to myself, as I helped my grandmother into her nightgown, Avram had
come back from his mysterious errand and entered the apartment calling, "Mayrke, my
love, marry me tomorrow; I'm back with the ring!" And maybe she quickly jumped into
her dress before he saw the nasty ruse she was planning. I knew my fairytale version was
unlikely, and my grandmother's quiet groans as she made her way back from the
bathroom were setting a somber mood.

"Bubby, do you feel okay? Does something hurt you?"

"I'm fine, my Sarah. I was just thinking, and I guess my thoughts escaped out of
my mouth. We'll just sweep up that bundle of misery and I'll tell you something happy."
I had a quick image of a pile of debris, like autumn leaves or the ashes that were left
when my father burned them, being scooped off the carpet in the hall into a big dustpan
and dumped instantly out the narrow bathroom window. Who was sweeping? I
narrowed my eyes and focused on the picture in my mind. It was the young Mary,
wearing her sister's embroidered coat, pulling open the bathroom window with ease, even
thought I knew it always stuck. "Just help me with this blanket," my grandmother

interrupted my thoughts, and I'll tell you what happened the next day, after I, well, after I did what I did."

So she really tricked Avram, I, thought. I didn't know exactly what my grandmother had done, and I didn't ask because my grandmother's reticence about that moment told me enough. I think children must be born with some sense of what sex is, or pro-creation, maybe, but they also sense it's something they're not supposed to know, so they make up explanations while they wait to be told the truth. A clear understanding of Mary's actions was the exact first thought I had when, just about a year later, Rikki had begun to explain where babies came from. My mother had handed me a little booklet to read on my tenth birthday, quickly explained the rudiments of menstruation and its implications and left me to think about any questions I might have. I had questions, for sure, but they had nothing to do with what would happen to my body. They were all about my mother's parents and what they had done that first night Mary had spent in London. But that story had been told to me in secrecy, and if there was one thing I knew how to do, it was keep a secret. Secrets were not only the bread and butter of my family, I thought, they were the meat, the salad, and the dessert.

I must have had some kind of doubt about the story; how could I think of my old and broken grandmother as some kind of sexual siren, after all? But twenty years later, I visited the Royal Hall of Records during a trip to London. And there it was, irrefutable proof: my grandparents' official wedding date, and five months later, Uncle Morty's birth written in spidery handwriting in faded black ink in huge ledger books with dates on their spines that divided each year into quarters. The truth of this story attested to the truth of all of them, I thought.

My grandmother began to speak before I had even finished putting on my pajamas. The light from the ceiling fixture illuminated the room brightly, and I leaped across the room to snap the switch off. Mary's stories were meant for a darkened room, I thought. I didn't think I could bear to actually see my grandmother's face as she explained what had happened next. I sidled silently into my bed, promising myself to get up when the story was done for the night to brush my teeth and wash my face. Everything had been out of order that day, from the turmoil in the basement to the impending moves to the story beginning too soon. I turned my attention to my grandmother's words.

"I never knew where Avram went out. Maybe he would have said if we had talked. But we didn't talk that night." There was a momentary pause as she seemed to think that over. "The truth is, we quickly learned never to talk to each other like civilized human beings. He taught me that when he sent me that letter telling me not to come, and I taught him the night I came anyway. A shandeh, was my life with him."

Shame? I knew the word, and found it profoundly tragic.

"There was nothing to talk about. He knew why I was there, in London instead of Ulla, and he knew I wasn't going back. But I still see his face when he opened the bedroom door and saw me. It was dim there because the lamp wasn't lit, but the lamp in the front room was shining over his shoulder, and I saw stars sparkle in his eyes. He stood there with one hand still on the doorknob for a few seconds looking at me, how I was lying there on the bed. And then he realized maybe his cousins could see me, which I didn't care, let them look, but he shut the door behind him, and we were in the dark.

"'Mayrke,' he said to me. But it was almost no voice he used, just breath. And he stepped in one step to the bed, and was on me."

The room was silent and I knew my grandmother was watching the scene in her head as if it were a movie that a projectionist was throwing onto a private screen. I waited quietly, not knowing quite what to imagine myself.

"And that was the beginning of my Morty. All I had to do was wait a few weeks, and I could tell Avram the good news. He fell asleep there next to me like he fell into a deep pit and banged his head. He didn't move the whole night, not once, and I know because I never slept for one minute, I just watched him. I was smiling, so happy, because I knew my life would now be perfect: Avram, so handsome with his black wavy hair and beautiful white shirt and his cane, and me, so beautiful I was glowing like a sun, together we would throw from us a warmth that people from all over would know about. And soon a baby would come who would be as handsome as his father, or as beautiful as her mother. But I knew really that it would be a son for Avram, because that would be the key that locked the promise."

I knew that my grandmother was talking about the promise that my grandfather had made back on the side of the hill at the fire in Ulla. I wondered if it seemed as far in the past to my grandmother as it seemed to me. My memory, after all, extended back five or six years at most. Mary was thinking of a moment that was as ancient as, well, George Washington, I thought to myself. No, I decided, it was the moment that had propelled the rest of her life. To her, it must have seemed as immediate as yesterday.

"So the next day, we came out of the room together to the parlor, and the cousins were gone. Avram had first on his face a very shy look, like he was afraid to look at me after what we did. But I was more bold. 'Look,' I said to him, 'we've been married in our minds and hearts since the day of the fire, right?' He was busy trying to make more heat come from the stove. I could see he knew nothing about that stove, not even how to scoop a few lumps of coal from the copper pail that was right there on the floor, and he was trying not to look at me. 'We'll go to a rabbi right away, and we'll have a marriage before God, with a ketubah and witnesses. And you'll have nothing to be shy about.' And then he looked up from the stove, and I saw in his face that he couldn't decide if he thought I was a whore that he hated, or a beautiful angel sent to him by a God that loved him because he followed all the commandments. There was a storm on his eyes, and his mouth opened and closed like a fish that was just pulled from the water. His hands were two white fists, and for a second I thought he would punch me. He took a deep breath and the air went in like a ragged edge of fabric getting caught on his tongue and teeth and throat. 'Mayrke,' he screamed at me, like a roaring beast, 'I think that, yes, we will marry, we must marry. And then we will live together and have children, beautiful children like you, maybe many children, as we are commanded by God. But we will all hate each other for the rest of our lives!' Those screaming words were the curse that we began with. Of course, I was used to curses. I'd been living with one for years."

Mary became silent. I felt the force of my grandfather's curse vividly. My grandmother's voice had been calm, and there was no sound of weeping or moaning floating from her bed like some sort of black storm cloud full of evil. But somehow that lack of emotional expression was so potent, so toxic, that it frightened me more than any part of the story had before. I could see glimpses of that curse growing like choking vines and breaking into suffocating flowers all over my aunts and uncles, even though I couldn't name their specific maladies and connect them with straight lines to that morning in London half a century earlier. It was as if they were all caught in the web of a lethal invisible spider that was throwing one silken tendril after another over them, binding them together, and they didn't even know how they were separated from the rest of the world and grown into each other. They nourished each other in that web, became each other's food and drink, but the more they each fed off the others, the more noxious the mixture became. For a second, I was relieved that I wasn't one of those caught in that web. But then, I realized with a gasp, that I was indeed one of them. But I also knew, dimly then, but with more clarity now, that it was the very knowledge of the true details of my grandmother's story that freed me from the choking control of that web. I could see the direction the story was taking, and in that moment, I abandoned completely the idea that this was any kind of happy fairy tale with a happily-ever-after ending.

"'No,' I said to him. 'Take that back! First my father cursed me and my life, and then my mother cursed me, and now you! No more curses! We must look to cancel the curses, not pile more layers on top. We will not hate each other.' Of course, I was screaming by then, too. I grabbed for something to throw, I was so angry. There was a plate on the table, I see it still, a small dish with flowers and leaves growing on it. I see it as it flies through the air, across the parlor, not near Avram, no, not near him. It smashed against the wall, near the door to the bedroom, and it shattered into a million sharp pieces. And the noise brought us to our senses. We looked at each other then, one on each side of the table, and then we moved around to meet, and we smiled, both of us, and laughed. It was the way we fought, always, screaming and shrieking and throwing, and then smiling. I think we knew a secret about each other, I don't know what, something that connected us somehow. And it held, the connection, like a knot it was, it held for years. For years and years and years. It almost held forever."

She was telling the story, I thought, as if it were the most ordinary tale. It was matter-of-fact as it came from my grandmother, but by the time it reached my ears, it had curdled and soured. How could she be so calm about it? Didn't she see the results as she sat every Sunday in her straight chair at the head of the table, listening and watching her children as they pinched and poked at each other with nasty words? Didn't she notice that her grandchildren were like a pack of unruly unsettled creatures, tearing apart any room they were in, hurling bad news at each other gleefully, and erupting in anger so intense that ordinary disagreements ended with bites that left black and blue tooth marks? Didn't she feel the least bit responsible or guilty? Maybe she thought it was the curse working its way through everyone. I couldn't sort through all my feelings fast enough. But my grandmother had been silent for a long time, and I thought that maybe the story was over for that night. I sat up and tried to see if she had fallen asleep. But as I squinted towards the other bed, Mary's voice began again.

"We left the apartment right away, and as we reached the street, Avram began telling me about the neighborhood, pointing out the stores and telling me what they sold in each, and where the shul was, and the theater, yes, a theater, and the mikvah, and everything I needed to know. Tomorrow, Sarah, tomorrow I'll tell you everything about Whitechapel Street. Now I'm tired. And I'll tell you about the hat store, in Saint James' Street, it was. And the present Avram bought me. I'll tell you tomorrow." And with that, she was asleep.

I was amazed at how she could weave in and out of misery and joy with such ease. It reminded me of an otter swimming. I had seen a nature show on television about otters, how they're so playful and sleek, and how they dart around the water as if they are equipped with propellers. That was my grandmother. It was almost as if her paralyzed body had to be offset by a mind that shifted moods as swiftly as Superman changed his clothes. And hearing my grandmother say, "Saint James," was almost funny. I didn't think she even knew the word saint; it was so far from her Yiddish accent I thought, as to be unpronounceable. But again I was learning that there were parts of that little old lady that were unexpected. By focusing on my memory of Bubby's voice saying saint, I was able to deflect the rest of the unsettling story. I thought for a minute about how maybe she did understand that she and my grandfather, but mostly she, were indeed responsible for the way their children had turned out. She believed in the curse, yes, but she knew that was only part of her legacy.

I turned over to my side, and set about falling asleep. I forgot about brushing my teeth.

Twenty-Three

Spring was nearly in place. It rained constantly, but one day, walking home from school, I realized it wasn't the kind of cold rain that seemed to seep through my skin and into my bones, but rather a soft warm bath that slid over my face when I tilted it up to the sky. It was a Friday, and Passover would start the following Monday, so I knew the weekend was going to be a frenzy of preparations. The aunts and uncles wouldn't be coming that Sunday because everyone would be busy putting away the everyday dishes and silverware and unpacking the separate Passover dishes that were kept in the back of closets the rest of the year. It would be even more complicated for them this year, because in addition to the usual upheaval of Passover, which required a major spring cleaning and purchasing of new spring dress-up outfits for everyone, they were all in the throes of moving. I had heard my mother on the phone with each of her sisters multiple times that week, but my mother's end of the conversation rarely included talking. Each sister was wound up in her own ways. As I splashed along in puddles, I ran over yesterday's conversations, which were typical.

"But Ruthie, why can't you just put the everydays in the boxes for moving, and don't use them again until you get to the new apartment?" went one of my mother's arguments. She listened to the reply, and I could hear my aunt's voice, loud but indistinct, rushing back her response. "But can't you just use paper plates for the few days after Passover ends and before the moving truck comes?" More blurry shouts from Aunt Ruthie followed. "I know they cost money, Ruthie, I know." Rikki tried to interrupt her sister's tirade, but it was useless. I watched my mother as she sat on the edge of her bed, smoking her cigarette with great concentration, her eyebrows knit together forming a deep v-shaped crease above her nose. The conversation ended abruptly, Rikki barely having enough time to say good-bye before Aunt Ruthie hung up. "Boy, was she in a rush," my mother muttered to herself, hardly aware of my presence. I nodded in agreement, but the phone was ringing again, so Rikki didn't notice.

"Hello. Oh, Esther, it's you. I was just talking to Ruthie. She can't figure out how to handle the Passover dishes and the move." Silence followed. I watched my mother's face go from passive even planes, to open-eyed surprised, to shock. There was a quick intake of breath, and her hand flew to her mouth. Then she crushed out the half-smoked cigarette, seeming to signal that she would spring immediately to action. She even stood up for a moment. What was this going to be? I stepped toward my mother, but when she sat back down on the bed, I backed away again. "Oh." Pause. "Oh." Longer pause. "Oh, that's terrible, Esther." Rikki's hand went to her forehead. "No, you'll have to." She kneaded her cheek. "Well maybe Joe can do it." Her hand dropped to her lap with a fast slap. "Well, then never mind. Right. Okay. Yes. Bye." Rikki replaced the phone in the cradle, gently, almost as if not to wake it.

I stood by expectantly, waiting for my mother to turn to me and explain Aunt Esther's problem. But she just stared out the window into the rainy backyard, her eyebrows trying to meet each other, and I knew not to inquire. My mother snapped back from her worry, picked up the dust cloth she had been using on the night table where the phone was kept, and began wiping the surface she had already cleaned. I gave up waiting for an explanation and almost announced my intention to go out into the rain and splash in the puddles when my mother sat down on the edge of the bed again and reached for the phone. I waited to see whom she might be calling.

"Jean, I just hung up from Esther," she began. "Okay, I'm sorry. Hello. How are you? How is Solly? How are the kids? Okay? Now, did you talk to Esther today?" And then what followed was as cryptic as the previous conversation. I tried to follow for a few minutes, but nothing coherent developed, so I backed quietly into the hall, and turned to go downstairs and outside. I opened the front door at the bottom of the steps to check on the rain, but found to my disappointment that it had stopped. No running around in the rain for that day.

But all that was yesterday, and now it was Friday, and it was raining again as I walked home from school. The drama of my aunts and their moving/Passover problems faded back into the general complicated and dense fabric of my family, and I kept tilting my head back to try to get a drink of water from the sky faucet, as I was thinking of it. I pictured a giant spigot just above the thick layer of clouds where it was attached to a pipe that ran somewhere up and out my consideration, and it was spraying torrents of warm water that were filtered through the clouds and down to the ground. I couldn't accumulate enough in my mouth to create a swallowful. Cousin Daniel had once told me, gleefully, of course, that ducks drown when they lift their heads up in the rain. I couldn't see how it could happen. I was so busy looking up that I nearly crashed into the mailbox on the corner as I made the last turn. I oriented myself just before grazing my shoulder, and ran the rest of the way home.

"I'm going out in the rain! It's so warm!" I banged through the kitchen door with unusual recklessness, transported by the newly warm air. My grandmother was perched in her usual kitchen seat, a cup of tea in front of her, and a cube of sugar planted between her front teeth.

"Sarah, my perfect. Your hair is wet. Didn't you wear your hood up?" She wasn't worried, though. I could hear joy in her voice, and a kind of admiration at this new abandon she saw in her granddaughter. "I would do it with you, if I weren't a crippled old lady!" I was usually brought up cold by remarks like that from my grandmother, but I could hear in this one a conspiratorial joy.

I let my yellow raincoat slide off my arms on to the floor, and sat down on the edge of the bunk seat to take off my shoes and socks. "I'm going barefoot for the first time this year," I announced to her smiling grandmother. "And no bees are born yet to sting the bottoms of my feet!"

"But what about your school clothes? Shouldn't you change into play clothes?" It was a good question, I thought, but after a very fast consideration, I decided no, my school clothes would be fine. I didn't see my mother around, and I could hear the muffled roar of the vacuum cleaner wafting down the stairs, so I knew there would be no immediate recrimination. It was almost as if some power had descended on me, depositing some new sense of intoxication. Even my face felt different, and I could see that my grandmother saw the difference, too.

"Watch me, Bubby, from the front door!" And with that, I hopped off the bunk seat and pushed the kitchen door open. I leaned out at first, face up to the sky, mouth open, and stuck out my tongue. I tested the feel of the first step with my bare foot, liked the coolness of the concrete that I felt, and jumped down the rest of the way. I looked to my right, down the breezeway toward the backyard briefly, but opted for the front yard to my left. The door banged behind me as I hop scotched along the flagstones that led me to the driveway and down to the street. I looked back at the house just as my grandmother opened the front door, caught her eye and we both waved our arms with glee. I paused

for a moment at the bottom of the driveway to check that no cars were coming. My quiet

street was slick and shiny gray from the rain, but there was no traffic. As usual, there

wasn't even a car parked along the curved street. There was a wide stripe of tar down the

middle, almost a seam where the two sides of the road had been knitted together, and an

occasional narrower cross stripe. On hot summer days, when the sun baked those tar

stripes into a soft gumminess, the neighborhood kids would finish their Good Humor ice

cream pops, sharpen one end of the wooden sticks along the curb, and lie down on their

bellies in the middle of the road where the stripes met, and dig up globs of black goo.

But this wasn't a hot summer day, so I was alone outside. I stepped off the curb

into the rush of rainwater on its way to the storm drain and marched through it, splashing

waves of water into the street, onto the lawn and up over my skirt. It was exhilarating. I

walked up and back in front of my house, trying different methods of creating sluices of

water. Every so often, I glanced at the front door where my grandmother was nodding

and smiling at me.

When the curbside river lost its allure, I walked back up the driveway to

investigate new possibilities. By now, I was soaked through, the outline of my cotton

undershirt clearly visible through my Friday School Assembly white blouse. Even the

little pink bow in the front of my undershirt was showing through the blouse, I noticed as

I looked down to examine the results of the water. I had never cared less about being

correct and controlled. I had never felt freer or been filled with more joy. And I didn't

even try to examine it, analyze it, or judge its implications. It was just plain fun. I tilted

my head back as a new outburst of rain dumped itself on my head. Rivulets ran down my face, and I pushed hanks of hair back. Then I saw the edge of the eaves next to the front door.

The sky faucet was on full force, and the accumulated sheets of rain coming off the roof were cascading down the front of the house like a waterfall. The wall of water that was created by the flow was falling right onto the chair that sat just outside the front door. Everyone in the family thought of it as Bubby's chair, and no one else ever used it. I looked at it and looked at my grandmother who was standing just inside the door looking back at me with approval. I signaled with a wave that Mary should come out and sit under the floodwaters and get soaked with me. The old woman reached across her chest and her withered hand to the doorknob, almost, it seemed to me, as if she would comply. But then she withdrew her hand, and instead waggled her fingers in response.

I walked over to the chair, turned around, pinched the sides of my nose closed as if I were about to jump into a pool off a diving board, and sat back through the runoff river into the nylon webbed chair. Never letting go of my nose, I steadied the chair with one of the two arms as I sat, and the water splashed onto my head, and down my face. A small puddle began to accumulate in my lap, and finally, I felt cold. It wasn't summer yet, I thought to myself. I stood up and walked up the one step to the front door that my grandmother propped open for me as I approached.

"Was that fun, my Sarah?" she asked.

"I loved it," I replied. But my teeth were beginning to chatter, and both of us were suddenly mindful of what Rikki might say if she saw what we were up to.

"Come right here into the bathroom," my grandmother said, conspiratorially, opening the door to the small bathroom that was tucked in behind the front door. "Take off everything and rub yourself dry with the towels there. Then, you can sneak up the stairs and put on something dry. We can throw the wet clothes down the basement steps, and maybe you'll go down later and hang them up there on the line."

I grinned through my shivering mouth, and nodded in agreement. It was like we were accomplices in some crime, aiding and abetting each other to avoid detection by the mother-police.

Everything in our plan worked perfectly. Dinner was the usual Friday night roasted chicken and Joe and Rikki chatted about his day and that day's spate of phone calls from her sisters. She didn't mention the mystery call from Aunt Esther, I noticed, but I supposed it wasn't important. David had heard from his friend's older brother that there were boxing matches on television on Friday nights, and he had launched a campaign to be allowed to watch. He seemed to know his mother would never agree, and so he was aiming his appeal at his father, who seemed interested himself. The phone interrupted the discussion and David raced to get it. As Rikki got up to take the call, I took the opportunity to leave the table, and Joe moved into the living room to consider the Friday Night Fights option with his son. Mary shuffled away toward the stairs, and I realized that she seemed to be going to bed earlier and earlier all the time. "I'll help you, Bubby," I offered. "I think it's Uncle Morty on the phone, so who knows when that call will be over."

Rikki was frowning into the phone, and with her free hand, she waved her mother and daughter out of the room. I could hear her side of the conversation over my shoulder, something about telling Mama, or maybe it was not telling Mama. Bubby didn't seem to hear. As we made our way toward the stairs, she whispered to me, "Wasn't the rain fun?

You reminded me of me, when I used to swim in the river in Ulla, remember I told you? I used to love to swim. I used to go with Rivka, my friend. Did I ever tell you, Sarah, that I named your mother after my friend Rivka?"

A shadow of grief descended over her face. Even after, what, fifty years, I thought to myself, she was still missing her friend. "Avram didn't want that name. 'After a friend, Mayrke? Who ever heard of such a thing? Name her, better, after my Aunt Liba, not your friend. No one is named for Aunt Liba.' But I didn't listen, who could listen to him, a monster he turned out to be. And anyway, maybe Aunt Liba wasn't dead. He didn't keep in touch with anyone." We were mounting the stairs slowly.

"But why was he a monster, Bubby? And anyway, where is he now?" I dared to try for information. My nerve must have come from the bond of our puddle-splashing conspiracy.

"Who knows, Sarah? The last time I saw him was at a wedding, someone's wedding, I forget whose. Ask your mother." We both knew that would never happen; I'd never ask my mother about him. Rikki acted like she had never had a father. There was no talk of him the way they talked of other dead people, like, "Oh, I remember when we used to go to White Lake to visit with your Aunt Gertie," Rikki might say to Joe. "She was a lovely woman. I still have the sweaters she knit for the kids when they were born." And there was also no talk of him like he was alive, but not until recently heard from, like, "I want to go with Ruthie to see her childhood friend, Faye. Suddenly, from nowhere, she got a call from her," Rikki might announce to Joe. There was simply no mention of her father at all. How can a human being just slip off the earth without leaving even one footprint?

But the discussion of Avram's current whereabouts was over. Mary was only interested in talking about him as figure from her past. I helped her get ready for bed, pulling off her shoes, gently yanking her nightgown over her head and easing her arms into the sleeves. I was eager to hear about the trip to Saint James' Street and the present Avram had given Mary, but I had one more chore to do.

"Bubby, I have to go down the basement and hang up my wet clothes before anyone finds out. Can you stay awake until I come back so you can tell me about the present?"

But it was already too late. My grandmother was half asleep already, moaning softly in her semi-conscious state. Oh, well, I thought. Maybe tomorrow. There might be time tomorrow to explore the monster Avram from before he turned into a monster. I turned off the light and crept as quietly as possible down the stairs and then through the basement door. No one heard me. My movements were masked by television noise. "And there's a left-right combination, ladies and gentlemen. And down he goes, and maybe for good!"

Twenty-Four

The next morning, Saturday, was clear and balmy. I woke to the noises my father was making outside my window, in the breezeway below. He was busy raking leaves out of the rose vines that were planted there against the adjoining garage wall. I loved to see how two spectacular profusions of rose-covered vines could emerge from the small crescent shaped cutouts in the concrete paving. As the summer progressed, those vines would grow up the white asbestos tiles of the garage wall, arch over the open top of the breezeway, and have to be anchored to the wall of the house to prevent them from draping down onto the heads of anyone walking there. They formed the most exquisite vault of red petals and green shiny leaves. In the fall, when my father would take out his sharp clippers and cut the spent vines back to the ground, I was always happily surprised at the surge of sunlight in the breezeway, even as I mourned the end of that floral canopy.

I glanced over to the other bed and smiled at my grandmother who was watching her granddaughter become wakeful. "Do you want to hear about the present now, the gift?" was my grandmother's greeting.

Thinking furiously about the implications of this offer, I said, "I'd love to, Bubby. But do you want me to help you to the bathroom first, or get your morning pills?" I was almost afraid to break the spell of this unusual daytime foray into the story, but I didn't want any ordinary needs to come along a few minutes later and interrupt, once the flow of the narrative got started.

"No, my perfect Sarah, I did all that while you were still sleeping. I've been awake for a long time already, and I feel like we'd better get right to work."

"Work? Why are you calling the story work, Bubby? To me, it's not work at all."

"Will you remember it all, Sarah?" my grandmother replied, ignoring the question.

"I'll remember, Bubby. I'll always remember. But what do you want me to do with my remembering?" It was the first time I had considered why my grandmother wanted to explain herself to someone. I had always understood that there was some relief in this act of unburdening that my grandmother was engaged in. But if I wasn't supposed to tell anyone the secrets of the story, what was the importance of remembering?

"You might need it, someday. You might need to understand what happened to me, maybe. Just remember it, my Sarah, and don't worry why."

This was typical of the cryptic moods my grandmother had been getting into lately, and I knew there was no point in digging around further, or trying to insist on a clear answer. And anyway, my grandmother was beginning to speak, so I put my question aside and propped myself against the headboard and smoothed out the top hem of my blanket, ready to listen. The noise of my father's raking faded as my grandmother's voice began.

"So Avram was explaining about where to find the chicken flicker, and the greengrocer, and we were walking along together, arm in arm, like a husband and wife, very modern we were. My hair was piled up on top of my head, very stylish, with my hat pinned down, on an angle over the side of my forehead. We weren't really a husband and wife, of course, and I had no wig or ring, scandalous, we were, but laughing together as we made our way to Saint James' Street. 'We'll go first to Lock and Company, my beautiful Mayrke, and we'll replace my hat that ran away from me yesterday.' Oh, we laughed at the memory, Sarah, how the hat fell into the gutter, and we kept looking at each other. His face filled me with pleasure, and my face filled him with pleasure. I knew I had been right to find him in London. I didn't ask then about Esther Bagoudis; I left her in the back of my mind for another time. I wanted to tell him about my journey, about the coat, and the train, and my friend, maybe even the conductor on the train who knew to take care of me just by looking at me, and walking right off Saint Katherine's Dock, that was the name of where we landed, Sarah! I just remembered it! But we were too busy talking about what he wanted to talk about."

Mary paused, considering the conversation she had had a half century earlier, I thought, and I found myself amazed again at my grandmother's capacity to sort through so many years, and events, and facts, and names of people, and things, and places she'd been, and pluck up just the word she wanted, often surprising herself. I pictured my grandmother sitting silently at the head of the table in the kitchen every Sunday, watching her family, looking like she might not be able to follow the thread of conversation before her. They all talked around her, and over her, and behind her, treating her, it seemed, like she was barely more cognizant than a woman in a coma. Mistaken, they all were, I knew. Mary was on to them all, an expert at blending into the furniture, a master at not reacting. I briefly considered why she let them all go on thinking she was slightly beyond being able to follow a conversation, but abandoned the question when Mary began talking again.

"We walked for a very long time. 'We could go on a streetcar, Mayrke, but this way I'll show you better what London looks like.' It was almost impossible for me to take it in. Once we left his quarter, where I saw all Jews, it was all different. Some streets were wide, wide like an ocean of stones, with carriages and horses and noise, such noise, like I never heard. And the air was black in London. Chimneys were everywhere; on every building I saw the roofs with chimneys poking through on every corner and in the middle, too. And from each chimney was belching black smoke that tried to escape to the sky, but the sky was too full of smoke from the other chimneys, and no more could fit. So it was all pressed down to the street where it curled around the peoples' legs, like strands of long curls or squash vines, maybe with those little fingers that attached themselves to fences or walls. But no one even noticed, it seemed to me as we walked along. So I never said a word. Some other streets weren't wide, and the air smelled sour, like everything that lived there was already partly rotten. Ulla didn't always smell so good, it's true, but the stink of London hurt the inside of my nose and my throat. 'Don't worry about the smell, Mayrke,' he said to me when he saw how I was turning my face this way and that to get a clean swallow of air. 'We're going after the hat store to another store I know, just for you.' I remember how I smiled then, to think he was going to take me to a special store. But I wasn't surprised, of course, just happy that he was paying attention to me, and thinking of presents that I deserved."

In the pause that followed that remark, I glanced over at my grandmother. She was smiling, her lips closed tightly around her toothless gums, and her eyes closed so she could examine her memory closely. She looked so old and decrepit. How could she have been beautiful? And how vivid the importance of that beauty was to her! It was the clearest thing in her memory, more important to her than anything else. I suddenly felt sorry for her in a new way. Then she began again, interrupting my thoughts. "Those side streets were little alleyways that you wouldn't want to look down for fear of what you'd see. Children with no shoes, their feet black with filth, wearing rags, no better than rags. The buildings had dark doorways, and windows you couldn't see through with shredding edges of curtains blowing from broken panes of glass. And rats, I saw, Sarah, rats walking along like they weren't even ashamed to be rats. Terrible." She shuddered at her memory of that walk. Then she was silent for a minute. I waited patiently. "But then we passed from this neighborhood, and the buildings changed, and the smells changed too. I saw women in gray dresses with long aprons down almost to the hems, on their hands and knees scrubbing doorsills and stairs, pushing steaming buckets of water along as they went. Every doorway had a black iron shape just to one side, planted in the stone, low down, maybe as high as a boot top. What's that, I wondered? But I didn't ask because I didn't want Avram to see how stupid I was, not clever like maybe Esther Bagoudis. And then I saw a man walk up the stairs to a doorway, and scrape the bottom of his boots on the iron thing, and I knew what it was for! Horses were everywhere in London, leaving behind them a trail of something you didn't want to bring inside a house. How smart were these people in London! In Ulla, we left our boots outside and wore felt slippers in the house to keep it clean from the animals. But here in London, they could scrape their boots clean at any doorway.

"And as we walked along, street after street after street, I thought to myself that London was endless, a city that stretched from the edge of the water until the edge of the earth. Sometimes we passed a park, and once we even stopped and sat down to rest. There were children playing, each one being watched by a woman who never took away her eyes from them. I saw also babies in carriages, the first time I saw a carriage. But in

London, they called them perambulators. Perambulators." She stopped and I glanced over at her. Her face was wreathed in smiles as she pronounced the antique word from far away in another life. I could see the pleasure that my grandmother got from remembering the big word. Her pronunciation was strangely perfect, not at all tinged with her usual Yiddish accent. I could imagine Avram sounding it out for her, showing off his newly acquired vocabulary, as if he were an established Lord of Parliament. And she still had it right.

"We walked for so long, hours, I remember. We walked on Piccadilly Street. Such a name, Piccadilly. Avram knew that name, somehow, and he knew Pall Mall, like Aunt Marly's cigarettes. I remember those streets. But they were far from where we lived, and there were no Jews there. We passed by buildings that looked like palaces, with statues carved right into the outside walls. I couldn't imagine what went on inside, and who was permitted to enter. And we passed statues that stood right by the sides of the streets, men on horses that were twice as big as real horses, with writing that explained who the men were. We didn't stop even once to admire them. And the streets were clogged with people, the wide streets were, and with omnibuses, we call them now just buses, pulled by two or three horses linked across the shoulders. And taxis, Sarah, but not like you see now in New York. Horses pulled these taxis, and they were carriages, sometimes with two wheels, and sometimes with four. The two wheeled ones flew through the crowds, this way, that way, like they would take off into the air at any moment. The drivers rode outside, holding the reins to direct the horses to go or stop, and people called to them from the street, just like you call for a taxi to stop in the city, but they were all pulled by horses. I think we passed five thousand horses that day, maybe more." The words were tumbling out of her with such delight that I loved listening.

"We talked sometimes as we walked along on the way to the hatters. Avram pointed out a famous building here, or a bridge there. But I think he didn't know too much. 'Piccadilly,' he kept saying, to make me laugh. He was puffing up his own importance. But I didn't let on that I saw his weakness. It was enough to be walking together, two handsome people, young and full of the promise of the future. And I saw the men who looked at me. I stretched out my neck, graceful I was, like a swan, and tilted my chin this way and that. Avram liked that the men noticed my beauty. He was proud to be with me. All the while, I knew a baby was growing in me, and that would be my insurance policy." Mary stopped talking, and when I looked over at her, she was swiveling her head right and left, imitating her preening behavior of half a century earlier. She remembered those streets names, I marveled, even though she probably hadn't said those words aloud in fifty years. Amazing. I wanted to know how she knew there was a baby, and why it would be an insurance policy. Weren't babies for married people? And wasn't insurance for people who were left after someone died? But I didn't interrupt my grandmother. I sighed quietly and waited for the story to resume.

"We turned at last into a quiet street, and Avram said, 'Here we are, Mayrke, Saint James' Street. And here is Lock and Company, my hatters. This shop was established in 1676, Mayrke. See how it is written here, right on the door?' Written right on the door? I think he said it to make be feel how much I needed him. Hatters, I thought to myself. He is so grand, my Avram. I was very proud to be with him. I pushed away from my mind that little remark about reading the sign. Whenever I felt the battle start up in my head between what I should do and what I shouldn't do, who I should be with and who I should run away from, what would be good now, later, always, what I wanted and what I didn't want, that growling fight between my brain that could think and plan, and my brain that only wanted, when that battle started up like my head was turning up the sound on the TV, louder and louder, I always pushed it away. I made my head turn that TV knob all the way to the left until it clicked off. And we walked right into the shop, one step up. Right away, a man came right over to Avram. 'Yes, sir?' he asked, 'How may I be of service?' Can you imagine? By that, I was impressed. I didn't know what his words meant, but I knew how they sounded. In Ulla, no one spoke like that to a Jew. I nearly laughed out loud with happiness. 'Yes, my good man,' said Avram, in English, hardly hesitating I thought, 'I'll have a new hat today.' I saw that man look at the other salesman there, and I knew then that they were laughing at us, two poor Jews in a neighborhood we didn't belong in. But no other customers were in the store, so they went along. Avram was dressed like a dandy, with spats and a cane, and I had on Dvorah's coat with the embroidery. I was too warm, but I looked beautiful, I knew. I stood up very straight, and I acted like a duchess. I don't know how I knew how a duchess would behave. But the looks between the two salesmen changed. Instead of looking to laugh at us, they were making Avram big to impress me, to win my approval. Can you understand my power?" Then in a rare acknowledgement of the fleeting value of beauty, she spat a side comment. "Look what happens to people, just look. What good did it do me?"

"But Bubby, everyone knows about your beauty," I tried to comfort my grandmother. Mary didn't respond because she wasn't really speaking to me, but more to herself. Or maybe to God, I thought to myself. Nothing I had ever heard about God led me to believe he'd be interested in laments about the value of having beauty, depending on it, or losing it. I hoped the story would continue, in any case.

"So in an instant, Avram was fitting hat forms on his head, looking for the correct fit. And then he picked out a Derby, black it was, or maybe dark gray, with a silky ribbon around. He handed over the coins, and we were out the door. We had walked for hours, and before I could catch my breath, we were back on the sidewalk, walking again. I think they didn't want us there, but Avram was very proud, haughty, about the whole thing. 'See, Mayrke, a wonderful new hat, from my hatter, even better than the one you made me lose in the gutter.' He was able to blame me for a trouble and take credit for the solution all in one breath. I should have seen clearly. But I kept my hand over my eyes, the better not to see what was right in front of me to see."

It was really such a sad story, I thought to myself. My grandparents had mean feelings about each other, inflated opinions about themselves, scorn from even store clerks, and blindness about it all.. But each one allowed for the other's hatred. They were like the parasites I had learned about in school, living by feeding off each other. It wasn't really a love story at all.

"Then, after we came out from the hat store, Avram said to me, 'So now we'll buy for you a present I want you to have, Mayrke.' And he led me away down the street, two blocks away we went. 'This is Piccadilly, Mayrke, a very fine street.' We both laughed again at the name. So I straightened my hat, made smooth with my hands the front of my coat, and watched the people as they went about their business. If someone looked at me, a man, I linked my arm through Avram's arm and busied my eyes in the store window displays. If it was a woman, I knew she was jealous, so I stared at her with a small smile. I was so clever. And they all parted to let us through. And then we came quickly to Regent Street, where we turned. And then right away into Rimmel, a store called Rimmel, where I saw for sale all kinds of soaps and perfumes."

Oh, I thought to myself, the lavender soap she always uses! Here's the beginning of the lavender soap. I had never understood my grandmother's demand for lavender soap before, and in fact thought it the strangest thing that an old woman who hopes for nothing more than a day with less pain than usual, who tries to attract no attention to herself, had always insisted that my mother keep a steady supply of lavender soap coming. Uncle Mayshe would sometimes show up with a case of it, brag about his "very important business connections," and drop the carton on the kitchen floor just inside the door. His mother would begin to giggle and cry at the same time, holding a bar of it under her nose and inhaling deeply, and I always thought to myself, over soap? Who cares what smell your soap has? But the whole family always carefully avoided using Bubby's special soap, and now I understood where it had all started.

"I looked around the store, and I saw that it was a beautiful place. There were many gas lamps with scrolling brass arms and etched glass shades, and the counters were glass topped, with dark polished wood trim. And behind the counters, against the walls, there were hundreds of small drawers stacked up to the ceiling that contained wonderful smells from all over the world. The whole store was like Bathsheba's bath, so thick with fragrances that were dancing with each other in the air. And fine ladies were shopping there, with hats that had feathers and netting, and hatpins with pearls on the end, and kidskin gloves with buttons from the wrist up the cuff. I wanted to stay in that Rimmel store for the rest of my life, but I was afraid that as soon as someone noticed two poor Jews there, they would throw us out onto the sidewalk. I took Avram's arm, and tried to remember how to be a duchess, but I was drunk from the smells all around me."

I giggled at the thought of my grandmother being drunk, even though I knew she didn't mean really drunk. My aunts' disdain for Aunt Marly's drinking usually made the idea of alcohol frightening, but somehow, applying it to my grandmother gave it a new deliciously happy spin.

"'Pick out which one you like, Mayrke, any soap you like, and I promise it will never run out. You will have that soap your whole life, and that fragrance will always be for you a reminder of how I love you, my beautiful Mayrke.' He was looking right into my face, so adoring, like I was a queen and he would bring me anything in the world I wanted. His eyes were shining, like he would cry any second from happiness. I almost fainted. I had to steady myself on the counter edge, but right away I saw that my glove had a smudge on the palm, and some of the buttonholes were frayed. So I grabbed my hand back and took a deep breath. A clerk was there then, opposite me behind the counter.

"'Yes?' she said, like she couldn't imagine what we were doing there. She looked around, maybe like she would find someone to throw us out, while I turned to Avram to speak. I didn't know one word of English then, nothing. 'A soap,' he said to her, 'Shoen soap, Miss.' After, when we went out from the store, we laughed together outside that he said 'shoen,' it means beautiful in Yiddish, Sarahla, instead of English. But the clerk, she understood him, and she turned to the little drawers behind her and pulled one open, and her hand rested in the air above the soaps inside, and then she closed that drawer. She pulled open a drawer in the next row, and right away closed that one too. What was she looking for, I couldn't imagine. And then, she opened a third drawer, near the bottom of the row, and took out a tray and turned around to put in on the counter. But as she turned, she also reached for a board, small like a school notebook, and covered with velvet, with tiny brass tacks around the outside, and she put that down on the counter first. On top of that, she put the tray with the soaps. Oh, it was so beautiful, what she did."

My grandmother fell silent. When I sat up and looked at her, I could see her toothless smile, and tears glistening on her cheeks. It was the memory of the most elegant moment of her life. It was attention that for once wasn't the result of a trick of her beauty, of the flirtatious click of her boot on the pavement, or the arrogant tossing of her hair. It was simply being treated as if she were loved and respected. Maybe it was a love story after all.

"'Lavender,' the clerk said slowly, sounding it out a piece at a time. 'Lavender,' I said just like she said it. 'Lavender,' said Avram. We each repeated the word, and then we said it together, like the chorus of a song. And we laughed, there in Rimmel, my Avram, the clerk behind the counter, and me. Avram paid her, and she went away to wrap my soap in paper tied with a ribbon. She gave me the package, and we left the store. So Avram had his new hat, and I had a present, too." I felt like I had been enchanted, somehow. I could almost hear the music playing from a movie about a beautiful princess who finally dances with the prince. My eyes were closed as I pictured the scene in the store.

Suddenly my grandmother sat up and pushed the blankets away. "Let's go have breakfast, my Sarah. Aren't you hungry?" The music in my head ended and the spell was broken.

"Maybe we'll have pancakes today, Bubby. Do you feel like that?"

"Pancakes, my Sarah? No, I'll have cottage cheese, maybe. You have pancakes. We'll see if your mother wants to make pancakes today."

Twenty-Five

The next morning, I woke up with a start, realizing that the usual sounds of Uncle Morty washing his car on the driveway were absent, and there was no smell of his coffee brewing. I went downstairs in my pajamas to watch TV in the living room, but David always got up earlier and he was already involved in a cowboy show. I glanced at the TV, and found the screen was filled with clouds of dust and men talking about forming a posse. Boring, I thought, and wandered into the kitchen. I made two pieces of toast and ate them at the long oak table alone, craning my neck periodically to see if anyone was pulling up behind my father's car that was parked on the street. I poured some orange juice into a glass and carried it upstairs to my grandmother's bedside.

Everyone upstairs was still sleeping. I worried briefly if they were all sick, but I had been warned that I should not wake my parents to ask if they were all right; sleeping late didn't mean you were sick. I yanked on a pair of soft corduroy pants and pulled a polo shirt over my head. I looked in the mirror above my dresser and tried to smooth the crumpled lace edging around the neckline, but it popped right back as if it had a mind of its own. The sleeves had grown too short, I noticed, and tried pulling them down to my wrists by hunching up my shoulders. I relaxed my shoulders and watched as the sleeves shrank right back up my arms to where they had been, but this time, the wristbands were stretched into uneven ovals instead of a neat ribbed band. I didn't even attempt to deal with the curls. I went back downstairs.

When I found myself back in the kitchen, I decided to try out a trick I had thought of one night when I couldn't fall asleep. I climbed up on the bunk seat right next to the door that led outside into the breezeway. I opened the door just an inch or two and put my left foot on the doorknob. Then I reached over, pulling my weight up the door by grabbing the wooden trims of the windowpanes as if they were ladder rungs. When I could reach the top of the open door, I carefully pulled myself into a standing position, all my weight resting on my left foot on the doorknob. Next, I shimmied as if I were on a swing, and finally I got the door to sway open wide enough that I could reach my right foot out, past the pantry cabinet and over to the door that led to the living room. I hooked my foot onto that doorknob and shifted my weight off the outside door. The same shimmying movement caused the living room door to slowly shut, and this attracted David's attention.

"What are you doing, Sarah?" he asked. I knew he'd find this much more interesting that a stupid cowboy show.

"I'm making my way around the kitchen without touching the floor. But you can't try it until I see if I can do it." He stood watching, his Davy Crockett coonskin cap cocked back off his forehead where it seemed to me to be permanently attached, as fascinated as if I were a circus performer.

"Now, I climb off the doorknob onto the top of the refrigerator, carefully avoiding this wooden bowl of oranges up here," I explained as I grabbed the top of the refrigerator and hugged myself onto it. I pushed the bowl of fruit back against the wall and clung to the front half of the top. "This next part is hard," I explained as if I were teaching how to work an arithmetic problem. My voice was more like a teacher's than a young girl's. I reached one foot across the space between the refrigerator and the wooden counter, took a breath and jumped. Some of the spice cans that were lined up in little cubbies along the back of the counter rattled as I landed, but nothing broke.

"Now I hop across to this other counter," I explained as I did just that. "And I walk along the edge of the sink, easy as can be, hop over the stove, being careful to miss the middle where the pilot light is, climb over this part here,' she continued, referring to the divider between the work part of the kitchen and the bunk seats and table. "I'm on the bunk seat, I'm on the table, I'm on the other bunk seat, and I'm done! Around the whole kitchen without touching the floor."

David had followed the path carefully with his eyes, not interfering with his sister's progress. "But you didn't step on the other door," he observed, pointing to the door that led from the kitchen to the hallway.

"Well there's no way to get from the top of the refrigerator to that doorknob," I retorted, annoyed that he had criticized my accomplishment.

"I can do it. You're just not strong enough. You'd have to take a jump and hang from the top of the door before you swing over to that counter." I looked at the space I'd have to leap across, considered whether I could hold myself as I hung from the door, and suddenly realized that this whole enterprise was entirely too dangerous. My mother, if she saw what I had done, would flare her nostrils, narrow her eyes, and scream at me.

"David, this was a mistake. I shouldn't have done it. She'll kill me. Please don't tell." I was beginning to tremble. But instead of obeying me, David hoisted himself onto the far bunk seat, and echoed his sister's journey but included the scary leap off the top of the refrigerator to the door that led to the hallway. He did it in half my time, moving and leaping and swinging like a muscular monkey. He laughed with glee at the end of the circuit, and started around again.

"Stop, David, stop. You're going to kill yourself!" I was becoming so overwrought; I couldn't stand being in the kitchen with this maniac I had created. I ran up the stairs, creating as much noise as possible so that my parents would wake up, but technically I wouldn't have intentionally waked them. But when I almost at the top of the stairs, I found everyone awake, dressed and walking around. My father stepped off the top landing, paused, and began singing about counting your blessings when you're worried, and my mother was holding my grandmother's arm as they approached the top of the stairs behind him.

"Why isn't Uncle Morty here," I demanded, trying to change the subject of acrobatics in the kitchen, a subject that only I knew was going on. But just then there was a huge crashing noise from downstairs, followed by David's voice. "Oops," he said. My father was the first into the kitchen.

"David, David! Where are you?" By then, I had flown down the stairs, skipping as many as I dared. My father and I discovered David's whereabouts at the same time, on top of the refrigerator, crouched against the wall. There were oranges all over the floor in every direction, and the wooden bowl lay on the floor right in front of the refrigerator split in two. "How did you get up there, David? Are you crazy? Get down right now!" Joe's voice was loud and angry, but I detected a hint of amusement, too. Was this what he had meant when he described his son as, "a real boy," a remark I had overheard when my father was on a rare phone call to his brother? I busied myself in collecting the oranges and storing them in my polo shirt top that I had pouched out from the hem. David jumped onto the wooden counter and flew into his father's arms from there shouting, "Superman!" as he leaped. Joe caught him and swept him onto the floor in one fluid movement. "Stay off there, young man. Your mother will be quite upset about her bowl, you know. And it's too dangerous," he added as an afterthought.

My mother and grandmother arrived on the scene then, but all the evidence of the disaster was gone. "What happened?" she looked from face to face for an explanation.

"Nothing."

"Nothing."

"Nothing."

"Anyone want to explain this totally useless bowl, or why Sarah has a bunch of oranges in her polo shirt top?"

"No."

"No."

"No."

There was a moment of silence, more looking at my family, all of whom were looking around the kitchen as if it had become the fascinating place on earth. And then they all dissolved into laughter. It seemed like the perfect time to change the subject.

"Why isn't Uncle Morty here?" I tried my earlier question. "Are we mad at him?"

Rikki's face changed. The laughter drained away like the last dregs of bubble bath going down the drain. "Why would we be mad at my brother? What makes you think someone is mad? You always think bad thoughts, Sarah. My family doesn't get mad; they just have their ways, and no one is mad." She bent down to find her coffee pot in a low cabinet, and for her the discussion seemed over.

I was momentarily confused. Didn't the absence of one aunt or uncle or another always mean there had been an argument? And how could she say they didn't get mad? I could think of millions of times they had gotten mad, said mean things to each other, stopped talking to each other, hung up on each other, millions. Why was my mother being so defensive? I looked at my father for explanation, but he had begun his song again about counting sheep, and he was patting his mother-in-law on her head gently to the rhythm of the song.

"But where is Uncle Morty?" I tried again.

"Tomorrow is Passover, Sarah, Passover. No one is coming. It's Passover. Everyone is busy. I'm busy. My sisters are busy. It's Passover. Get it?"

The angry words spewed out all over the kitchen, ricocheting off all the walls like a pinball machine gone berserk. I felt like I had been slapped, and my hand flew involuntarily to my face. I turned and ran from the room, through the hall and up the stairs, hot tears coursing down my face. I heard in the distance my grandmother's voice speaking Yiddish to Rikki in an admonishing tone. I was too far away to hear the reply.

I resolved to stay in my room all day and eat nothing. I was considering leaving home, but there was no place to go. My aunts and uncles were busy with Passover, that had been made clear, and they were in the process of moving, as well. And the atmosphere in any of their houses was even more contentious than in my own house.

Once, I remembered, I had gone to stay with Aunt Jean for the weekend. I slept with my cousins in their crowded bedroom, sharing cousin Sherry's bed with her one night, and cousin Melissa's bed the next. We slept head-to-toe, just like when Rikki was growing up, sharing with Aunt Ruthie. "Aunt Ruthie always came to bed much later than

I did," my mother had remembered fondly, "and her last words each day were always, 'Move those feet over, Rikki.'" Why was that angry scolding a warm and cozy memory for my mother, I always wondered? When I shared with my cousins, it was more like an adventure, like camping out inside somebody's house. But the fun of sleeping with my cousins did not make the experience of staying there pleasant because no one spoke at a normal volume in that house. Aunt Jean screamed at Uncle Solly because he had left a burning cigar in an ashtray in the living room and because she wanted a bigger household allowance than he could provide. Uncle Solly screamed at Aunt Jean because there were no clean socks in his drawer and because she had bought new lamps with turquoise shades that had patterns of swirls and sprays pierced through them, when the old lamps with the gold shades with fringes along the bottom were just as perfectly beautiful as when she had bought them only last summer.

And in that house both parents screamed at their children to clean up the mess they had left in the hallway, to stop opening the refrigerator, to stop hitting each other, and to stop bothering them with whining. Cousin Melissa screamed at her older sister to be allowed to play with her dolls, to share their mother's costume jewelry, and to stop pinching her. Cousin Sherry screamed at her younger sister to get away from her, to get off her side of their room, and once, she was so angry at Melissa that she bit the side her own index finger while wiggling the rest of her fingers and screaming in frustrated yelps. Cousin Melissa screamed wordlessly at the end of a wave of breathless unresolved crying, leaving me amazed and frightened by the lungpower of such a small skinny person. No one seemed to pay the slightest attention to anyone else. I backed into the corner of whatever room they were in at the time, cowering in fear of being the next victim. I wanted to call Rikki to come pick me up, but I was afraid to touch the phone; all four of them might start screaming at me at once, and I knew I'd dissolve if that happened.

So going there to escape was out. Aunt Ruthie and Uncle Milt were always threatening to slice each other up or throw the other off the roof, especially when they were staying in their tiny apartment in the Bronx rather than an equally cramped bungalow in Rockaway. Cousin Stacie had to come stay at my house more than once because of their battles. Somehow the atmosphere at the beach calmed them down, but this was the spring, not the summer. At their house, it wasn't just screaming, either. I had listened with alarm to my mother on the phone with Aunt Esther once as they talked about Aunt Ruthie grabbing a kitchen knife during a fight with Uncle Milt. It was incomprehensible to me that these eruptions seemed totally forgotten once they were over. Not only did Rikki and Aunt Esther seem blasé the next Sunday when they all crammed together into the yellow bunk seats, but even Aunt Ruthie and Uncle Milt arrived together, laughing as they took turns interrupting each other's recounting of a fat woman carrying an enormous red patent leather pocketbook they'd seen crossing the Grand Concourse that morning. I wondered if I had dreamed the conversation I had heard earlier in the week. I was sure if I went to stay with Aunt Ruthie, I'd never close my eyes for one second in case there might be another knife threat. My mother had claimed that no one in her family got mad, really, that they just had their ways. But escaping to Aunt Ruthie's house would be like trading my sandwich in the school cafeteria that I just didn't feel like for one that was green with mold.

And going to Aunt Esther's house was not an option at all. No one was ever invited there because Aunt Esther ran her house like an Army base. Children were not allowed in the living room. Eating was not allowed anywhere but sitting at the kitchen table, and crumbs were not allowed at all. Combing your hair in the bathroom was dangerous, because if you left any hair in the sink, there would be trouble. Brushing your teeth there had similar perils. Children had to be in bed by 6:30 in the evening, because Aunt Esther said that after she fed them, she was done with them for the day, and she did not want to see them or hear from them again until the next morning. And morning at Aunt Esther's house began before the sun made its appearance. If you slept later than 5:30, she'd snap on the glaring overhead light and snarl, "What are you still sleeping for? The whole day is wasting away. I have to make these beds, I have to vacuum here, and I have to take the laundry down. Do I look like a slave who wants to work all day?"

Years later, when I read *Jane Eyre*, Bronte's description of Jane's years at the Lowood school were nothing short of a recounting of being a weekend guest of Aunt Esther. It wasn't that Aunt Esther would actually starve you or beat you or let you languish until you died of consumption. It just felt like those things might happen. I had no explanation of how Aunt Esther's husband or children survived there, but I knew I didn't want to go.

Staying with my mother's brothers was unthinkable. It had been made abundantly clear to me that the women they were married to ran filthy inhospitable homes. Aunt Rose Aronsky, who seemed like a sweet sad lady to me, was only interested in eating. My mother and her sisters repeated the same negative stories about her endlessly. One was about the time they all went there together to visit Uncle Morty who had had a tooth pulled and was recuperating in bed. I remembered that my father had questioned at the time why dental surgery required bed rest and sick bed visits from relatives, but that wasn't the part of the story they dwelled on repeatedly. They loved to examine and discuss from endless new angles the scene that they encountered on their unannounced call on their convalescing brother. "And you remember Rose Aronsky's outfit? A full slip with Morty's old house slippers. Hasn't she got a housecoat?" Aunt Jean had housecoats and matching mules in every color.

"Yes, but what about the sandwich? A mayonnaise sandwich on a saucer on the floor. I didn't believe it." Aunt Esther would rather die instantly than eat anything that was near the floor, even her surgery room clean floors.

"My favorite part is why it was on the floor: she was cleaning the floor on her hands and knees, she claimed, and she pushed it along and took a bite every so often to give her strength. Strength from mayonnaise on Wonder bread? If that's what she feeds my brother, he'll be dead before he gets old." My mother held that white bread was really cotton in large slices, and she wouldn't feed it to the dog.

"But did you see that bathtub? The white porcelain finish was scrubbed right off it. She used so much Clorox on it, it was plain black cast iron. That's clean, by her? What's the matter with that woman?" This was the part of the memory that they practically said in unison.

I could not see myself escaping to Aunt Rose Aronsky and Uncle Morty's house. The reports of the Cloroxed bathroom were enough for me to abandon the idea even without the poisonous bread threat. Once, my mother had hired a cleaning lady to help with spring-cleaning, and the hapless woman had mixed Clorox with ammonia to create a potent cleaning solution. The resulting chlorine gas had knocked her off her feet and nearly killed her. Clorox vapors held terrifying power to me, and I avoided that smell carefully. Even swimming pools that gave off chlorine fumes from their purification chemicals did not seem at all inviting to me even though other children were eager to jump in and out of them until their eyes were bloodshot red, lips turned blue from the cold, and their finder tips withered into flesh colored prunes.

Uncle Mayshe and Aunt Marly's house was even more nefarious in my mind. The reports of Aunt Marly's having boyfriends who visited while her husband was at work were simply terrifying. What if while I was visiting, a strange man turned up and spoke to me? What would I say? Wouldn't Aunt Marly be so embarrassed that she'd run out of the house wearing only a white satin robe with feathers along the hem and high heeled white satin slippers with a rhinestone studded buckle? And then I would be stuck alone with the strange man, and he'd have on black pants and a black silk shirt with a white satin tie, and his shoes would be mostly black but with white where the tongue and laces should go. And he'd speak to me out of the side of his mouth, "Hello, girly. What's your name?" The utterly menacing scene that I had witnessed at cousin Danny's Bar Mitzvah said enough to me about Uncle Mayshe that I could barely bear to be in the same room with him, even when the whole rest of the family was there, too. But to go sleep at his house, even if every story about Aunt Marly were fiction, was completely out of the question.

And how could I stay at a friend's house? I'd have to explain that I wanted to run away, even though it would be temporarily, and I'd have to explain why, and that would entail revealing things about my family that I always kept carefully to myself. I knew no one would understand their ways; I had only the slightest understanding of them myself. The friend would tell her mother, and soon everyone in the neighborhood and then the whole school, and then who knows who else, would know that I came from a bunch of crazy people, so I, too, must be crazy. If that dam broke open, I would be soaked with a shame that I couldn't even get clear in my own mind.

I lay on my bed, and my thoughts turned to my grandmother's story. There was some connection between Mary's tale and Mary's children's lives. Rikki always remembered her childhood as a continuing cycle of delicious food prepared by a warm and loving mother, a religious father who revered knowledge and studying holy books to learn how to live a better life according to God's desire, and a troupe of funny siblings who adored and respected each other and their parents. She used those very words: "loving mother," "religious father," and "funny sisters who adored their smart handsome brothers."

But the stories she told, or that slipped out when she let down her guard, did not support those words. The sisters shared their beds or their possessions with nasty reluctance. The parents yelled at each other or threw dishes at each other with so much venom that Rikki was afraid to bring home a friend lest they have one of their screaming matches and frighten the friend away forever. Mary pronounced each child worthless. "'Jean, you're a filthy liar,'" she quoted her mother once, "and she said over and over until everyone called her Liar instead of Jean." And Mayshe, my mother told me, was kicked out of the house at 13 for refusing to go to school and hanging out with gangsters. "'Get out from my sight, gonif,' she railed at him, 'and never do I want to see your face again,'" my mother sadly repeated her mother's words. One of her brothers was accused of slapping a teacher, Aunt Ruthie was derided weekly because she had crossed eyes, and, "Me?" she asked aloud about herself. "I have a dark complexion so I was called a slave. The only child she was proud of was praised simply because he was handsome, but he disappointed her by eloping with his pregnant girlfriend, a woman she called a whore." Mary was expected to feed seven children on less than dollar a day that their father supplied reluctantly, while he had a car and driver to chauffeur him around to his appointments. "She called him a goat," my mother said of her parents. The vague reference was unsettling to me, even as I tried to make sense of it. Were any of the stories really true? I couldn't imagine Bubby saying such things. And Sidney, the son who was never mentioned, well, what about Sidney? When did he leave, and where did he go?

As I turned over these worries, trying to make connections and ferret out explanations, time ticked by. Before long, I realized that the two pieces of toast I had eaten hours earlier were long ago digested, and I was hungry. And as I tried to think of a way to go downstairs and ask for lunch rather than run away, I heard my mother's voice. "Sarah, sweet Sarah! I made you lunch, so come down before it gets cold! It's French toast with jelly! I want you to help finish the bread in the house before Passover. Are you coming?"

It was forgotten. The verbal slap that had sent me upstairs in tears had been swept away, seemingly over and done for my mother. There would be no talking about it, no resolving it, and no getting beyond it by each person explaining her position. It went to the place all the fights that happened in my mother's family went, wherever that was. I was both relieved and uneasy. That place that held the arguments must be getting so swollen. I pictured my grandmother's hot water bottle as my mother filled it with just the right amount of water, pushed out the air and capped it. If they kept stuffing more and more arguments into it, it was one day going to burst and spew those hot words all over anyone who was standing in the way. I imagined it like the fallout that had poisoned the Japanese people after the atomic bomb had dropped on them. Was there going to be anyplace safe to stand?

"Here I come." As I moved down the stairs, I thought of Alice falling down the rabbit hole on her way to Wonderland. I wondered what the tea party would have been like if no one had attended.

Twenty-Six

The most difficult part of Passover for me was eating lunch at school. Bread was forbidden, of course, so peanut butter and jelly sandwiches were out. Peanuts were forbidden too, for that matter, so ants on a log, the favorite snack in my family, was out, too. Ants on a log was peanut butter spread thickly into the groove of a stalk of celery with a row of raisins walking along the top. "So what's wrong with a few hard-boiled eggs and a board of matzoh?" asked my mother when I said there was nothing to take for lunch, and I'd just eat an apple.

"I don't like hard-boiled eggs," I lied, not looking at my mother as she spoke.

"You eat them all the time, Sarah. Since when don't you like hard-boiled eggs? I'll give you soft-boiled instead. Let me see what to put them in." She bent down to search in a lower cabinet for a container that could accommodate soft-boiled eggs.

"No soft-boiled eggs. No eggs of any kind. And no matzoh." My voice was beginning to tremble.

"You're not going to school with no lunch, Sarah, so you can just dismiss that idea from your head. What's wrong with matzoh? It has a lot of meaning, you know." I was afraid my mother would begin the entire story of Passover as if I didn't know it as well as my mother did.

"Okay. Give me matzoh with butter. But also an apple, please." I was picturing myself removing the apple from the brown lunch bag and tossing the matzoh into one of the big garbage cans that stood sentinel by the door of the multi-purpose room where they ate before I got to my lunch table. I knew that explaining to the rest of the girls there what the big flat cracker was and somehow sweeping up the shower of crumbs that would result if I tried to eat it were too much. I couldn't stand to feel like I was defending myself in any way, and that's what a lunch of matzoh would be. A week of apples and hunger was preferable.

My grandmother had a constant upset stomach that seemed unlikely to abate before the end of Passover. "My insides are as paralyzed as my outsides," she complained. "Nothing is moving. It lays like a stone in my belly." Everyone attributed it to matzoh, which was notoriously difficult to digest. I was sorry to see my grandmother suffering, but there was a certain air of resignation in the house. By the time seven days had passed so would the upset stomach. I was disappointed, however, that the nighttime stories were interrupted. Instead of tales of Mary's time in London, mournful moans came from the other twin bed in my room.

"Bubby, you don't have to obey the holiday if it's a matter of health," I counseled.

"Please, Sarah, my perfect, I have this every year. It will pass. I'll talk fast next week when I feel better."

The week went on, and the family soldiered through it. I felt like they were the ancient Israelites crossing the desert, deprived of anything good to eat. Aunt Esther always made Passover cake for everyone in the family and made sure everyone had enough for the week. But one year, my father said what no one had dared to say before. "It all tastes the same, and the taste is exactly like sand." It was like the story of the emperor's new clothes, and my father was the little boy who told the truth about the naked emperor that everyone was trying to ignore. I could never again eat Aunt Esther's cake without thinking of the beach. At the Seder, the celebratory meal, I was told to think as if I myself had escaped from slavery in Egypt. With the menu they followed and the moans of gastrointestinal distress I heard all around me, it was easy to follow those instructions.

On Friday, a phone call came that changed the focus drastically. I was having a snack in the kitchen after school. It was a plate of the soup greens that had stewed for hours in my mother's chicken soup. The dish of steaming limp vegetables included pale green celery, creamy parsnips and sweet white onions, and it was always saved for me because I loved the rich broth and soft almost unrecognizable solids. My mother ladled the snack into a soup bowl for me with the phone cradled between her ear and her shoulder. "Who called you?" She put the bowl down on the table in front of me, and interrupted her conversation. "Did you wash your hands?" But she didn't listen to my reply before going back to it. "Who is going? And you want me to tell Mama? Am I supposed to bring her? And who says she'll want to go?"

I slurped my soup and listened. What was my mother going to tell Bubby? And where were they going? This better not be another one of those visits that ended in screaming and carrying on.

"I have no intention of going. This happened years ago, as far as I'm concerned. Have I seen him in the past fifteen years?"

My stomach dropped and my interest in the soup green broth ended with a lurch. The only person I could think of that my mother hadn't seen in years was Avram, my missing grandfather. What happened fifteen years ago that really didn't happen until now? I dropped the spoon into the plate and stared at the scraps of boiled onion that floated among the shreds of green parsley. Rikki was running water into the sink, the phone still propped up to her ear.

"Will that woman be there?"

Woman? What woman? I sifted through some possibilities, all of which fell away except Esther Bagoudis. But I had no idea if Esther Bagoudis was in America, was in touch with my grandfather, or was even still alive. This is silly, I told myself. I didn't even know for sure what my mother was talking about, and here I was, making up stories about a woman who had gone her own way more than half a century ago. I picked up my spoon and stirred the vegetables around.

"Well, fine, I'll get her dressed, and I'll tell her he's very sick and asking for her. You can come get her and tell her the truth in the car on the way. I don't want to be involved."

I put down my spoon. It must be about Avram, and, he was dead and they were going to lie to Bubby. I carried my bowl to the sink where my mother took it absentmindedly, poured the liquid into the drain and tossed the vegetables into the trash. I left the kitchen before my mother could ask questions. As I went around the turn to the stairway, I heard the end of the phone conversation. "I'll see you Sunday morning by 10:00." She hung up without saying goodbye.

Friday night and Saturday crawled by, and somehow I avoided talking to anyone. I had questions but I knew I wasn't entitled to answers. There were phone calls from various family members, but the halves of the conversations that I heard were incomprehensible and gave me no information. My father spent Saturday at the lumberyard and in the basement, David was nowhere to be seen, and my mother went on cooking and vacuuming as if nothing new had happened. At some point, she must have interrupted her chores and had a conversation with her mother that explained something of what was going on, because Mary was unusually silent as she shuffled through her daily routines. She sat outside in her folding chair by the front door, her right hand gripping the side of her face with shuddering spasms. I was unsure about what to say, so stayed away from her.

Sunday brought an outright spring day. I kept myself in bed as late as I could, and only when everyone was already dressed and downstairs did I rouse myself. I dressed absentmindedly and crept down the stairs as invisibly as I could. I slid out the front door at the bottom of the stairs, grateful that no one had noticed either my absence or my late appearance. The giant pine tree on the front lawn had not been pruned, I noticed, and most of the lowest branches were below my eye level, creating an accommodating retreat. I backed into the embrace of the green needles, trying not to notice the ones that were sticking me as I went by. I watched my house, sure it must be 10:00 by now. Who would come to pick up Bubby, I wondered? I sat down on the bed of brown pine needles that formed a round carpet around the trunk. The sunlight was spattered on the path along with dark patches of tree shadows.

And then a long black car sailed down the street slowly and turned into my driveway. It was Uncle Mayshe's car, and there he was driving, sunglasses covering most of his face and a long cigar clenched between his teeth. He was alone and he did not seem to be getting out of the car. I watched as if I were seeing a movie with no sound.

The front door of the house opened, and my parents both appeared. My father propped the door open, and Rikki turned to grasp her mother's arm.

"No, Ma," Joe was saying, "I think you're wrong about that."

Rikki was walking along the flagstone path with a dressed-up old woman whom I could barely recognize as my grandmother. She had on her gray coat, but it flapped open as she hobbled along, and I could see her navy blue best dress peeking through underneath. The white lace collar and her hair were exactly the same color. Her hair was neatly combed and caught up in a tidy blue felt hat that hugged the top of her head and curved around the top edges of her ears. She had on her navy blue suede shoes with the fringes that just brushed the toes, her only shoes whose backs were not broken. I couldn't see from this distance, but I knew they were decorated with a scrolling pattern of tiny holes around the laces and down to the fringes.

"He's dead already, I know it," she was saying to her son-in-law. But she was smiling, like she was in on a joke or a secret of some kind. "Mayshe is taking me to a funeral today, I already know. So now I'll be really a widow, instead of pretending to be one."

"Ma, I'm telling you, he's only asking for you. Don't you think someone would tell me if he was dead?" My father spoke without looking at his mother-in-law, but he too had some kind of a smile playing around his mouth.

"Pay attention to where you're walking, Mama," instructed Rikki. "Mayshe, don't you think you could get out of the car and help your mother?" she called to the car. How many people need to help her, I thought? It was clear she was trying to change the subject. Bubby was walking very carefully, and didn't need to be scolded.

The car door cracked open and Uncle Mayshe spoke with his head tilted up so his mouth faced the opening at the top of the door. "Hurry up, Rikki, I got things to do after this." He pulled the door shut.

This is astonishing, I thought to myself. Everything about it was strange, from the secret part, to the smiling part, to, well, I couldn't articulate the strangeness. I watched as my father pulled the door open and stood out of the way so Bubby could turn around backwards and sit into the seat. I saw him bend down behind the open door and scoop her feet up and into the car. I stared at my mother who had let go of her mother's arm and was standing like an accidental observer who happened to be passing the scene of an accident and had nothing personal to do with the shocking events that were unfolding in front of her. She had stopped on the curve of the path with her arms folded tightly around herself watching an elderly lady as she was escorted into the car. Then my father backed up to my mother and put his arm across her shoulder and they waved as the car slid in reverse down the driveway, tooted its horn in two fast beeps, and then proceeded down the street. I followed the car until it turned the corner. My parents had gone back into the house and shut the front door heavily behind them.

I felt like I was an excluded or maybe even forgotten figure. I had followed the scene as it played itself out before me, unnoticed by the adults. And now I was alone outside, protected by the huge prickly branches that drooped around me and enveloped me in green piney fragrance, but barred from knowing the truth of what I had observed. I sighed as I went over the pieces of the puzzle I had just seen enacted, reviewed the parts that had been inadvertently revealed earlier in the week, and came to the conclusion that I'd never truly understand. I climbed out of my green alcove and made my way around to the kitchen door.

"Oh, there you are, Sarah-sleepy-head. Do you want eggs for breakfast? It'll be lunch time soon, you know." Rikki seemed blissfully unaware of what I knew, and she certainly was unaware of what I didn't know. For her, I thought, the day of her father's funeral was a day like any other Sunday. I wondered if the aunts and uncles would be coming later. No, I decided. They come to see their mother, but she had gone to her husband's funeral that day. They wouldn't be there.

"Scrambled eggs, please. And when can I have toast? I'm tired of Passover."

From where I am now, looking back at that day, I'm filled with some kind of hollow anger. I was so confused, so uninformed, so ignored. Did adults back then look right past children, as if they were deaf, or blind, or not really there? Or was it just my family? I felt uneasy that day, and many others as well, I think, because the stuff I made up to fill all the blank spaces in my understanding was far more painful than the truth would have been, if anyone had thought to explain it to me.

Twenty-Seven

I went to bed before my grandmother came home from the funeral. I did not want

to have to greet her and ask how her day was. The entire subject of what had actually

gone on that day was too troubling, and just thinking about it had made me feel anxious

and eager to escape into sleep. Breakfast had been so late that there was no lunch, and

dinner was pizza brought home from the Roma Café at 4:00 in the afternoon. By six, I

felt like a little man with a sledgehammer was breaking rocks in my head. Rikki was

folding the paper box from the pizza so she could stuff it into the garbage pail under the

sink, and my father and David were practicing boxing moves in the living room. "I'm

going up to read in bed," I announced casually. "When is Bubby coming home?" I tried

to affect the same indifferent tone I might have used to remark on the whereabouts of the

dog: I was interested, I wanted to convey, but I was certainly not worried.

"What book are you reading?" Rikki chose to answer the part of my comment

that was not the question.

"I've been reading *Little Women*, so I'll probably read that. But I really like *Mrs.

Piggle-Wiggle* better. Those cures she invents for children who visit her on her farm are

so funny. And the sisters in *Little Women* are not really funny. More like sad, really."

"You'll love those sisters before you know it. You're getting to be too old for

*Mrs. Piggle-Wiggle*. Rikki kept the focus off the question of Bubby. She turned back to

the pizza box. "This box is so greasy. It leaked through to the counter." She became

incredibly busy scouring the counter, and seemed to dismiss me from her thoughts.

On my way to the stairs, I ducked into the small bathroom by the front door to

look out the narrow little window that faced the front yard. There were no cars coming down the street, and no sign of any life out there at all. My pine tree hideout was empty now. If it was really a hospital visit my grandmother had been taken on, they must have very late visiting hours, I thought. And if it was a funeral she had gone to, where in the world was the cemetery? It was nearly dark out. I turned away from the window and walked up the stairs, wedging my right shoulder against the wall as I climbed.

Once I was in bed, leaning against the headboard with my *Mrs. Piggle-Wiggle* propped up in front of me, I found I was simply too sleepy to keep my eyes open. I dog-eared the page corner, turned off the light, and slid down into my comforter. I fell asleep instantly and dreamed of my youthful grandparents floating in the air above bright yellow flames that were consuming a village of small peasant huts alongside a meandering river. I floated next to them, my bird's eye view of the burning village somehow not frightening at all. Then voices in my bedroom cut into the dream and I gradually woke. I kept my eyes closed and listened.

"He's really gone now, Rivka, not just gone from me with another woman," Bubby was saying, using my mother's real name. Her voice was not really sad, I noticed. It sounded strong and almost triumphant.

"What's the difference, Mama? Gone is gone. Stop thinking about him. He never gave you a good day in your life. Nasty, he was, and cruel. No, really he was crazy, crazy like a dog with rabies is crazy. And he infected everyone he bit. Look at Sidney, Mama. Look what he did to Sidney." I lifted my eyelids just enough to see through my lowered lashes what was going on. Rikki was poking her mother's arm into her nightgown as if she was angry at the arm, or the nightgown, or the old lady.

"My Sidney!" My grandmother slumped forward, her posture suddenly sadder than I had ever seen it. And her voice was like a strangled wail. "He's dead and living together at the same time, my Sidney."

"And how did he get that way, Mama? I lay that right at the feet of that man who is finally lying under the ground, Mama. So you can just stop thinking about him." Rikki puffed up her mother's pillows as if she was angry with them, too. Then her anger suddenly deflated like the dust bag of the vacuum cleaner when she flipped off the switch. "I'm sorry, Mama. I'm really sorry. And don't worry about Sidney. He doesn't know what world he is in, and he's not suffering, I'm sure of it. Maybe he found a good way to escape his father. That's what I think." My grandmother was tucked neatly into her bed by then, the top hem of the blanket folded tightly across her chest almost as if she wasn't even under it. "Go to sleep, Mama. Tomorrow we'll end Passover. It's only one day more, really. Sarah is tired of it, and so is everyone else. What do you think?"

I snapped my eyes all the way closed because I knew they would both be looking at me. I heard my mother leave the room without waiting for an answer, and I could sense through my shut eyelids that the light had dimmed, so I knew that my mother had shut the door most of the way behind her. My grandmother began moaning softly.

"Bubby, are you okay? I'm awake, Bubby."

"Ah, Sarah, my beautiful Sarah. Let's talk about happy things. Let me talk to you about another present I once got. Are you really awake?"

"I'm totally awake. What present do you mean? Tell me all about it." There was an unspoken agreement to pretend nothing unusual had happened that day, it seemed to me, and as if the discussion of the mysterious Uncle Sidney had not just taken place.

"Well, you remember the soap, right?" Mary rushed on without waiting for my reply. "I had the package of soap, wrapped in green paper and tied with a ribbon just like she gave it to me, the clerk, and we began to walk again when we left the shop. I remember one thing like it was yesterday: when we left the store, we left the clean smell inside and went back outside into London, where the smell pinched the inside of my nose. I held the package of lavender soap up to my nose, but all I could smell was the paper smell. 'Mayrke, my beautiful Mayrke, now we will go to one more special store,' said Avram. 'You will soon have a gift that you will keep all your life, something delicate and precious, just like you.' I stood up straighter then. Where was all the money coming from, I was wondering for a moment? He loves me just like he did at the fire, when I saw him from the hillside, I thought to myself. Who cares what woman he knew before I came here? She's a rotten cabbage leave, stinking in the gutter, now that I'm here, I thought to myself. He must prove to me what he thinks of me, by buying me gifts, and I must accept them to prove I forgive him, I thought to myself. It would all be easy.

"'A man I know, my beautiful Mayrke, a very religious man, has a shop where he trades in precious jewels. He buys, he sells. He has watches, brooches, combs with sparkling rubies and pearls from far away lands. And there I will find something for you that will be a sign of my love.' I blushed, I think, to hear such talk. We were walking, passing ladies in beautiful fitted jackets with velvet piping around the edges, I can still see them, and hats with feathers and netting and silk flowers. And gentlemen we saw, with silk ties and stickpins with stones that threw out beams of light like stars shining. And then we came to a couple standing near each other. They had just stepped down from a carriage, and she was waiting as he paid off the driver. We were passing by them, and she looked at me, and I looked at her. Her dress and jacket were the color of the wine we drank on Rosh Hashanah, deep red, with embroidered flowers down the button placket, so delicate they were, finer than even I knew how to make them. Her nose opened for a second, like she was smelling something she didn't like. And I saw at her throat, tucked into the ruffles of her silk shirtwaist, a beautiful cameo carved with the image of a lady who looked just like the lady wearing it, with a sparkling diamond hanging from a golden chain around the neck of the carved lady. It was pinned into place, like a mirror image of its owner, I saw, and my mouth opened before I could stop myself. 'That is it, Avram, that is what I want.' We were speaking Yiddish, of course, so the lady didn't understand me, but she was looking at me like she would order the gentlemen to beat me with his walking stick. He finished with the driver then, and took her arm to lead her to safety, away from us. But Avram was quick, and he saw the cameo. 'A cameo, my Mayrke? A carved jewel you would like? From Italy they come, and my friend I know will sell me one for you.'"

I was transported by this part of the story. It was better than any fairytale I knew about princesses or Prince Charmings. I could almost hear an orchestra of violins swelling around my young grandparents as they walked together, no, floated together, down the sidewalk in London, on their way to find the perfect symbol of their love. I pushed from my thoughts the intrusive knowledge of the misery that I knew would follow. I pictured the horses and carriages making their way past on the street, and I could almost hear the clip-clopping of the hooves. Each one was a gleaming bubble with golden engravings and liveried drivers, and the street itself a pristine ribbon of scrubbed and glowing paving blocks. I could almost hear the sound of a string orchestra swelling.

I watched my imaginary version of the scene, the various couples on the sidewalk dancing graceful patterns around my grandparents who were bathed in the warm glow of sunshine. And then my grandmother's voice interrupted my wandering reverie.

"Avram and I walked quickly then, on our way back to the East End where he lived, or rather where we lived. He said that his friend's shop was in Commercial Road, right by the mikvah. He wanted to show me where the mikvah was, he said, because married women would need the mikvah. You know the mikvah, Sarah?" she interrupted herself, suddenly remembering her listener's age and lack of knowledge. "It's where married women must bathe once a month. But everyone has forgotten the rituals, I think. Maybe you don't need to know."

I was more interested in the present my grandmother was about to receive than the fine points of the ritual bath. For the moment, it was yet another thing I filed away as currently unavailable information. "I could ask my mother, Bubby. But what about the cameo?" I was eager for the story to continue.

"We came at last back to streets where Jews were going about their business. I didn't care that the houses were grayer, and the roads were dirtier. I wanted that cameo. I deserved that cameo. I must have been hungry by then; we had been walking all day, it felt like. I didn't think about food, though. I kept touching the hollow part of my throat, the place where my cameo would soon be, like the lady near the shop of soaps. We came at last to a doorway, a tiny shop it was, dark inside. We went in and a bell tinkled, but at first, no one was there. And then a man appeared from behind a black velvet drape, with a white beard and a hat with a broad brim. He looked at me for a blink, I saw, and then talked to Avram, pretending like I wasn't there. I stood near the door; I didn't want to make him uncomfortable. I knew he wasn't allowed to look at me even though I also knew he wanted to look." Mary made a noise with her tongue like the memory annoyed her. I feared for a second that she would be derailed by her memory of being ignored by the man. But she began speaking again quickly.

"Stupid man, he was. What, I would poison him? Anyway, Avram asked him for a cameo, and I watched as he moved some boxes around that were stacked near the drape. He was muttering, something about God, I think, but I don't remember. He finally found what he was looking for, and he brought a flat leather box, dark green, onto the table. Avram leaned over as he opened it, blocking my view. 'Avram,' I said, at least twice I spoke, to try to get him to move out of my way. He waved his hand at me from behind his back. 'Be quiet,' the wave said. So I stood still and brought my package with the soap up to my face again. They spoke to each other, mumbling so I couldn't hear, and finally Avram brought out his money, gold coins it was, and in an instant, the leather box was handed over to him and we left the shop.

"'Did you get it? Is it a cameo? Can I see it?'" I tried a million questions; I was almost dancing around him like a dog hopping around his master who is holding a bone just out of the dog's reach. He didn't answer me. And then we were home. The hallway inside the house was dark, but by touching the wall as we went up the stairs, we found our way to our door without having to light our way. And now, here's the strange part: I cannot remember how he handed over the cameo, or what we ate for dinner, or where the two cousins were, or anything else until the day of the wedding. A drape, a dusty moldy drape fell over my mind, and every memory is hidden behind the drape. It's gone, the whole memory." She paused. I had more time to look at the scene as I imagined it.

"I'm sorry, Sarah. It's gone. All I can remember is we went to the rabbi. It was the Plotzker Shul, the Plotzker. Avram went there all the time to doven. He used to say to me in the beginning, 'Mayrke, I'm going to the Plotzker Shul, 45 Commercial Road. He said it so often, like I was too stupid to remember where he was going. Or maybe he was going someplace else, and it was a lie. I don't know. But for the wedding, we went to the Plotzker. Was it the next day? Maybe the next week? Was it before he found the outwork job for me, finishing ladies' mantles, or maybe after? I think and think, and I can't remember. I know that I stood with Avram in a room, along with the rabbi's wife and a few others. I wore the cameo that day; I can still feel it under my fingers pinned at my throat. Somebody signed the ketubah. I must have marked with an X, but I don't remember. You know it, the ketubah? It's the marriage document, and then someone else signed for a witness, I don't know who they were. Or maybe I knew then, but I can't remember now. And I was wearing the cameo. Did I already say that? I remember the cameo. And we ate something after together with the rabbi and the others, maybe herring, but I don't know where the food came from, or who paid for it, maybe a society that paid for poor girls' weddings. The Marriage Portion Society, I think it was called."

Her voice sounded like she was actually squinting to see someone from the Marriage Portion Society handing over some money. "And then we went home. We couldn't afford a wedding photograph. The rabbi said, 'Go to Boris Bennet, right near here, in Stepney. He'll make you a picture and you'll show your grandchildren.' But we couldn't afford."

My grandmother was quiet then, and I thought the end of the story had come for that night. I sighed as I thought over the anticlimactic ending. Plotzker sure was a funny name, but there was really nothing happy about the story. And she even remembered the name of the photographer. So how could Bubby have forgotten all the details of her wedding? I was quite sure I would remember every second of my own wedding, whenever it came. I slid down into my blanket and turned toward the wall. I had never seen the cameo Bubby had been given to celebrate her beauty. What had happened to it? Could one of my aunts have it? Did Bubby lose it? Sell it?

After a few minutes, my grandmother spoke again. "It was the end, Sarah, not the beginning. It was the end of my hope, my peace, my happy plans. It was the end of good, and the beginning of evil. The beginning of punishment, of a cursed life, of being paid back for expecting something that would erase what my father was. Nothing was ever sweet again, especially my hope." And then she was done for the night. I opened my mouth to remind my grandmother about having children, moving to America, sharing a room with a loving grandchild.

But I pressed my lips together at once, because for each thing I could think of that might have given my grandmother pleasure, I also saw how it brought misery as well. There was no point in looking at the bright side, I saw. My grandmother could only see that a beautiful young woman who thought she had engineered a perfect future had become instead a crippled, betrayed old woman who had lived a miserable painful life. I felt tears well up and spill down my cheek. One slid into my mouth, and I tasted its saltiness. I sniffled a few times, wiped my face with the edge of my pillowcase, and tried to fall asleep. But there was one question I couldn't resist asking.

"What happened to the cameo, Bubby? I would love to see it."

"I don't know. It's laying in hell, where I'll maybe be one day, my Sarah, I guess. I forgot it years ago."

There was nothing further that night.

Twenty-Eight

The weather right after Passover was warm, misleading everyone into thinking it would stay that way. School was closed for Easter vacation, and on Monday morning, the street outside my house was filled with kids who were bursting with the energy that had been pent up all winter. The curbs that ran along the street by the front yards featured a motley tangle of discarded winter jackets, abandoned there by over-heated bike riders, roller-skaters, and tumblers practicing summersaults. The bright reds, blues, yellows or greens that the jackets had been back in the autumn were faded to a nearly uniform gray, and the cuffs had become so tattered and short that gangly wrists poked through. Any parents who had hoped to pass on a jacket to a younger sibling had only to glance at the collection to realize that they were all too stained and shabby.

I was riding my old red bike up and down the street, from the far corner where the Molloys lived with their two almost grown children, to the opposite end where Mr. Rosenthal lived. The Molloy's children were already in high school, and I often saw them late in the afternoon walking past her house on their way home from the high school bus stop. They each carried huge piles of books, she holding them right in front of her hugged against her chest, and he balancing them casually under his arm, braced against his hip. The sight of them had created in me a terror of the obvious impossibility of high school. All the kids called Mr. Rosenthal The Lollipop Man because if they summoned the nerve to knock at his door, he would usually reach into a box of Tootsie Pops he kept and hand them out, one each. The problem was that sometimes, he'd growl at his callers, demand to know why they were always bothering him, and stare at them menacingly. Then he'd slam the door so hard, the brass knocker would rattle for a few seconds and the terrified kids would run across his lawn to the bikes they had left at the edge of his property.

As I peddled furiously up and back, I saw that no one outside was my age, and no one seemed to be engaged in a game I was interested in. My grandmother had come outside in her gray coat with a silky floral scarf tied on her head, knotted loosely under her chin. She sat in her usual place, next to the front door, and she nodded and waved at me each time I rode past the house. I had grown bored with the repetition of my route so I called out, "I'm going around the block, Bubby. I'll be right back." I didn't hear any reply, and wasn't even sure I had been heard, but rather than wait to be told I couldn't go, I sped up, and turned left at the corner. I stood up to pedal up the hill, and breathless but pleased with myself, I continued, eventually making three left turns and reaching my house again. Having completed this challenge, I felt emboldened to try for a longer ride.

"I'm going to the duck pond, Bubby. I'll be back later," I called as I sped by my grandmother who was enjoying the spring sunshine in her chair. I too had thrown off my jacket earlier, and my cheeks felt warm and must have been glowing with a healthy pink blush. This new destination, I knew, would have been forbidden without doubt, had I asked for permission to go. It involved crossing Reed Avenue, a four-lane thoroughfare, and venturing down a very steep and winding road where drivers might not see a young girl on an old red bicycle. I wasn't even completely sure I knew the route, but somehow, in the glowing warmth of the day, I had thrown away my usual caution and I flew past my house as if I were in an exuberant trance. I could almost imagine my conversation with Bubby later. I'd tell her all about my glorious adventure before anyone had a chance to scold me for it. She'd love to hear about, I thought. I focused straight ahead as

I came to the Molloy's corner, turned right, and peddled effortlessly down the three blocks that would lead me out of my safe little neighborhood, to the Reed Avenue intersection.

When I came to the traffic light, I got off my bike and bounced it up onto the sidewalk that ran along Reed Avenue. The whole world sounded different once I left my innocent self-contained little community. The reverberations of children's voices faded away replaced by cars and commercial traffic. I could actually feel the growl of trucks as they rumbled along busily. I felt my stomach lurch for a second, amazed at my daring, but somehow I was not interested in going back home until I had first accomplished my impetuous goal of riding to the duck pond. I suddenly had a thought that had never occurred to me before: if only Bubby were not paralyzed and old, she could have come with me to the duck pond. For a moment a wave of sadness at my loss of an imaginary possibility swept over me. I shook my head to dismiss the thought and concentrated on my journey.

The duck pond was nestled in the lowest lying section of the entire area. All the rainwater that collected in the neighborhood sumps traveled by gravity through underground pipes and emptied into the man-made pond in the middle of the old village. I had been taken to this park from the earliest time I could remember, to feed the ducks cubes of stale bread my mother saved, and to have cinnamon toast and juice at the Old Mill House Tea Room that was located at the edge of the park. In the spring, when the rain and melting snow filled the pond to its banks, the excess would rush into an overflow stream and cause the old waterwheel at the mill to turn. As I rode along Reed Avenue, I was imagining that the waterwheel must be spinning furiously, sending splashes of water into the air and onto any children who had been brought there to feed the ducks.

I passed a small strip shopping center that had a bakery, a dry cleaner and a stationery store. I rode under the parkway, testing my echo with a tentative, "Hoot, hoot," and I passed a gas station and a Chinese restaurant. I crossed each street with elaborate caution, thinking about the sound of the water as it would be tumbling over the rocks in the streambed and lifted over the top of the waterwheel. It was as if I had on blinders that blocked my view of my mother's disapproving face, had I asked for consent to take myself by bike across the whole town to visit the ducks and listen to the water on its way out to the Sound.

I knew I had to cross Reed Avenue and make my way east through the old village, but I wasn't sure which cross street would lead me correctly, so I guessed. Garden Drive seemed promising, and it had a traffic light. As I rode further and further from home, the houses were less and less familiar. I had only seen this neighborhood out the window of the car, but now everything looked bigger and more alien. There were sidewalks along Garden Drive unlike my neighborhood, so although I felt a bit lost, I knew I was safe. Or rather, I sometimes thought I was safe. As I peddled along, I studied the houses. They were much larger than the ones in my neighborhood, and older too. Many had front porches that were filled with tired old living room furniture, like dilapidated floral sofas and side tables with legs missing. Some had large areas of bare wood where the paint had peeled away. The street was lined with huge old trees that even with no leaves created so much shade that the lawns were scraggy and bare. There were no children anywhere. For a moment, I couldn't remember how long I had been riding; it suddenly seemed dark enough to be almost dinnertime. I wondered if my grandmother was still sitting outside by the front door, and then I wondered if she had heard me when I had announced my plans as I soared by.

The street began to tilt down, the tree canopy parted and the world brightened. I regained my composure as I recognized the route to the duck pond. I turned left just before the train station, and then left again, and there, just around the last bend, was the duck pond, looking just as tranquil and picturesque as always. I nosed my bike onto the path and peddled right up to the edge of the pond. A bunch of ducks spotted me standing there, and swam over for the bread they expected me to toss for them. "I'm sorry, duckies, but I didn't bring you a snack," I apologized. "I didn't know I was coming to visit you today." The ducks paddled around aimlessly for a minute or two, but when they understood that no food would be forthcoming, they pivoted their upturned tails around, and swam away.

Suddenly, I didn't know why I had come. The idea of visiting the Old Mill, listening to the waterwheel, or following the stream to see it empty into the Sound seemed silly. And the park seemed deserted, emptier than I had ever seen it. There were no mothers pushing babies in carriages, no toddlers chasing geese in wild circles, and no park workers raking up bits of uneaten bread or forgotten wrappers. I was alone, abandoned even by the ducks. And then I began to think of the ride home, which would be the exact opposite of the easy glide downhill that had brought me here. Gradually, I realized how tired my legs were, and how my knees were aching from all the peddling I had done on this first warm day of the season. And what had become of the warmth, anyway? A breeze had picked up, dropping the temperature back to its pre-spring reading. I pictured my jacket ditched at the curb in front of my house in the middle of a colorful jumble of all the others. I could almost see it in the hodgepodge of red and blue and green and pink, tangled up with one sleeve inside out and one straight. By now, their owners had probably collected all the others, and there was mine, alone and maybe wondering why I had forgotten it. I remember being very avid about anthropomorphizing everything. I swallowed hard and mumbled, "I think I'll go home now."

And then I was suddenly surrounded by a group of boys. There were probably only three or four, but I felt like it was an uncountable horde. They too were on bikes, their legs straddling their boy's bikes crossbars, their sneakered feet planted on the grass on either side. They were older than me by a year or two, and as my eyes swept around them, I saw that I didn't recognize any of them. The sky had become darker, almost instantly, I thought, and the temperature seemed to have dropped even more. Goose bumps stood up along my arms and I hugged myself reflexively. The picture of my lonesome jacket popped cruelly into my head for a split second.

"What are you doing here?" the leader of the pack demanded. His black hair was slicked back from his face, but he had teased one curl onto his forehead where it lay demanding that viewers notice its supposed disobedience. The sleeves of his lightweight jacket were pushed up to his elbows. I knew he wasn't feeling the cold like I was.

"Yeah," repeated one of his sidekicks. "What are you doing here?" This one had blond hair, but his attempt at creating the errant forehead curl was not as successful. The effect was more like an uneven row of menacing bangs. He had on dungarees, I noticed, and his belt was buckled to one side. The buckle was big, too big, and made of dull silvery metal.

All the boys walked their bikes closer to me, encircling me. I looked over my shoulder at the one behind me. He was smaller, maybe my own age, wearing a brown felt hat with the brim cut short into a circle of peaks and turned up. It looked to me almost like a king's crown wedged down over a skullcap. He wore a cardigan sweater that was too big for him, like an older brother had passed it down too soon. Somehow I found him more sad than scary.

"This isn't your park, you know. You don't belong here. It's our place. These are our ducks." The leader bumped his front wheel into my bike creating a slight clang of metal against metal. "Where's your money?" His question sounded like an afterthought, like it had just occurred to him that he had stumbled onto a good opportunity.

"This is my park, too," I replied, my mind scrolling quickly through all the times I had come there with my parents on weekends, or after visiting the library that was just on the far side of the pond. But then I realized how frightened I was and closed my mouth and looked at the fender of my bike where it touched the leader's bike.

"He said, 'Where's your money.' Didn't you hear him?" demanded Blond Bangs.

"Yeah, where?" echoed Cardigan Sweater.

All three bikes were touching my bike by then.

"I have to leave now. I'm late and my mother will come looking for me with my big brother any second." My voice trembled a little, but I was amazed to hear myself lie with such self-possession.

There was a moment of silence as the boys looked at the leader for directions. The leader was looking around for signs of my mother and brother, it seemed, so I seized the moment, and pushed my bike right between two of the boys' bikes and began pedaling away from them. I knew they could overtake me in a second if they wanted to, but I made for the path that led out of the park as if I had a chance. Silence followed for a moment, but when I glanced over my shoulder, I saw them coming toward me. They took turns pulling up on their handlebars and forcing the front wheels up off the ground, like horses rearing in wild frenzy. I stood up on my pedals and propelled myself as fast as I could. My heart was rattling against my ribs and my knees burned with pain, but I could see when I snuck a look back that they had abandoned the chase. By the time I passed the train station and was making my way up Garden Drive, my heartbeat had returned to normal and I was beginning to feel proud of myself. This story was going to make a great tale for Bubby, if I dared to tell it. She might be angry with me for taking such risks, I thought. But, no, I concluded. She knew all about taking such risks, and maybe she'd think I was getting braver and stronger every day. Or maybe not. I couldn't decide.

The breeze had washed the remnants of the warm day away completely, and I felt even colder as I wheeled along Reed Avenue. But I also felt a warm glow as I thought about how I had stood up to those mean boys. My response was totally unlike me, I knew, but I had no explanation for it.

I rode along still considering whether to tell anyone in my family. My mother, I knew, would be upset that I had ridden so far alone. And she would want to drive right to the duck pond and find those boys to give them a scolding. I liked the fact that I had handled the situation myself and didn't want my mother to go stand up for me. My father would agree with my mother, or maybe he'd even want to call the police so someone official would straighten those boys out before they really hurt someone. But what about

Bubby, I asked myself again? Maybe Bubby would be proud of me, happy that I didn't let some boys take advantage of me. Maybe she'd remember how she had been taken advantage of when she was young, first by her father in a horrifying way and then later by her husband in some as yet unexplained way. I reached the turn into my quiet safe neighborhood. Yes, I thought. I'd tell Bubby about it that night before her story started. Bubby would be proud of me.

My street was empty. What time was it, anyway, I wondered? I drove up alongside my tangled jacket and bent over sideways and picked it up. I bumped my bike up the curb and wheeled it into the garage. I suddenly realized that the car wasn't there, but as I gazed down the street, I saw it coming down the road, driven by my mother. I stood by the side of the driveway as my mother pulled in and stopped next to me.

"Sarah, I have groceries in the back seat. Would you please start bringing them in while I run in and begin peeling the potatoes? I'm late getting dinner started." Rikki slammed the car door shut and dashed into the breezeway and opened the kitchen door. "Why aren't you wearing your jacket, young lady? It's not summer yet, you know. Do you want to get sick?" And then she disappeared into the house.

I made my way to the car door, and looked into the back seat to see how many bags my mother had bought. I spoke to myself aloud, as if I was there with an equally incredulous friend. "Can you believe it? She didn't even realize I was gone! Maybe I'll just keep the whole thing secret. She didn't even realize I was gone." I grabbed the first bag and hugged it to my chest. The fragrance of oranges wafted up into my face. "I wonder where else I should ride," I mused as I walked into the breezeway. When I reached the kitchen door, I banged on it gently with one foot and waited for my mother to realize I was there.

## Twenty-Nine

That night, when my grandmother and I were tucked into our beds, I didn't even wait to see if she was in the mood to speak. "Bubby," I whispered conspiratorially. "Listen to what I did today. I rode my bike all the way to the Duck Pond." I gasped at my own daring when I heard myself say the words aloud. "And I stood up to some mean boys who were bothering me, and I rode right back home, and even though I was a little afraid, I got braver and braver as I went along, and my mother will be angry if she finds out, but I'm glad I did it and I'm thinking of other places to ride to. What do you think of that?" I found myself sitting up straight after I had poured out my escapade, looking over at the other bed and waiting for my grandmother's response. She was quiet for a minute, and I began to fear that she hadn't heard any of it, that she had fallen instantly asleep as soon as she had gotten into bed. But then she cleared her voice and spoke almost like her words were part of a ceremony.

"Sarah, you have crossed an important bridge today. You are no longer a helpless little child. You have become a woman, a small woman, but a woman who will never be taken advantage of, who will never be too weak to act for herself, and who has learned from what she's been told. I am very proud of you. But, Sarah, if you tell your mother, you will frighten her and she will punish you. So you and I will have to be two brave women together, but apart. Do you understand?"

I sunk back against my headboard and smiled in the dark. I was nearly grown, I thought.

Emboldened by my adventure to the duck pond, and deeply bonded to my grandmother, I didn't wait for my grandmother to offer the next chapter of her life. I demanded the details.

"Bubby, I want you to tell me about what it was like after you got married. When was Uncle Morty born? And what about the others? Who was born in London? Did you keep living with the cousins? Did you say you had a job doing outwork? What's outwork? Does that mean you worked outside? How did you get to America?" I had to stop to take a breath.

"So many questions, my Sarah, my perfect! What did you eat for dinner that makes you so full of questions? I'll tell you, I'll tell you. I said already that we have to hurry. I want to finish soon because I, well, never mind because. I'm talking now."

The mysterious reference to some impending event that would come along and stop the story unnerved me. "Well, don't worry, Bubby, if you don't feel like talking. We can always talk tomorrow, or the next day. We have tons of time."

"I'm talking, Sarah, I'm talking now! Are you ready?"

"Go!"

"So, where was I?" She paused, thinking, and I almost piped up with the answer, but I held my tongue, not wanting to interrupt my grandmother's thought process.

"Oh, yes, now I remember. The outwork. I'll tell you about the outwork. Avram knew a man who arranged for ladies to do work at home so they could also take care of the babies. And I told you I was a wonderful sewer, right?" She lengthened the word wonderful so that it sounded like part of a lyric, like a waltz, maybe. I could hear the smile in her voice as she remembered her embroidery skills. "So he brought for me home some ladies' mantles, like cloaks they were, made of silk and rich fabric, for very rich ladies, very fine. He brought for me five at a time, at first, and I made on each one designs like flowers along the edge, each one the same, with many rich colors. And I was very fast, so he brought more, and then even more. I stayed up into the night, because by then, Uncle Morty was there, to work on those tasks, yes, tasks, they called it." Her voice had taken on a dreamy quality as the particular vocabulary came back to her. "Tasks of outwork, late into the night. And Avram took them away back to the man, who paid him. I never saw one penny of that money. Never a penny." These last words were spat in a kind of instant fury, followed by bitter silence.

"But later, years later, when Avram went to America without us, without me and his three sons, I had to go myself to the man, Shimon, his name was, Shimon something, to bring the finished goods, or how would we have something to eat? Once, I remember, I went at night, after the babies were asleep. I left them together in the bed, and I went with the bundles for Shimon. And a bobby stopped me, a policeman. He saw me on the street, and he asked me what I was doing out alone at night on the street. 'You are looking for men, Miss? You'd better go home, Miss, before I take charge of you.' He thought I was a prostitute! A prostitute carrying bundles of finished mantles! What, he was too stupid to know I couldn't go with three babies in the daytime? But I said to him, 'I'm taking mantles, Sir, you see them here?' And he took them from my arms, the bundles, and carried them for me to Shimon who lived nearby, in Old Montague Street. 'I would love to carry your burdens, lovely lady,' he said to me. 'You are like a lovely flower I came upon in the forest, a surprise for my eyes.' I remember still how he was laughing at his rhyme. Yes, even then with three babies to wear me out, a man still saw

my beauty." As always, any mention of her youthful beauty brought a certain
haughtiness to her voice that disturbed me. How could she care about that when she had
just said she didn't have enough to eat?

"Did you still live with the cousins, Bubby?" I broke my normal silence if only to
draw my own mind away from the conflicted feelings I had about my grandmother's
values. Somehow, my grandmother had realized I was there, and she replied.

"No, my perfect Sarah. They were both gone by then. One went earlier to
America, to Chicago, I think, to be a tailor. Chaim, he was. He must have gotten tired of
the junk business. And the other got married to a woman who wasn't religious. Can you
believe? No wig, no mikvah, no Sabbath. He went with her to Wonderland every
Saturday.

"Wonderland? Like Alice's Wonderland?" Bubby isn't making sense, I thought
to myself.

"A music hall it was, Wonderland, in Whitechapel Road. It had shows in
Yiddish, Yiddish actors, and they played on Saturday afternoons, and even Friday nights.
That cousin, did I tell you his name? I don't remember at this moment his name." She
paused to think, and I was afraid she'd lose the thread of the story. But I knew I couldn't
interrupt to tell her his name was Faivel. That wasn't our routine. And then I heard her
hand slap her lap. "It was Faivel! That nasty Faivel! He and his wife went every week.
He forgot all about the Sabbath because she wasn't interested in the old ways. So he, a
weakling he was, he wasn't interested either. First he had to make my life there in that
apartment an agony, and then he met her, Henya, she was called. And so, that's how it
goes." She sighed.

"Go on, Bubby," I prompted.

"I complained to Avram, of course. How did that cousin judge me, and then go with Henya to shows every week on Shabbat? Avram told me that the Jews are like a tree that remains alive even though it may shed its leaves. So his cousin forgot the Sabbath, he said. 'If you'll dig a hole in the sand by the seashore, by the time the morning comes, the hole will be filled. The sand will return. One Jew who forgets is not the end of the Jews, Mayrke.' So I knew I should stop complaining. What good would it do? Who would listen to me?

"So I worked, and I had babies, one every two years. A goat, he was." Her voice had slid into a snarl at these words. In my mind, I saw a man in an old-fashioned suit, carrying a shiny cane with a silver tip, and as I watched him, he morphed into a bleating goat whose long yellow teeth protruded from his open mouth and straggly beard waved up and down with each bleat. But I didn't understand the relevance to my grandfather. My grandmother continued, unaware of my vision.

"And Morty, my miracle, went to school to begin to learn his letters, English in the morning, and Hebrew in the afternoon. He called his father, 'Gov'nor,' which made Avram happy. He liked to be the supreme ruler of his family, but he was never the supreme ruler of me. And then one day, Avram told me he was going to America, to Brooklyn, New York, and he would send for the children and me soon. It was 1911 then. I remember. 'You liar!' I screamed at him. 'Now you will leave me alone again and forget about me! And where is Esther Bagoudis? In Brooklyn, New York also?" She was screaming her words with strength that caused me to bolt up straight in my bed.

"Bubby, Bubby, don't scream, or my mother will come! Shhhh!" I had swung my feet around so fast that they got caught in the blankets. I was trying to step out of the tangle and reach my grandmother before Rikki became alarmed.

"Okay, Sarah, yes, I'm shh now." I smoothed out my bed and climbed back in. "It didn't do any good, you know, when I screamed at him. He had to go, he said. Bad times were coming. His friend Herschl, an anarchist he was, don't worry, doesn't matter what that means, Herschl was in a meeting in his club in Jubilee Street, against the government they were, in his club. And someone fired a gun." I gasped. "Like the Wild West it was," my grandmother chuckled at the memory, but then caught herself, seeming to realize that it wasn't funny at all. And Herschl ran out because it was just like the time when three policemen were killed, he said, after they raided his newspaper. It would be a battle, he told Avram, and Avram ran right away to buy a ticket, steerage he bought, underneath the ship, under the water, I don't know what was his hurry. That's how I remember it was 1911. Everyone was saying, 'Oy, 1911 and the world is over.' What idiots." It was too much information for me to grasp. I had no idea what an anarchist was, or why, if it had become dangerous in London, he would leave his wife and three children in the middle of danger.

"What does it all mean, Bubby? I don't understand the story." I began to whimper. But my grandmother didn't seem to hear me, because she went right on.

"Avram, he left on January 4, on the SS Adriatic. I had just come from Mrs. Levy's Nursing Home; it was a place where you could go when a baby was born. In Underwood Street, she was, Mrs. Levy. With the other babies I was home in Whitechapel Road. I don't know why I went to Mrs. Levy for Mayshe. I can't remember. But January 4, I remember also because he used to say, 'January 4 was the end of my second life, and the beginning of my third life, in America.' He sailed for more than a week without seeing the sky. The ship rocked and the sea threw it around like a matzoh ball boiling in soup. He told me later when I came with my three babies. He never had one minute of peace for the week. Green, he said he was, and vomiting day and night. He thought God was punishing him for something, but never did he figure out what it was. I would have told him if he asked me. A week of punishment was a gift. He should have had a year, or maybe fifty years." Her voice was triumphant at that pronouncement. By then I was thoroughly confused by the rapid unfolding of the story. My grandmother had left me to my own devices to understand what she was talking about. I was sure that she had forgotten her granddaughter was even in the room.

"Avram's friend Herschl was right. It wasn't the end of the world, but there were three days of riots then in the streets all around. For the only time in my life, I thought maybe I should have stayed in Ulla with my mother. It was winter then, a quiet time in Ulla, and I was thinking about the czar and his family, dead in the revolution, the little czarovitch, murdered with his sisters. No, I think that was later, the murders. But I was thinking of the black bread, how delicious and wonderful it was, and the rich black earth there. I didn't even know if my mother was alive or dead. And then I thought of my sister, Dvorah, my baby sister who would never see her nephews. I cried, then I cried plenty. The tears I never had when I came, I found them then."

Czarovitch? Revolution? Murdered later? I didn't know whether my grandmother's words made any sense, or if maybe she didn't know what she was saying anymore. But the sorrow in her voice, and the talk of crying were perfectly clear. And I wept too. What could I do with this information? Where could I keep it? Who could I

talk to about it? My cousins, after all, had the same relationship to this old woman as I

did. Maybe they had a right to know too. Why had I promised to keep it all secret?

Secrets were so painful. It was so difficult to know what to say, or what to do. I felt like

a storm was tearing through my head. Maybe I wasn't so brave or grown up as I thought.

My grandmother was talking about winter, but even though it was spring right outside my

window, there was a frigid wind ripping across my bedroom. I thought maybe I should

ask Uncle Morty about it. He would remember the whole thing, right? I could meet him

outside when he came to wash his car on Sunday. I could talk to him quietly, and ask

him to keep it just between them. I pictured myself pushing open the kitchen door just

when the blue Ford pulled into the driveway. I'd bring the detergent and rags outside for

him. He'd smile at me, chewing his cigar, and push his hat back off his forehead and

make the whole story clear. He'd explain the riots in the street, and maybe he'd even

remember Herschl. Uncle Morty could be nice, right? He'd crouch down and look right

into my eyes and tell me what a czarovitch was, and who killed him and his sisters, and

everything.

I sniffled. I realized that my grandmother had stopped speaking. I listened,

waiting for her breathing to tell me if we were done for the night.

When Mary resumed, her voice was quiet and composed. "While Avram was

gone, I waited for him to send money for me, or tickets for a steamship. And a man, a

sweater he was, Avram knew him, he gave me sewing work to do at home, at night, while

the children slept. I worked on the ladies' mantles, or I made buttonholes, or did felling

until my fingers were red and swollen. You heard of felling, Sarah?" My grandmother posed the question as if they had been having an ordinary conversation while sharing a snack together in the kitchen. It was as if she had forgotten all the misery she had been talking about moments earlier.

"No, Bubby. What's felling? And what's a sweater? You don't mean to keep you warm, do you?" I replied in kind, sniffling but struggling to hold up my end of what had become a perfectly ordinary conversation.

My grandmother ignored the question about the sweater. It landed in the pile of unanswered questions. She took up the one about felling. "You sew a seam, and then you turn it over and stitch down the raw edges. Does anyone do it anymore?"

"I don't know, Bubby. I never noticed. Should I look at a dress inside out right now?" I asked as if getting out of bed to check on the construction of a garment was exactly what I did every night.

"No. It doesn't matter. Felling, that I did at night. The gaslight was bright enough for me. My eyes were young. And my babies had what to eat, and I had what to buy coal with so they wouldn't freeze to death. So, at night I sewed. And during the day, I scrubbed with Sunshine washing soda the clothes and bed linens on a wooden board with boiling water. And I put Reckitt's blue dye to make the shirts white, and I twisted them to wring them out. I had no mangle. Avram left me with nothing but lavender soap and a cameo. I heated irons on the stove. I made soup from water and rocks."

"Rocks?"

"No. Not really. But almost rocks. We ate beans and then lentils, and then beans. I don't know why we didn't starve. But don't worry, Sarah, because then the tickets came. A letter came from America, and it was tickets, steamship tickets to come.

I ran right away with the letter to Mrs. Rosenberg who ran the mikvah. I knew her, of course, the closest mikvah it was. And she read to me, 'Come, my Mayrke, with the babies. Come right away. I have a new kind of work here with cars, certain parts.' It was after the winter. The spring was finished, too. Passover was gone and the time of year when the trees begin to be green, like blushing green instead of red, you know? That was finished, too. And it was summer then, the hottest summer I ever knew. The only creatures that were happy were the bedbugs and the flies. You never saw so many flies. I had flypaper hanging from the ceiling, curling down and covered with dead flies like poppy seeds on a bagel. The children were too hot to play, too hot to eat, too hot to sleep. But nothing mattered because I had tickets to America! Oh, it was a new world, Sarah. Avram had sent me tickets to America."

I began to cry again.

"Don't cry, Sarah. Sometimes life was wonderful in London, you know. We went, before Morty was born, to plays sometimes. I saw Charlie Chaplin, Sarah, once, in a show at the Paragon. Do you believe me? He was sixteen years old, and I went with Avram. My belly was getting big then. But I wrapped myself with Dvorah's coat, and no one saw. We ate oranges there in the theater, I remember. Everyone ate them. We threw the peels right on the floor. No one cared!" She laughed at the memory of her young self, so carefree and careless. "Look how much I remember! The Paragon Theater in Miles End Road it was. I remember the good parts, too, you see."

"We ate roast chicken every Friday, and I always stuffed the neck; Avram loved that, the stuffed neck roasted with the chicken. He went to Frumkin's in Whitechapel Road for wine. Can you imagine? I remember Frumkin's; I knew his wife, Yenta, she was called. Her son was the same age as my Morty, Irving he was, a very modern name she gave him." At that she laughed outright. "And we ate cholent on the Sabbath. We gave it to Mrs. Schwartz, in the bakery, up three steps she was, and she left it in the hot ovens all night. It was delicious, Sarah. I wish you could taste it." My grandmother was smiling, I knew, and it was joyous to hear. "And I remember that Avram went to Lazarus, the barber. But sometimes I cut his hair, right there in the kitchen. And we played cards, Sarah. Or at least the men did. The women didn't play. We drank tea with sugar and lemons, the Russian style, or sometimes we put jam into the tea. And we noshed on herring and black and green olives and salami and Russian black bread. We didn't have olives in Ulla, that, I can tell you. The bread, it wasn't as good as the bread in Ulla. But the butter! I never had such butter as the butter in England. I would go back there right now for a taste of that butter. And I remember how we worked to get ready for Passover. We burned sulphur candles all night to kill the bedbugs, and the children had new clothes. The shoes, I remember the shoes for the children. The shoes had patent leather toecaps, so adorable they were. We worked so much for Passover, but we loved it. Passover time we loved." I found myself smiling again. But the seesaw of emotions was taking its toll. I yawned loudly.

"Okay, my perfect Sarah. I know you're tired."

"No, Bubby," I recovered quickly. "I'm not tired. Really. You could tell more."

But my grandmother seemed to know better. She had exhausted her granddaughter. "You're as limp as a washrag, Sarah. What a day you had! And I'm tired too. Let's just go to sleep now, and maybe tomorrow, I'll tell you about coming to America with three little boys. Okay?"

"Okay, Bubby. Maybe tomorrow." I felt like the dog had dragged me across a huge field. I was relieved that Bubby had left me with a few happy memories. But the echo of the earlier ones, the grinding poverty, the seeming abandonment, the one about being mistaken for a prostitute. I wasn't completely sure what that meant, but there was no doubt it wasn't good. I focused my thoughts on the young couple peeling oranges in the balcony of a huge theater, and far away, on the stage, a young actor dressed like a poor tramp was squeezing gales of laughter from them. I fell asleep.

## Thirty

On Sunday morning, I was awake just as the sun began to lighten the sky. It was as if an alarm clock had rung inside my head, bringing me to instantaneous alertness. For a second, I couldn't remember why I had awakened so early, and why I felt so edgy, but quickly the plan I had settled on to question Uncle Morty about his memories of London gushed into my brain like an incoming wave inundates a sandcastle. I couldn't focus on anything else but how to speak about his childhood to Uncle Morty in a way that wouldn't reveal any of my grandmother's secrets.

I folded back my blanket silently and carried the clothes I had worn the day before into the bathroom so I could start the day without waking anyone. Someone had closed my parents' bedroom door for some reason, but I was too involved in sneaking around noiselessly to start worrying about the reason for that unusual incidence. One worry at a time, I thought to myself. Luckily the closed door would prevent them from hearing the water running or the toilet flushing, I thought. I made my way down the stairs, stepping over the fourth one down which I knew groaned when it was stepped on.

The downstairs of the house seemed eerie at this early hour. The kitchen had been straightened up the previous night as it always was, but by the time I usually got to it in the morning, signs of use would be obvious. There would always be a few coffee cups left on the kitchen table, the wooden counter would have a shower of toast crumbs and a smear of butter or jam, and the juicer would be propped open with the pulpy remains of someone's squeezed orange beginning to dry in the crevices. Rikki would be putting everything to rights as I left for school.

But today, it looked like a stage that had been made ready for the first scene of a play, and I was witness to the unused set before my family came into it to enact the morning plot development. I boosted myself up against the edge of the sink, balanced on my straightened arms and peered out the window to see if Uncle Morty's car was parked in the driveway yet. It wasn't. I lowered myself back to the floor, briefly considered making my way around the kitchen without touching the floor, and decided I wasn't in the mood for a game. I opened the refrigerator, peered inside, but closed it without taking anything out. I opened the bread drawer and examined the contents of a folded down white waxed paper bag from the bakery, but it was only some stale rye bread that didn't interest me at all. I opened the kitchen door and leaned out into the breezeway, checking the driveway again. Still empty.

Maybe this was really too early, I considered, even for Uncle Morty. And then I heard an engine outside. I pushed the door open the rest of the way, and saw the blue Ford nosing its way up the driveway and stopping.

I darted through the kitchen and into the hall where I yanked open the door to the basement. Right on the top landing of the stairs was a bucket of rags and a box of Spic and Span. This will be perfect for washing a car, I thought, and grabbed them both. I was out the kitchen door with my offering in an instant.

"Someone is up early today," said Uncle Morty as he pushed his straw fedora back off his forehead. "Bed bugs get you?"

"We don't have bed bugs, Uncle Morty," I said, astonished at my good luck. He had given me a way to begin my conversation with him about his childhood in London. "Did you ever have bed bugs?"

"Sure. They bite you all night long, and suck your blood. Then you itch the next day like you want to tear your skin off. I had 'em plenty." He took the bucket of rags from my hand as if I offered them to him every Sunday.

"In your house now there are bed bugs?" I watched him as he began unwinding the hose from its coil behind the bushes. I was carefully manipulating the conversation. I knew I had to progress slowly, but the idea of bed bugs was making my arms feel itchy. I rubbed them, and considered abandoning this thread as too uncomfortable to tolerate for long.

Uncle Morty dumped the rags out of the bucket and poured some detergent powder in. He stuck the hose nozzle into the bucket. "Hey Sarah, give me some water here, will you?" I stepped over to the faucet and struggled with the wheel until I got it on. "More. I need more pressure," my uncle instructed. I spun the wheel easily now, and I heard the water caroming off the sides of the metal pail. The pitch became lower as the water level rose. When the suds appeared at the top, he lifted the hose up and released the nozzle trigger, shutting off the flow.

"Did you scratch a lot?" I returned to the topic I thought might get him talking about his childhood. He was dipping the rag into the sudsy water and slapping it onto his car.

"Scratch what?"

"You know. From the bed bugs."

"I haven't seen a bed bug in nearly fifty years. Or maybe I saw them when we lived on the Lower East Side. What do you care so much about bed bugs for?"

"I don't. But did you have them in London?"

Uncle Morty picked up the hose and began spraying the soap off his car. He considered the question carefully, almost as if he were weighing the significance of his answer. I busied myself with picking a few dandelions that had sprung up overnight, trying not to look too interested. What if he figured out why I was digging around for information? I almost abandoned my quest. I was determined to keep my grandmother's secrets.

"In London? What we had in London was complete misery. We had too much heat in the summer, too much cold in the winter, and too little to eat always. We had no hot water, no money for keeping the oil lamps lit, and no peace in the house." I watched his face go from calm and thoughtful to bunched up and boiling red. I backed away from him a few steps, suddenly afraid of what I had unleashed.

"My mother and father screamed at each other like crazy people, and they screamed at their children too. They got mad at little things, like where he put down his prayer book; they screamed at big things, like how she couldn't feed three children on tuppence, or thruppence, or whatever it was. It was all the same. No one came to visit; no one could be trusted. That was my father. 'They'll steal from you, they'll look to betray you,' was his comment about anyone I talked about. And my mother, 'Go to your whore, Esther Bagoudis, go,' was her response to him every time he asked for something, food, a clean collar, anything."

The water was accumulating in a huge puddle, almost a pond by now, beside the driveway. He had forgotten all about the car washing, it seemed. I had backed myself almost into the breezeway. It was like I had tapped gently on an abandoned beehive, but thousands of angry bees had come swarming out in response. The tirade continued.

"I was in the street every minute I could. And so were my brothers, even the baby. I took him down with me, both of them I took, because the both of them would start wailing whenever the screaming started. "He would storm out and slam the door, and disappear. Mama would look at herself then in a mirror by the chest of drawers, and she would be sobbing louder than the babies. She would get in the bed and lay with a red swollen face until eventually, he'd come home with a package of that lavender soap, and she would get up. She would do up her hair, long, black hair she had then, and coochie-coo with him. Until the screaming started again. When my father left for America, that was the only time I remember that the screaming stopped."

He stopped talking then, and looked down at his hand that was holding the streaming hose. He stepped back from the pool he had created, and dropped the hose. I must have slipped completely out of his consciousness, because the next thing he did was walk around to the driver's side, open the door, and get in. He turned the key he had left in the ignition, looked over his right shoulder, and backed the car down the driveway. Without waving to me, or even looking at me, he pulled the brim of his hat forward, shifted the gears, and drove away down the block.

I felt like I had been slapped across the face, or maybe even punched in my belly. One hand went involuntarily to my cheek, and the other to my stomach. Some of the water was spilling down the driveway slowly, and the discarded hose was lying in a muddy pool. I stepped towards it in a kind of trance. I bent down and reached for the nozzle. My feet were bare, I suddenly realized, and wet and cold, too. I pulled the hose toward the garden, and began coiling it back the way it had been before Uncle Morty had come. The bucket was lying on its side, somehow, with a scum of suds spilling out next to it. I went and collected it, and stuffed the rags back inside. I retreated into the breezeway, and holding the handle of the bucket over my arm like a purse, I pulled the screen door open, and walked up the two steps into the house. I dried my feet on the rag rug by the door, still operating on automatic pilot, and deposited the bucket back on the basement landing. I left the rags inside it, unable to think of what to do with a pile of wet soapy rags.

I quietly closed the basement door, and began walking up the stairs to my room. My parents' bedroom was still closed, my brother was still sleeping in his room, and the house was as silent as it had been when I had gone downstairs to wait for Uncle Morty to come and fill me in on the details of life in London when he was a boy. I went into my bedroom and found my grandmother lying in her bed with her eyes open. I went right past her, crossed the room, pulled back my covers, and got into bed. I grabbed for the satin binding at the top of my blanket and pulled it up to my chin as I turned over to face the pink wallpapered wall. I stared at the whimsical furniture pattern, the chair with the feet that looked like they might walk, the chandelier with the circle of lampshades, and the footstool with the multicolored cushion. Then I eyes closed quietly.

A few big fat tears escaped from under my eyelids, but I wouldn't have been able to explain them even if my grandmother had noticed and inquired. I think now that it must have had something to do with my fear that my whole family was crazy, and this was just the evidence for Uncle Morty's insanity. Eventually, I must have thought, I'd have evidence for each person. But my grandmother was silent in her own bed, maybe thinking about why she had heard the running water for so long. If she had heard any of the conversation through the open window, she didn't say. Maybe she had, and was remembering what a poisonous childhood she and her husband had given their three sons, and maybe she was regretting it quietly. Or maybe she had heard neither the water nor the conversation, and was only half awake and not fully aware of my having been out of bed longer than it might have taken me to simply visit the bathroom for a moment and come back to sleep.

There was no explanation for her silence. And there was likewise no explanation later for Uncle Morty's absence from that Sunday's visit. He didn't reappear for weeks, but there was no explanation for that either. No one mentioned the fact that he didn't come to visit his mother. It seemed that his sisters and brother didn't even notice. Maybe they thought he was in Cuba on business. Maybe they thought he had had a fight with someone. And my grandmother didn't ask anyone where her son was, at least not that I had heard. It was like she thought she didn't deserve an explanation. A person evaporates, I thought, every Sunday for the weeks he doesn't come, and no one thinks anything of it.

Who the czarovitch was, what the anarchists did, how my grandparents had made their separate ways to America were all unanswered questions. I knew what to do with unanswered questions: swallow them down into some secret closet deep inside where I kept them for all the years of my childhood.

Thirty-One

I was barely awake the following Saturday when I became aware of my grandmother's voice. It sounded like she had been watching me for the first signs of my wakefulness. She spoke quickly, as if trying to say as much as possible in the closing seconds of a radio program. "This is the same weather as when I came to America, Sarah. At least I think it was the same. I know Avram left me in the winter, that I remember. And I know I was alone in London with three babies in the cold. But I don't remember Passover alone. Maybe it happened, maybe it didn't. I think I went to the steamship in this weather, the spring."

I pulled up my pillow and arranged it against the wooden headboard. I remembered that she had said she was alone in London with her three children in the hottest summer she ever knew. But I also knew it wasn't the season or the weather that really mattered, and I didn't want to stop her from speaking by correcting her. I settled my head against the headboard, my eyes still closed, partly from sleep, partly to envision the scene that would be momentarily spread out before me. I didn't comment on the unusual time of story telling. I was getting used to the unexpected. I sensed my grandmother's hurried tone, as if she was late for a train that she had to board as a matter of life and death. I waited quietly. The voice continued.

"I carried bedding with me, rolled up. Can you imagine? A huge bundle I carried because it was the most valuable thing I owned, not counting the cameo, of course. But you can't sleep in a cameo, and a cameo won't keep you warm. How could I set up a home in the new land if I had no bedding, I thought? Everyone had bedding. The dock looked like a feather bed sale was going on. What fools we were! Did we think there were no feathers to be had in America? Bundles tied with ropes watched over by knots of men in hats and women in kerchiefs pulled down on their foreheads. Ugly we looked, everyone.

"I stood straight up, proud and brave, with my three sons right there with me. The other children were too frightened to run around like children usually do. Morty, he was six years old, I think, he had to behave like an adult. He carried bundles, too. The baby, I had him, the other followed his brother, his feet shuffling along. He was crying, the middle one, I remember. 'What are you crying for? Pick up your feet; I have no money for new shoes when you scrape off the bottoms.' He never stopped crying for a minute the whole voyage, my middle one."

She stopped talking. Couldn't she say Uncle Sidney's name aloud? I almost seized the moment to ask what had happened to Uncle Sidney. I opened my lips and took a deep breath, but the sound I began to make froze in my throat and I converted it into a short cough. I didn't want to know what had happened to Uncle Sidney just then. The image of the sobbing child trailing after his bundle and baby laden mother and his older brother morphed into a sobbing adult wandering along some vague street scene. Luckily, the cough did not distract my grandmother.

"We rode in a cart, I think. It must have been, because how did I get to the steamship if I didn't ride in a cart? A carriage, maybe? Why are some memories gone? And was the steamship right there, by the Tower Bridge? Or, no, I think I went first in a train. I don't remember anything right." She groaned a few times.

"Bubby, don't worry about all those details. They don't matter now, right? Tell me about the steamship instead. If you remember later, you can just back up a little." I nearly got out of my bed to go comfort my grandmother. But I didn't have to because my words had just the right effect.

"So smart you are, Sarah. The steamship I'll never forget." Her emphasis on the word "never" was full of pain and wonder. "I remember it every time I feel a little dizzy. That reminds me. Or if I feel like maybe I'll vomit, like I'm sick. Then, right away, I'm back on that ship. I still see it in dreams sometimes. Nightmares, really." She shuddered and paused, seeming to examine the scene in her mind.

"The men and the women in steerage, they lived separately. But I think families could be together. I wasn't a family, of course. I thought I would soon be one, but I wasn't a family on that ship, and I wasn't a family ever. You need a husband, a father for the children, to be a family. An old story. Anyway, on the ship, I had a berth for me and my baby together, and the other two had a berth right above me. We had less than three feet above our heads. I couldn't sit up straight in that berth." She hesitated a moment, considering the scene. "No, wait, I forgot something. In London, before I could get on the ship, that dark sewer, it was, first there were questions. I was in a room, very high ceilings, it had. And light was shining in through the windows, coming in in wide bands, like big, flat bars of butter, painted across the floor, and the tables. There was crying there; I could hear someone crying." She stopped as if she was listening to the crying, trying to remember who was crying.

"There were twenty-nine questions. Why do I remember twenty-nine? Because I was twenty-nine years old. Yes, twenty-nine. One question for each year. The inspector said, 'How do you do, Madam? I must ask you twenty-nine questions.' 'Oh,' I said to him, 'One for each year of my life,' I said to him, laughing, like. I don't know if I was really twenty-nine, who knew such things? But I was trying to be friendly, more friendly than those other people, the ugly ones, you understand? So he would help me, you know? They looked like potatoes in clothing, those others. Anyway, it worked. 'You have the bloom of a spring rosebud, you have,' he said to me. I was holding the baby, and Morty was telling his brother to stop crying for one minute. But that man, that inspector, he saw only me, how beautiful I was, even in the middle of the turmoil there. So he said, 'I'm sure I don't need to go through all these questions. You're going to relatives, right? And you have some money, I'm sure, to pay your way when you arrive? You couldn't be an anarchist or a polygamist, so let us shift you right on to the doctor for a quick look.'

"I didn't know half the words he spoke. He had a little Yiddish, I had a little English by then, and there was an interpreter there, but they were too busy to take too much time. And then, I gathered my bedding. He watched me, I remember. He stood up into that butter light, and I was embarrassed for him to see all my bedding, like he was looking under my dress. So then the doctor looked at my eyes; he pulled down my eyelids. And I marched straight up onto the ship. And then down into the belly of the ship where another man showed me my berth."

I tried to envision the bowels of the ship. I pictured tiers of cots, stacked up along the sides of a big room, each one filled with skeletal people wearing gray striped shirts, staring blankly at a cameraman who was capturing their horrific situation. No, I suddenly realized, that wasn't a steerage image I had conjured; it was a photo I had seen of a concentration camp and its wasted inmates, a photo taken right at the end of World War

Two when the camp was being liberated. I had to interrupt my grandmother. "Was it like a concentration camp, Bubby, in your ship?"

My grandmother didn't answer immediately. I looked across the room at her, trying to determine whether the pause was for thinking about the answer, or if the story was over for that day.

"The camps came to the Jews only twenty-five years later, or maybe thirty. But they were worse, Sarah. The ship was carrying me to freedom, I knew. First I would suffer, but I had always suffered. And then I would reach the Golden Land. It was part of the price. I only had to live long enough to pass through that misery. The camps, the camps, Sarah, carried people to death. And no matter how they tried to live through the misery, they couldn't. They disappeared from this earth, smoke going up chimneys and then blown away. My baby sister, Dvorah, maybe, with them. No, it wasn't like a concentration camp. But I didn't know the camps were coming, so at the time, it felt almost impossible to live through."

Neither of us spoke for a minute. I considered my grandmother's words. I could barely imagine a span of thirty years, and my grandmother's ability to look back over forty years, or fifty years or more was an impossible feat. I thought how each decision my grandmother had made, each movement, led directly to a result, one threaded and woven into the next, locked together like fabric. From the vantage point of fifty years, it was easy to see how the choice she had made at each crossroad led her down from her forsaken hovel in Ulla to her bed in this room on an island east of New York.

I thought about my aunts and uncles and cousins, their faces riffling through my mind like a flipbook you make to animate a story. Each relative was like a product constructed from the threads of this fabric that was itself constructed from decisions and considerations that my old crippled grandmother had made for more than half a century. Yes, I told myself, other things were in their mixes; it wasn't all from my grandmother. But that half-century of choices was unmistakably there, woven through their personalities, influencing the choices that they themselves made at their own crossroads. If someone wanted to pick out the threads from their own pasts, the ones they didn't like, the colors, sort of, that they didn't want there, could they do that? I pictured my mother sitting on the sofa with a bolt of multicolored cloth in her lap, holding a tiny pair of scissors, snipping out little bits of the fabric and brushing them onto the floor, and the accumulating pile of ragged scraps growing around her feet. I knew I would have to think about this more later.

"Do you want to hear more, Sarah, more about the steamship?"

"Please yes. Tell me more." I unconsciously ran my fingers back and forth across the satin hem of her blanket. I stared at the ceiling.

"So I pushed all the bedding into the berths. There was no place like a closet or a trunk. The bundles made the berths smaller, but I just bent up my knees to fit. The children fit better. I was lucky to have two berths. Some people had to fit their children in with them, into one space. When I first got there, the worst part of it was the dark. There was a smell, like if you fold up wet laundry, or maybe it's almost dry. But it wasn't yet the smell, the stink that grew there as we sailed. That smell, feh, that smell was a stink."

Her lips were pursed, and one side of her mouth curled down as she remembered. "For twelve days we sailed, not steady and even for even one of them. Hundreds of people were there, and everyone was vomiting. Even if I didn't feel the ship throwing itself around the ocean, it was all the other people vomiting that brought up my stomach."

My grandmother laughed for a second. How was this funny, I thought? I sat up, beginning to feel nauseated myself just by listening. "Was it terrible! We thought we would die." Then her voice turned sober. "No one came to clean the floor. And those floors! In some places, they were wood, which would never dry even if they wanted to clean them. And in some places they were sheets of iron, cold like a frozen river. They gave us each a blanket when we got there, and the man said, 'Here you are, Madam, a gift for you from our steamship line. Please take it with you when we arrive in New York.' I thought then to myself, this is a wonderful steamship Avram bought my ticket on. But I soon learned. The blanket was rough, like needles almost, and too thin to do anything. And by the time we came to New York, I never wanted to see that blanket again.

"But didn't you have bathrooms, Bubby? Or bathtubs?" I was trying to transpose my life onto the ship. "And what about food? Did you have to bring all your food? But was there a refrigerator?" I heard my grandmother snort at those questions.

"There was a room with toilets. They clogged up and we couldn't use them by the second day. There was a tap to get water to wash with, but it was cold salt seawater. A woman, Pnina she was called, was next to me, in the berth next to me. She went to the tap to get water the first night, to wash herself, and I watched her. She stood away from the tap and leaned over to it, a washrag in her hand. Very proper she was that first day. She turned the tap and held the washrag under the stream of water, and then she brought it to her face, leaning over, not to wet the front of her shirtwaist. 'Ach!' she screamed. 'It's salty, like pickle brine!' She dropped the washrag and it fell onto her skirt that she was trying to keep dry. 'I'll dry stiff like a corpse!' She ran back to her berth, sobbing she was, and trying to wipe the water away from her clothing with two hands. She was weeping the whole night, moaning and calling for her mother who she left behind. I knew she would never last, and I was right: she vomited for days, grew weaker and weaker, and then she died right there in the berth next to mine. Two men took away her body, who knows where."

I gasped. My grandmother was so casual about watching a woman die. Yet another side to the grandmother I thought I knew, I thought to myself. "There was no refrigerator." This last piece of information was nearly spat out. Her tone felt like a dismissive rebuke, like I would never understand, and her efforts to impart the facts of her life would never succeed.

"Maybe it's time for your morning medicine, Bubby? Should I get you some juice?" I had had enough of the ship part of the story. Was any part of my grandmother's life pleasant? Thinking back over all the tales I had heard, I couldn't think of anything funny or pain-free in my grandmother's life since her early childhood in her village. Yes, there had been stories of her getting what she wanted, like the beautiful coat or the trip out of Belarus or the cameo. But even those good stories were overshadowed with misery. The coat had been stolen and never really made her happy. The trip may have gotten her away from rural poverty and her cruel father. But it brought to urban poverty and a cruel husband. And the cameo brought delight for a mere instant before it became the symbol of the only gift she had ever received from her poisoned marriage.

"Good idea, wonderful Sarah. You get my juice for me, and I'll go and wash my teeth. Then I'll be able to chew the toast, instead of gumming it down to a pulp," she laughed, making exaggerated sounds of gnashing her tongue against the roof of her mouth. How is she laughing now, I asked myself silently? Where in her old gray head does she keep all the black melancholy so she can lock it away safely and allow laughter out? I threw back my blanket and set off for the kitchen.

"I'll finish the story about the steamship later. I have to tell you about the goddess in the harbor, don't forget. That was something amazing." I looked at my grandmother as I passed her. Her eyes were shining and she was smiling a toothless smile at the memory of finally arriving in New York.

Thirty-Two

"How is it fine by you to steal thousands of dollars worth of furniture, Esther? Either you paid for it or you didn't. I can't follow your logic," Rikki was talking to her sister on the phone as I came into the kitchen and reached for the refrigerator handle. "What do you need, Sarah? I'm on the phone here." I looked at my mother who was leaning across the stove and stirring the contents of her big aluminum pot with a long wooden spoon, the phone cradled between her ear and her shoulder. The scent of garlic simmering in oil filled the kitchen.

"I'm getting juice for Bubby for her morning pill," I answered, my tone nearly sarcastic, since what I was doing seemed so obvious to me. I knew that what my mother's words really meant was, "Stop eavesdropping and go away." Aunt Esther is a thief of furniture? I pulled the refrigerator door open and ran my eyes around the inside looking for the container of orange juice. I knew where it would be; it was always in the same place. But a short look around the inside of the refrigerator might yield more information about Aunt Esther, the thief. My mother was silent, obviously waiting for me to finish my task and move out of earshot.

"No, she's getting juice for Mama," Rikki spoke into the phone. "No, I'm not interested in how you rationalize it, Esther. You accepted the delivery, and now you're refusing to pay. I call that stealing." She paused, and I could hear the muffled phone voice of my aunt spilling tinnily out of the speaker that Rikki had propped at an angle. "I'm not discussing it later Esther." Another pause while she continued stirring and watched me boost myself up against the counter high enough to open a cabinet door and extract a juice glass. I shook the juice container, spilled a few drops of its contents.

"Sarah! Be careful! I don't need orange juice spilled all over the kitchen!"

"Sorry," I said in two distinct syllables. I could hear my aunt's voice again.

"Meat sauce," my mother said into the phone. More tinny burbles followed. I replaced the container into the refrigerator and left the kitchen with the glass of juice.

"No, no veal chops. I said meat sauce, not plain sauce. Morty likes meat sauce. If he comes. . . ."

I mounted the stairs watching the orange juice slosh around the glass dangerously. I walked across the hallway upstairs to my room with my shoulders hunched up nervously, trying to balance the liquid.

"Here, Bubby, here's your juice. Do you know why Aunt Esther is stealing furniture?"

"Stealing furniture? What stealing furniture?"

"Something about not paying for some that got delivered."

"I don't know anything. The stores are the real thieves, though. They charge too much and it falls apart. Good for her if she got it for free." My grandmother was not taking the position that I had expected. "Maybe your mother can help me get dressed, Sarah? Go ask her, please, beautiful Sarah."

I knew that was the highest compliment from my grandmother. Beautiful me forgot Aunt Esther's crimes for the moment and went back downstairs to summon my mother.

"When all the cousins come later, can we walk up to George's Candy Store, Ma?" Rikki's phone call had ended. My mother murmured an unintelligible reply. "And

Bubby wants you to help her get dressed." I leaned out the kitchen door to test the temperature, stuck my bare foot out into the spring air, and finding a balmy day, went outside into the breezeway. The rosebush vines had climbed part way up the garage wall and I could see bits of daffodil clusters around the crabapple tree in the front yard.

"Please don't walk around outside in your pajamas, Sarah. And put shoes on. It's not summer yet." Rikki's voice fell away as she left the kitchen the other way, on her way up to her mother.

By the time the sun was as high as it was going to go, the house was humming and buzzing with relatives. The adults sat in the yellow bunk seats, as usual, slurping noisily on long strands spaghetti dripping with tomato meat sauce. They ate in uneven shifts, as usual, some just beginning on heaping bowls, while others sopped up the dregs with heels of bread, and still others sipped coffee and broke off hunks of coffee cake they had brought with them from whatever bakery they were currently touting. Invariably, the best bakery in the world from a previous week now sold poison, and this new one was where they intended to shop forever. The cousins rotated in and out of the house, sometimes floating aimlessly and sometimes tearing through with a vengeance, absorbing themselves in a string of games that could only flourish in a backyard or basement that they didn't have at their homes.

I stationed myself at my living room listening post, interested in hearing more about my aunt's perfidy. If everyone in the kitchen knew about the furniture theft, could it be long before the police found out, and Aunt Esther was carted off to jail? What would Uncle Jack do then, or their children Darlene and Jeffrey? The older two children, Veronica and Judith were already married and living with their husbands, so I figured they'd be all right, even if their mother went to jail. Maybe no one in the family knew except Rikki, and she would keep it a secret because it would be too shameful if everyone found out. Secrets were a specialty of the family, and this one was big, not just what one sister had said about another. This was a crime, like in a movie. I knew I was working myself into frenzy, but I couldn't stop. I crept close to the door into the kitchen, hanging on every word that wafted through.

"Who taught you how to make sauce like this, Rikki? You cook like an Italian woman from the Bronx." Having moved from the Bronx themselves, anyone who still lived there was somehow beneath contempt, low class, and not worthy of their company. The aunts and uncles, I noticed, never bestowed a compliment without pairing it with an insult.

"Mama taught me, it so happens," replied my mother haughtily. "While you were painting new make-up on top of your old make-up, my darling sister, I was watching Mama cook and learning. Mrs. Russo, remember she was that neighbor from Rockaway years ago, when we rented on Beach 83rd Street? Before Bobroff. She showed Mama, and Mama showed her gefilte fish in exchange. Am I right, Mama?" They rarely spoke directly to my grandmother who usually presided silently from her chair at the head of the table. There was a moment of uncharacteristic silence while all the heads turned toward the matriarch and waited.

"Mrs. Russo, that's right. She showed me." The quiet space filled up instantly with all their voices like water filling up a hole you were digging by the shore. I caught snatches of personal memories of Rockaway. "Was that place crowded!" And, "No, it was not 1932. It was before because I know when I met Faye Greengold!" And, "The hottest summer on record." And, "Hot? You're crazy. It rained cats and dogs the whole summer. We never took off our raincoats." And, "You couldn't pay me to go there. There's a certain element now."

The conversation paused for a moment. That was one sentiment they all agreed with. I recognized that word, element, but couldn't imagine what the sneering tone that had uttered it had meant. "They would steal your laundry from the line while it was still wet," said Aunt Ruthie. Everyone laughed at the instant scene Ruthie had painted. I could see shadowy people skulking around clotheslines full of pinned on sheets and undershirts that flapped in the wind.

"They would steal your sandals from your blanket while you were in the water," countered Uncle Solly. I saw a crowded beach littered with tattered pastel colored chenille bedspreads spread out on the sand and orange and green striped umbrellas leaning this way and that. The bedspreads had been abandoned by their owners, women were standing ankle deep in the surf, leaning over and splashing water up onto their abundant bosoms, and men who were standing near the women in knots of two or three, cross-armed and lobster red with zinc oxided noses. Furtive figures were sidling from one bedspread to the next, stuffing sandals into huge Santa Claus sacks that they dragged behind them. More laughter followed. Now they were all trying to outdo each other.

"They would steal your chamber pot before you emptied it," bellowed Uncle Mayshe. I could hear hands slapping the table as they roared in response. Chamber pots? They still used chamber pots in Rockaway? Maybe those people really were backward. Is that what element meant?

"What happened with your living room furniture, Esther?" Aunt Jean's voice changed the subject.

"I'm not talking about it," came the snooty reply. She patted her new hair-do, a coppery series of finger waves rippling up and down her head, both checking it and drawing attention to it.

"So don't talk," retorted Aunt Jean. "But I know Macy's will never see their money from you."

"They would see it if they delivered on the day they said," snorted Aunt Esther. "I know what a contract is. They said they're coming Tuesday. I waited Tuesday. They didn't come. Wednesday morning, the bell rings from downstairs. 'Furniture,' says the guy. 'Where were you yesterday?' I say. 'I'm here today,' he tells me. I'm not paying. That wasn't the deal. So now, they can bust." Aunt Esther harrumphed triumphantly.

"She's right," put in Uncle Jack. "Why should we pay? They broke the deal."

"Jack, you're sitting on a new sofa, you're eating off a new table, and you're watching a new TV. You took the furniture; you have to pay," Rikki said, with the kind of slow logic she might have used to explain something complicated to a five year old.

"No, Rikki, you're wrong. When you make a deal with a big outfit like Macy's, and they change the deal, the deal is off. She does not have to pay. I agree with you, Esther," said Aunt Jean.

"That's right, Rikki, Jean is right," said Aunt Ruthie.

Grunts of agreement erupted from all around the table. Rikki tried to counter them. "What's the matter with you people? Why did she accept the furniture if she wasn't happy with the deal? She could be sued by Macy's, you know. They have teams of lawyers. They'll yank her right into prison, and it'll serve her right! You think they have beauty parlors in prison, Esther?" I gasped. My aunt in prison? For a split second, I had an image of the whole family visiting Aunt Esther who was behind bars and they were all right up next to the bars, sitting around the kitchen table as usual on the yellow bunk seats. My grandmother was in her regular chair, but instead of sitting there serenely, she was sobbing into her good hand, crying, 'Esther, my Esther.'

My thought was interrupted sharply. Someone had heard me gasp. "Sarah? The eavesdropper is here again. Go outside, will you please? Every other child is getting pink healthy cheeks, and you're in here getting yellower by the minute. Send her out, Rikki! What's the matter with her?" It was Aunt Jean. There were other voices of concurrence. I left my perch but not wanting to confront them all, I walked around the long way and out the front door.

I considered a quiet retreat into the big pine tree hideout. I thought I should spend some time alone to consider how life might change with an aunt who was a prisoner, a guest of the state, as I'd heard the phrase on a TV detective show. But solitary thinking time was not going to happen. A bunch of cousins had discovered the pine tree hideout, and were sitting cross-legged on the bed of pine needles deciding what to do next.

"Let's play jacks," suggested cousin Stacie, her thin fine hair escaping from the barrette that was sliding over her ear. She looked like someone had just rumpled her head. She was really too old for jacks, but she was very good at it, and probably wanted to show off, I thought. Darlene responded instantly, her two fat braids flying behind her as she darted her freckled face toward Stacie.

"No, Stacie; can you grow up? Do you see any sidewalk to play jacks on? Do you even have jacks with you?" Stacie pulled her arms and legs around herself and scooted back from her cousin Darlene. Darlene was two years younger than Stacie, and loved to point out her inadequacies. I knew that Stacie was much brighter than her younger cousin and easily outdid her at school, but Darlene talked louder, weighed more, and had enough hair for two people while Stacie had barely enough for one. And Darlene used her brash personality against Stacie's timidity like a muscle-bound lumberjack. Stacie could outsmart Darlene and send her wailing to her mother by using her far better vocabulary, or by simply icing over and refusing to respond. There was a constant battle of wills between the two of them, and during an ordinary Sunday visit, each new skirmish drew them a step lower down the scale of human unkindness. By the late afternoon, each of them would have had at least one screaming, weeping breakdown that required adult intervention.

I looked around at the group of my cousins in the pine tree warren. It was only the girl cousins. Two were younger than I was, and two were about my age or a little older. But the boys, including my brother David, were not there. I wondered where they were. Sherry was explaining a complicated activity she had thought of, one that required paper, pencils, scissors, a blackboard, chalk, and chairs. I began imagining my art supplies scattered all over the yard once this game was abandoned, which I knew would happen moments after they got it all set up and realized that Sherry's explanation was simply a complicated way of saying, "Let's play school." I knew my mother would be unhappy about replacing things that were not really used, but merely ruined by neglect.

And my father would not be happy to find scraps and bits of a game all over the yard, blown into the shrubs and forgotten.

"Would you like to walk up to George's?" I ventured as a suggestion.

"Who's George?" asked Melissa, the youngest cousin. She was so thin that I could see and understand her entire skeletal system just by looking at her in her shorts and sleeveless blouse. Her mouth opened so wide when she spoke that it created a hole that was at least half the size of her face. Her mother, Aunt Jean, pulled her hair back into a very tight ponytail on top of her head, making her look like she could be lifted straight up by anyone taller the way you'd pull a teabag out of a cup of hot water.

"No, it's not a person. Well, it is a person. But we might not see him," I stumbled over my explanation, and Darlene lost no time in capitalizing on the error.

"Well, smarty-pants Sarah, is it a person or isn't it? Make up your mind before you tell us we should go there."

Momentarily stung by my cousin's rebuke, I considered backing out of the group and returning to my spot in the living room. But Sherry, who did not seem at all upset that her suggestion had been rejected without debate, rescued me.

"Let her talk, Darlene. Do you have to be so bossy? Tell us about George, Sarah, and ignore Darlene." Her tone balanced between condescension and sympathetic support. I didn't want to find myself in the middle of a new clash involving Darlene whose temper was unpredictable.

"Well, George's is a candy store up on Reed Avenue, and it's owned by George, so you see it's a person, but it's really a place." I smiled around the group, trying to undo the negativity. There was an momentary pause while they all looked up and back at each other, each assessing the other's opinions of my suggestion; it looked like no one wanted to be the only one who didn't agree with the group's decision. Sherry took the lead.

"That's a great idea, Sarah. Do they have only loose candy in a showcase, or do they have regular packages, like of gum or Almond Joy or Snicker's?"

"I hate Almond Joy," complained Darlene. "They better have Bazooka, or I'm not going."

"They have Bazooka, Darlene. Every candy store has Bazooka," explained Sherry as if she had been the one to suggest George's, and had examined their stock just the day before to compare it with all the other candy stores in her experience.

"I'm not sure about loose candy," I said apologetically. "Maybe just licorice, or Dots."

But by then, they were all chatting happily about what candy they liked, and what candy they wouldn't give them one cent for, and which candy maker was lying on the packaging about how delicious his product was. A lively debate ensued on the definition of "all day sucker."

Melissa went through the breezeway to the kitchen door and called inside that they were all leaving for the candy store. Her father, Uncle Solly, who had been standing just next to the door, handed her a handful of coins, admonishing her to share with everyone.

"Let's see how much we can get without paying," suggested Darlene.

"Yeah."

"Without paying?" my stomach lurched as I followed my cousins down the driveway. I recognized all the cadences of their parents. It was easy to connect the dots between my cousins' views of the world and how to negotiate and their parents' views.

Trust no one, get what you can, keep your defenses up, and expect negativity. And

where, I thought as I trooped after them, did this come from? That was easy, too. I

quietly but regretfully laid the responsibility right at my grandmother's feet. What a long

reach she had.

And so we were off.

Thirty-Three

The trip to the candy store was an adventure in misery. I couldn't stop thinking about it later. The thought that it had been my idea to walk up to George's sent waves of guilt washing over me, even though I knew I had not been part of what happened. My cousins had acted like a seasoned gang of criminals, I decided, and I wished I knew what to do about it.

On the way there, we had passed the huge tree that marked the back way into my neighborhood, a tree that I called The Lollipop Tree. It wasn't shaped like a lollipop, I knew, and in fact had no connection to lollipops. These facts had never disturbed me until that afternoon. As we turned the last corner that led up to it, I, in my most articulate tour-guide voice, had said, "And now we will pass, as you all can see, The Lollipop Tree, just ahead of us on our right." The response was relentless.

"And now we will pass," mimicked Darlene in a nasally sing-song voice, "the Lollipop Tree, as Miss Priss can see."

I stopped walking for a beat. "Well, that's what we call it."

"What, it grows lollipops?" questioned Sherry with disdain.

"Yeah, that's right, lollipops," laughed Darlene. "Or sometimes, Almond Joys."

"No, I think I see Bazooka packs, hanging from that branch up there," joined Melissa, the youngest, grateful to be able to join the jeering.

"No, it's Nonpareils, stupid. See those white dots?" chimed in the usually quiet Stacie.

"That's not candy, moron. That's bird shit," Darlene shouted, relishing her choice of words.

They were all laughing except me, slapping their thighs and each other's shoulders. I was frozen out of their company, suddenly smaller and as helpless as a naked featherless baby bird that has fallen from the nest. I had completely forgotten whatever strength my trip to the Duck Pond had given me. I considered turning back. But explaining to the adults in the kitchen why I was back so soon and my cousins were not with me would have been too difficult.

We came to the one square block of trees left untouched by housing developers. "That's the woods," I tried in a whisper. They never heard me. I was relieved to have been ignored.

The cousins walked the last few blocks to the candy store repeating their mockery and ridicule of me ruthlessly. I walked alone, several paces behind them, unable to counter their callous cruelty. The clear sky seemed to glare menacingly.

When they pushed open the glass door and entered the store, though, the cousins took on new personas. They became jovial but compliant children, and only by carefully watching the furtive looks they flashed each other, something George, the candy store man failed to do, could you see that they were practiced delinquents. George was very tall and he held his head thrust forward a bit, probably from years of feeling too gawky and ungainly. He nodded at them meekly, wiping the already clean counter with a frayed cloth. They split into pairs and wandered around the candy displays discussing what would be good to buy, casually displaying the coins they planned to use so that they would not be suspect them of any nefarious ideas. George was either too trustworthy, or maybe even intimidated by them. He said nothing. I said nothing. Each distraction by one pair of children enabled another pair to stuff handfuls of unwatched candy into their pockets. At the end, they paid docilely for one candy bar each, and exited the store. I followed, red-faced, trailing after them in mortified silence.

Out on the sidewalk, they erupted into hysterical howls, dancing around each other in triumph. I was ignored.

As they reached the woods, Darlene had a new idea. "Let's go in those trees and pee." This was a new low, I realized, and began to tremble.

"No! That's not right!" I gasped.

But my cousins were too stoked on the adrenaline that their candy heist had produced. A chorus of mocking, "Not right, not right," erupted in shrill shrieks. And before I could even consider what to do about this horrific behavior, they had scampered a few feet along a wooded path, squatted down, yanked their panties out of the way, and urinated with exaggerated cries of relief. I didn't know where to look.

That night, I was stricken with a spate of seemingly inexplicable trembling. Rikki was sympathetic, but her comments only made it worse.

"What could this be about, Sarah?" She sat down on the edge of my bed. "You spent a lovely day with your cousins, walking up to George's, playing in the backyard. We ate six boxes of spaghetti, would you believe so much? I'm glad I made enough meat sauce. If I tell you what the butcher charged for ten pounds of chop meat, you won't believe it!" She was trying to distract me, it seemed, but any mention of my day with my cousins renewed the trembling.

"Leave her, Rivka," advised my grandmother from her bed. "I'll tell her a story and she'll go to sleep."

My quivering hands paused as I considered the surprise of hearing my grandmother say aloud that she would, or even could, tell a story. Rikki nodded and left grandmother and granddaughter together.

"I'll tell you about how we came to New York, Sarah, how we saw the goddess in the harbor. Will you like that?"

I took a deep breath, held one unsteady hand in the other and bobbed my head up and down, barely perceptively. "Okay, Bubby. Yes, tell me about when you saw the Statue of Liberty."

"I knew we must be close to New York, you see, because some men came along with mops and buckets of soapy water. They were cleaning and fixing because there would be an inspection from the government of America. I knew about it because a woman there told me. She had a letter from her husband, Chaim, or Cheval, something, anyway. That husband, he was already in New York, and when he sent her, I forgot her name, Pesha, yes, that's it, Pesha, he sent her the tickets, he wrote about the inspection. He said, I remember this, he said, 'Pesha, the trip, maybe it will kill you. But when they come with the mops and pails, you know it's almost over.' So I knew, too." She stopped talking, and my trembles, which had subsided, started up again.

"Where did Pesha go, Bubby? Did she live near you in New York?" I said, trying to distract myself.

"Pesha? Brooklyn, maybe. I don't remember. Some went to other places once they got off the steamship. There was a boat that had trains on it, like a barge. I don't remember how they got to that boat. They went all over America. My brother Simon, when he came here, they sent to South Bend, Indiana. An agency, a Jewish agency, they

met us on the docks and grabbed people and said, 'Here Mister, here Missus, here is a
ticket to go to a new place where they are waiting for you with a job. You're a tailor,
maybe? I know they want you in Chicago if you know from men's trousers.' So I don't
know where that Pesha went. She's laying dead now, maybe."

"Bubby! Why do you think that?"

But my grandmother made no reply to my mild reproach, because she had picked
up the thread of the story. "So after that, the next morning, we put on clean clothing for
the first time in almost two weeks. Everyone, I think everyone, had special clean clothes
bundled up, ready to wear for the new world. Oh, wait, some kept the clean clothes
hanging on the ironwork of the berths, draped around for privacy. But I had clothes in
my bundle. We came up to our part of the deck. It was a very small place; we could
hardly all fit. But everyone wanted to see that Golden Land when we got there. It was a
beautiful bay we saw, big and wide, and the water was not quite calm, but rippling like a
sea of long curly hair. And I remember the ripples made the water look like it was
shining, sparkling like diamonds were just below the surface, pinned into the hair.
Someone said, I remember, 'Look! They have diamonds in the water in America!' An
idiot, she was. What, she never saw water sparkle in Europe?

"And then there was the big woman standing there with the spikes on her head.
No one spoke, not a word. We couldn't, couldn't speak, couldn't believe we were there.
And then the weeping began, sobbing and praying, 'Thanks to God! We're here in
America!' Oh, how I remember that crying. We sailed right straight past the Lady
Goddess, right to Manhattan. I didn't know where I was going. But we gathered our
bundles together, everyone did. They tried to give us the blankets to take, but I wouldn't

take mine. I left it there on that foul straw-filled mattress, a gray woolen blanket laying on a blue and white gingham mattress. That was the last sight I had of that ship. I looked back once over my shoulder as I carried the baby up the steps, very narrow, steep steps, it was. The other two dragged the bundle. And I shivered, I remember, when I looked back for a second, back down the stairs into that hell. But then, I stood up straight, took a deep breath, and walked right down the gangplank into New York."

"And then Avram met you? Was he right there waiting?"

"Waiting? No, Sarah, not waiting. Not then. First, they marched us right back into boats, no, barges, and in no time, we were sailing again."

"What? But weren't you there already? Where did you go?" I considered the possibility that my grandmother's memory might have clouded over. This didn't make sense.

"Ellis Island, we went. Right across the bay. They didn't just let us in to America, the ones who came steerage. The first-class and second-class passengers went right off the ship and disappeared into New York just like roaches disappear when you turn on a light and surprise them. But steerage people, we went to a waiting room first, got a name tag that they tied onto a button, and we went in groups, they counted us off, groups of thirty maybe, or maybe twenty-five, and right onto a barge to Ellis Island. That's where the trouble really started." She stopped and moaned a few times. My hands began shaking again, and I waited quietly in my bed, to hear more.

"We had to walk up a steep stairway to the Registry Room. Men stood at the top watching us. Some people they pulled to the side by the time they got to the top of the stairs. Lame, you were gone. Blind, you were gone. Scabs, gone. They marked people's coats with chalk, an X, and X in a circle, some on the shoulder, some on the

waist, some got a B, some something else. It was a code for I don't know what.

"The cries were different there, I can tell you. Families were divided up. If the

doctors pulled you out, that meant you had to go back where you came from, right back

onto those ships. And if it was a mother, her children screamed with grief. Or if it was a

child, someone had to go back with him. Who would go? No one wanted to go; no one

wanted to stay behind alone. Terrible, it was there. They had one doctor, he looked at

the eyes. Trachoma, he was looking for. Everyone feared that one. If he found

trachoma, they sent you back. And do you want to hear something funny, Sarah? Later,

years later, a doctor discovered the cure for trachoma. And do want to know who he

was? Well, I'll tell you. He was an immigrant himself! Can you imagine?" She

chuckled then.

"But if you passed the doctors, they sent you to another line in a big hall. We

were standing there like cows lined up for a slaughter, it looked like. Oh, that hall, I'll

never forget it." She stopped talking then, and when I looked over at her, she was staring

off into space, as if she were looking straight through all the decades right to that big hall.

Her lips were pursed, as if in deep thought. She nodded her head abruptly, as if the

image was focused and fixed, and she began to talk again.

"The windows were very high, right up to the ceiling, made of lots of panes of

glass stacked up and up and up. And the light came in, a gray light it was, gray like pale

ashes, maybe, and it filled the hall with some kind of a chill. The noise there, it was a

hammer in my eyes, in every language. I never knew there were so many ways to talk.

And also, I remember metal rods the separated the lines, with lamps hanging from them, I think. Or maybe no lamps; it was so dim there. But the thing I couldn't get over was the birds. Yes, there were birds inside, a few only, but birds. They were sparrows, I think, or something else small. Gray, like the air, almost. First, I heard one calling, a very sad song it was singing, like calling for its mother, maybe. So I looked up, around, but I didn't see anything. And then, yes, there it was, high, near the ceiling, swooping and flying, looking for a window to fly out from that hall. Up and back, higher, lower, to one side, to the other, it raced around, desperate to escape from there. And crying the whole time. But it was trapped in a trap it had made itself. That bird and the others too, they came in to see what this place was, and could never escape until they died there of starvation. I never forgot those birds.

"The line moved forward, slow like a funeral. There, inspectors sat on high stools, and one by one, they asked questions. Your name, your age, who you were going to. They looked down at papers they had, the papers with the same questions they had asked in London, it seemed like. Up and down, they looked. And they compared your answers to find the liars and the cheaters. It took two minutes. Two minutes. If you passed, that was it. You were in. They gave a landing card, you changed your money, and they gave you a box lunch for the ferry back to New York. It had an apple, I remember. It was the most delicious thing I had ever eaten. Sweet liker sugar, I remember." She paused then, as if to relish the memory of that apple.

"And there's one thing more. When I passed out of that building onto the dock where the ferry was waiting, there was a sign. I couldn't read it, of course. But many could. And everyone who read it, read it again out loud, over and over, until everyone, even the children and the ones who couldn't read, was saying it together, 'Welcome to America.' And that's it."

I began to cry then. It was a combination of forces that brought the tears. I wept with joy, first of all. My grandmother's tale of suffering that ended in triumph was gloriously cathartic. Hold out, it said, endure misery when it presents itself, and the rewards will be sweet. But my tears of happiness brought on tears of another sort next. I thought of my difficult day: the prospect of Aunt Esther being a thief and ending up locked away in a dark prison, probably as poisonous and miserable as that steerage compartment had been; my cousins' derisive laughter at my childish name for the tall tree at the entrance to my neighborhood; the stomach churning experience at the candy store where I had become an abettor to a shoplifting ring; and the mortifying stop at the woods where I had watched helplessly as her cousins defied all decency and urinated publicly, defiling that one small square block of natural landscape that was left in the area. I felt like I could never go back to any of those places; they were altered forever.

But eventually I cried myself out and fell asleep. My grandmother must have heard me tossing around all night, tangling my blanket into knots that I wrapped my legs around. And when I awoke the next morning, I found myself damp from sweat, and completely unrested. Some wisp of a dark dream was receding, but I couldn't bring it back enough to think it through. I could just remember trying to run away from a policeman who was holding out his handcuffs menacingly. I was running as fast as I could, but I was on a tall stack of newspapers, and each step I took reduced the pile by one sheet of paper that flew out behind me and fluttered into the officer's face. He never reached me, but I never got away either.

"Time to get up for school, Sarah." It was my father, standing at my bedroom doorway. "Have fun today, Sar," he called as he started down the stairs. I could hear him singing and then whistling quietly. "When the red, red robin comes bob, bob bobbing along, along. . . ."

I flipped back the cover and went to brush my teeth.

Thirty-Four

Mrs. Pappalardo, my school's art teacher, did not have her own classroom. She had a huge gray metal cart with fat tires and it was stocked with all kinds of art supplies. She wheeled it around the corridors, making her way from classroom to classroom on a regular schedule. She was a tiny person, the size of an average sixth grader, and I worried that one day, she'd get run over by her tremendous supply cart, and we'd never have art again. Mrs. Pappalardo wore dresses that she must have bought in the children's department, because they all had ruffles around the hems, or white cotton collars that framed her face, or high waists that anchored smocked bodices. She wore her hair in a ponytail that hung down between her narrow shoulder blades, with a thick fringe of shiny bangs across her brow. She wore shiny penny loafers every day, and I begged Rikki to buy a pair just like them for me, until finally she relented. If I was lucky enough to be called on to hand out supplies, I could get close enough to Mrs. Pappalardo to breath in her scent, which was definitely Johnson and Johnson's baby powder. I adored her.

Tuesday was Art day for my class, so it was my favorite day of the week. Each week, Mrs. Pappalardo presented something new for the class to work on, always related to the coming holiday or some unit of study they were pursuing for Science or Social Studies. Mrs. Pappalardo would appear at the classroom door, tap her signature rhythm, and pull her cart through the door calling, "Hello, hello, hello, my favorite class of this exact moment!" She would reach into her cart at this side and then that, bending to reach inside, or standing on her tiptoes, the backs of her penny loafers flipping off her heels, to reach across the top, and another project would be explained and demonstrated. And then the class would get to work.

But there was never enough time for some children. If you couldn't think of an idea, you might spend precious minutes with your chin in your hand, furtively glancing around at the projects that were blooming around you. That was never my problem. If you weren't good at cutting straight, or using just the right amount of paste, you might create such a mess that you'd have to ask for additional supplies, and start over. That wasn't my problem either. I always feared I would need more time because I had a million ideas, complicated detailed ideas that were comprised of layers of paper, complex folds or pleats, and lengthy drying time. And the truth was, I wanted to please Mrs. Pappalardo enough to have her hold up my finished project to be admired by the whole class. This race against the clock generated anxiety, and the only thing that prevented me from becoming paralyzed with fear was the quiet signals I got from my teacher, the nods and smiles, that told me I was doing a good job and I was right on schedule.

Thinking back on it, I realize that my love of Mrs. Pappalardo was all about how different life was in her class, under her guidance, than it was with my extended family. I spent my childhood worrying about how disturbed my relatives were, and exactly how much like them I might turn out to be. The approval that came from my art teacher was like a balm that soothed the discomfort they had left each week.

The Tuesday after the painful trip to George's came two weeks before Mother's Day, and Mrs. Pappalardo explained, that would give us just enough time to complete our Mother's Day gifts: clay plaques that would be embedded with small mosaic tiles and painted after they had had a week to dry and harden. "Finally, we will attach strings to the back so that each mother can hang her beautiful gift wherever she thinks it will look the best," chirped Mrs. Pappalardo, looking around from face to face, a model of a plaque hanging from her thumb and forefinger. "What to you all think?"

There was a moment of silence, which was followed by a chorus of general assent. I remember that I wasn't the only one who liked Mrs. Pappalardo. Everyone greeted her project introductions with delight. But one other child also adored her as I did.

Rosemary Mullen was often chosen as the teacher's helper, which made her blush with happiness. She was the thinnest, palest child in the class. She had sparse lank hair and a mouthful of crooked teeth that were fighting with each other for prominence and lips that were always fighting with each other to keep the teeth hidden. Her dresses, all hand-me-downs from her three older sisters, never fit her right. Some were too small, the hems falling inches above her knees, and some were too big, the sashes that tied in the back pulling the side seams nearly together along Rosemary's spine. They were all faded cotton, washed and starched stiff, but a bit frayed or mended and somehow shabby. The previous summer, Rosemary had become one of the first children to have successful open-heart surgery to repair the holes she had been born with in the walls of her heart. She had to miss the first few months of school that fall, and I was too frightened of her to speak to her since her return. But there she was, well enough, according to Mrs. Pappalardo, to hand out balls of wet clay to each child.

Everyone began to knead and pinch the clay as we had been instructed, flattening the balls into round flat plates. The room rang with the sound of hands slapping clay. There was something completely joyous about being allowed to make noise in school. There were even several rolling pins available to facilitate the task, and the children took turns guiding them over their clay. No one had the skills, however, to create a truly round disk of even thickness like the model, so the room began to fill with cries of frustration. Mrs. Pappalardo's voice rang out above the sounds of disappointment. "Oh, I love this one! It's so original!" and, "Look at this clever oval! What a good idea you had not to make it perfectly round!" and, "Children, glance this way to see how wonderful Glen's is. It looks like an egg, or maybe a football. I bet he wanted it to look like a football, right, Glen?" And their unhappy voices were quelled. Then she came to my desk.

"Oh, Sarah, this is the most perfect circle in the class. Did you trace it out first?"

"No. I just did it freehand, Mrs. Pappalardo," I defended myself, a bit uneasy about having my honesty questioned.

"Well, I'm very impressed by it. You certainly are skillful at modeling clay."

I glowed with pleasure. I saw Rosemary peek over at my disk and quickly bow her head to her own imperfect circle. "Mrs. Pappalardo is going to like yours, Rosemary," I whispered. "She said she likes the ones that are not really round." I felt good to have said something encouraging to Rosemary, but I only vaguely realized it was not as generous a comment as it might have been.

I chose the mosaic tiles I liked from the supply box and pressed them into the perimeter of the clay. And finally, with a thin pointed wooden stick, I began to draw an image of a rooster in the middle of the circle. I went a bit too far as I rounded the line of his back, but with my finger, I was able to press the mistaken line out. I etched his two legs and his jagged comb into the clay, careful not to go too deep. Then I carved a circle around his feet so it looked like he was standing on the ground instead of floating in the air. I pulled my hand back and admired the finished design. Mrs. Pappalardo stopped behind my chair just at that moment. "Sarah, that is wonderful work. Your mother is going to love her Mother's Day plaque, I know it," she chirped. "Next time we have Art, it'll be dry and you can paint it." And with that she slid it off the desk surface with a large spatula she was carrying, and onto an outsized metal tray. In a matter of minutes, all the plaques had been collected, and the desks were sponged off and dried with brown paper towels.

Mrs. Pappalardo positioned herself behind her huge cart and called out, "Goodbye, goodbye, goodbye, my favorite class of the moment! Someone dash up here and open the door, please. I'll see you clay sculptors soon!" She pulled her cart through the open door, and off she went, down the hall to her next class. To me, it felt like she had pulled all the joy out of the room with her.

There was always a momentary letdown when Art was over and Miss Sullivan, the regular teacher brought her stern no-nonsense demeanor back. She strode imperiously through the door and she was already instructing the class. "Take out your Arithmetic books, class. And fold the paper I'm handing out into eight boxes. We're having a quiz." I felt my stomach drop as I followed my teacher's directions, and I glanced at the clock to see if it was almost time to go home.

Just as Miss Sullivan turned to the blackboard to write out the quiz problems, the sound of an ambulance siren filled the room. It had arrived silently, but the attendants were now wheeling a stretcher across the parking lot and the driver had started up the siren in preparation for taking off for the hospital. My classroom faced the front of the building, and I could see easily into the parking lot at any vehicle that was parked there.

Miss Sullivan put her chalk into the chalk tray and walked briskly to the windows. "There is no call for my students to be staring out at whoever is unfortunate enough to be in need of that ambulance," she scolded as she began to drop the blinds, one by one across the wall of windows. But before she got the last one down, I was able to see, just for a second, as the stretcher was being pushed through the open back doors of the wailing car, the face of the young boy who was strapped onto that stretcher. It was David, I was almost completely sure. The blind dropped over the picture with a bang, and now I could only look at the image that was burned into my brain: my younger brother, with a webbed belt across his chest, tossing his head back and forth, writhing in pain.

"Number each box on your paper," Miss Sullivan instructed, "one to eight, please. The problems will be on the board. You must show all work. There is no talking during a quiz, Carol and Diane. Begin now." She turned to retrieve her chalk.

I was frozen. It couldn't be my brother, I thought. He was fine this morning. What could have happened to him? The wailing siren was fading, but the picture I had seen just before the blind had closed was vivid and unmistakable. I could see the two ambulance attendants, and they were on either side of the stretcher, and it was tipped back just enough as they were pushing it into the back of he ambulance so she could see light glinting off her brother's teeth. Maybe you imagined it, I cautioned myself. You're always imagining the worst. He was fine this morning. Perfectly fine. Do your quiz. Do you want to get a U in Arithmetic? I looked at the board. The problems swam around, unfocused. Do your quiz, I repeated to myself. Concentrate. I listened, bending my ear toward the window. The siren sound was gone.

"Pencils down," intoned Miss Sullivan. "Pass your papers forward, please. Pencils down, I said, Jeffrey. Put an X next to your last problem; it's automatically wrong when you write after pencils down has been called." How could it be over, I asked myself in a panic? How did time go by when I didn't know it? The atmosphere of the room had chilled. I passed my blank paper forward.

"You may speak to each other in whispers while I grade your quiz. We will have our Arithmetic lesson, the last lesson of the day, as soon as I am done with these quizzes." Miss Sullivan sat down at her desk and bent her head to her work.

Somehow, the school day ended an instant later. I could not remember a single second of it. I stuffed papers and workbooks into my schoolbag without thinking, and sped to the bike stand. There was my bike, the same one that had provided such a thrill of happy abandon when I had ridden it to the duck pond, now a different kind of transportation entirely. I peddled home as if my hair were on fire, racing through intersections wantonly, ignoring the part of my brain that was cautioning safety, and dismissing the voice that was telling me I was being silly, that it had not been David.

But it had been David. When I came tearing around the final corner, my house came into view, and the driveway was empty. The car, which was always parked in the driveway by the time school let out, was gone. And so I knew: it had been David. But what had happened?

I jumped off my bike and let it fall to the ground, scraping my shin as I abandoned it and tore through the kitchen door. "Bubby! Bubby, where is my mother? What happened?"

My grandmother was sitting on the yellow bunkseat, a cup of cold tea in front of her, and a half eaten bowl of red borscht pushed to the side with coagulated white streaks of sour cream pooling across it like sickly clouds. My grandmother was alternating between out of control wailing and frantic shushing. "Oy! Oy! Oy! Sha, Sarah, don't worry, sha. He'll be fine. Oy! Oy! Oy!"

"What happened, Bubby? Where are they?" I was half crying, but also trying to get information as well as calm my terrified grandmother. I was afraid of what could happen to a sick old lady who got herself too upset. "Just tell me what happened, please. Calm yourself, Bubby."

"David has an appendix, Sarah, an appendix. He ran in the school yard, and he hurt himself," she cried, and then the wailing returned.

"Bubby! Stop yelling. Where is my mother?"

"In the hospital is your mother. With David. He broke open his appendix. He's emergency in the hospital to take out his appendix." Her command of English had slid away from her in her terror. But I understood enough. Somehow, there had been an accident on the schoolyard, and David had injured himself enough to need an operation. As soon as the situation was clear to her, I began to tremble. I tried to tell myself that my brother would be fine, but my out of control grandmother made it impossible to believe it. "Everything around me is cursed," she was crying. "Nothing of mine will come to good. There is nothing but black misery on this earth. Better I should be dead."

I snapped to my senses. "Nobody is going to be dead, Bubby. Just stop it. It would not be better if you were dead. It would be worse."

"If I'm dead, Sarah, the curse will be over. Finished. The curse is from my father, and from my husband, and from my own self. This is the evil that's been following me, spreading like a cloak around me and all the children that are mine, and now the ones that are theirs. It's like a well, like a fountain that throws up poison, and everyone drinks it, and no one can escape until I am dead. I wish I could be dead right now; what's the use of living for me? Now David, little David, is poisoned, another one. It's a punishment for me, God's punishment. What my father did, and then I stole the money and the coat and ran away. And my trick; I regret that trick now! What can I do now but die?" And then she began keening again, like some kind of a tribal lament that bemoaned all the malevolence and iniquity of the earth. Her superstitious mind was so toxic. She sat alone with her thoughts, afraid to ask anyone to help her relieve her pain because everyone was just waiting for ammunition to use against her. Or maybe like she liked the pain because she thought she deserved it.

I reached my hand towards my grandmother, but then drew it back to my chest. I watched my grandmother tear at the flesh on her cheek with her one good hand, and it seemed like she might gouge out her eye. I took a step back, turned and darted out of the kitchen. I hurried up the stairs, barely touching the treads as I went, ran into my room and slammed the door behind me. I dove into my bed and pulled my pillow around my ears, trying to drown out the shrieks that were erupting from my grandmother.

And there I waited for my mother to come home.

## Thirty-Five

It was still light outside when my grandmother called me to come for dinner that night. "Sarah my perfect, come down," Mary yelled up the stairs with her quivery nervous voice. "I'll give you something to eat. Come down because it must be time to eat dinner. The sun is dropping behind the houses, Sarah, so come down to the kitchen." The afternoon had been punctuated with her keening cries from downstairs at her seat at the kitchen table. The slice of sky outside my bedroom window was clear brilliant blue dotted with pillows of white clouds. That happy sky was as ill fitting, I thought, as shoes from last year.

"I'm not hungry, Bubby. And I'm waiting for the phone to ring, so I don't want anything to eat." I knew that didn't make sense, but I couldn't think of how else to refuse my grandmother. I reluctantly thumped down the steps, stopping to look out the small window that was halfway down. My grandmother's voice called from the kitchen, more strongly than before.

"We'll have cold cereal, Sarah, like the animals ate in Ulla. People in America eat what we fed the geese. Such a rich country, and they eat animal food here. But your mother doesn't want me to turn on the stove anymore. So, come down to me Sarah, and we'll eat animal food together."

I giggled in spite of my state of anxiety. I rounded the corner into the kitchen. There was a pot on the stove, the metal one my mother used for French fries. I glanced into it as I passed it; it was filled with oil and a mass of sodden potatoes. The image of my mother listening to someone talking to her on the phone, telling her about David and the ambulance flared across my brain. I saw my mother reach for the knobs on the front of the stove, turn off the flame under the pot of frying potatoes, and hang up the phone. I shook my head back and forth a few times to dismiss the image. It had been hours since I'd come home from school, and my mother hadn't called yet. But it had been even longer since I'd eaten lunch, and I had to admit that eating "animal food" with my grandmother instead of the usual dinner my mother prepared sounded like fun.

"And we'll start with apple cake, I think," continued my grandmother. "We'll start with dessert, and then we'll have the breakfast of ducks and geese. And I can tell you about 326 Madison Street. And soon your mother and father will be home to say that David is fine. Okay?" Just the mention of David brought waves of terror washing through my head. My stomach lurched around wildly. And why had my grandmother's keening stopped?

"What's 326 Madison Street?" I asked. I tried to focus on my grandmother's words, allowing myself to be somewhat mollified by her new optimism.

"That's where I went to live with Avram and the three children. On the Lower East Side, Sarah. Didn't you know where we lived? Your mother and her three sisters were born right in that house. No, I'm wrong. Jean was born in a hospital, Gouverneur Hospital, right around the corner. She was the only one born in a hospital. The others were born right in the bed where they were started. But with Jean, I went to the hospital. I forgot why I did that." Her voice was wandering at the end. She was distracted by a vague memory, and the pause gave me the opportunity to worry about David again.

"When do you think my mother will call, Bubby?"

"What are you thinking about that for? It takes time to take out an appendix. Give them time, Sarah! I'm trying to tell you about 326 Madison Street!" Her mock anger distracted me from my thoughts.

"Okay, Bubby. I'll give them time. Tell me all about 326 Madison Street." I sat down on the yellow bunkseat in the seat my father usually sat in so I could see easily the clock that hung above the refrigerator. My grandmother hobbled to the cabinet with the dishes and brought down two cereal bowls.

"We stayed there until Aunt Rose Aronsky came along. She came from Monroe Street, a coalman's daughter, she was. Not refined at all. And then we moved to the Bronx into six rooms. But that was later. Now, I'm telling about the Lower East Side. I can see that house right now if I close my eyes." She had opened the silverware drawer and was reaching in for spoons. But she stopped and closed her eyes, smiling. "A stoop in front, Mrs. Greenblatt on one side, Mrs. Pearlmutter on the other. And in the back, Mrs. Cohen, very religious, and Mrs. Chait, a wild screamer, she was. She threw out her husband twice a week, Nathan was his name. A butcher. She took him back twice a week, too, because he brought home meat. How could she ignore that?" She considered what she had just said and harrumphed. Her mouth was set into an angry scowl.

"There was screaming all over that building, all over." She sighed resignedly. The scowl melted. "Her children had to eat, right? And we were one flight up. I had four rooms there, so small you could fit the whole apartment into this downstairs of your house, Sarah. The main room was the kitchen. I had a big round table there, oak, and I had a white tablecloth on it, heavy white lace it was. Once, your mother took scissors, she was very little, I think right after Jean was born, and she walked around the table and

cut off the whole lace hem that hung down. 'What did you do, Rivka?' I gave a scream.
'I didn't do it,' your mother said. She was standing there with the scissors in her hand,
and a big round lace circle in a puddle around her feet. 'I didn't do it,' she said."

"My mother?" I was incredulous. I had stood up and taken the bowls and spoons
to the table. I was reaching into the refrigerator for the milk, but the idea of my mother
doing such a mischievous thing made me laugh aloud. I could only imagine the Rikki I
knew, all grown up, a mother, but wearing a little girl's smocked cotton dress, holding
her big pinking shears.

"Walked around the whole table and cut off the lace hem, your mother. I gave her
such a smack! But she wouldn't admit it. I don't know why. It took me two weeks to
sew it back on, and it was never the same. I left that table right there in the kitchen with
the repaired tablecloth, right in the middle of the kitchen floor when we moved to the
Bronx." She sighed, almost longingly. I put the milk on the table and my grandmother
brought the box of corn flakes with her, wedged under her paralyzed arm. "You like this
kind?" she asked as she sat down and pried the box away from her involuntary grip. I
nodded and glanced at the clock over the refrigerator. It was 7:45. When would she call?

"And we had there a parlor. We used that room only for a special occasion, like if
my sisters came from Brooklyn. We had a green velvet sofa there with long twisted
fringes that hung down to the floor. Like Aunt Ruthie's when she was in the Bronx. Do
you remember that sofa?" She didn't pause long enough for me to answer.

"Did I tell you, Sarah, that my sister Tova and my sister Fanny came soon after I
came here? But they went to live in Brooklyn. Fanny and her husband had a grocery;
they lived in the back. Tova's husband was a buttonhole maker." Images of sofas with

curving backs shaped like violin bodies competed with images of Tanta Tova and Tanta Fanny carrying their old lady canes and handkerchiefs.

"A buttonhole maker? That was a job?" Sometimes Bubby's stories were too strange to believe, I thought, or too funny.

"They had piecework in garments. Everyone had a small special job. Remember I told you about the mantles I made in London? I worked on them here in America too, in my kitchen, at night when the children slept. I never slept. Who had time? But Tova never worked." She stopped then and grunted. Did she disapprove of Tova's not working, or did she envy it? I couldn't tell.

"Tell more about the house, Bubby. How many bedrooms? How many bathrooms?" The sound of crunching corn flakes was so out of place in this evening kitchen that I giggled and drooled some milk down my chin.

"What's funny? I had bedrooms; I had two bedrooms. I slept in one with Avram, and we had there with us a cradle for a baby. He was a goat, Avram. 'Beauty,' he would say, 'We'll make more beauty.' Pah!" A goat? I was momentarily confused. But the story went on. "First Esther was there, then Ruthie came, then your mother, and then Jean. In the other room, the other bedroom, I had two beds, for the girls. They slept there, two to a bed, head to foot. The boys were in the kitchen, on three beds I folded out at night, and closed during the day. Later, there were just two. Just two. I had a cover to spread across them. Every house had this.

"But why didn't you use the parlor, Bubby?" I ignored the comment about the number of foldaway beds. I knew it was about Uncle Sidney, somehow, but the taboo against speaking of him was too strong to violate.

"The parlor? That was the parlor. No one slept there. What kind of question! Anyway, the stove was in the kitchen, so it was warmer in there."

I was momentarily chastised. I glanced at the clock again. Where were they? Then I yanked my brain back to my grandmother's story, turning my face back to her before my eyes were willing to follow along. I tried to picture the arrangement my grandmother was describing. Years later, when I visited the Tenement Museum as an adult, I walked into what was an exact duplicate of my grandmother's description, including a round wooden table with a lace cloth over it, and burst into tears. The docent nodded knowingly. Many others had cried on seeing the room before me. "What about the bathroom, Bubby? Where was the bathroom?"

"In the hall was the bathroom. But it wasn't a bathroom. It was the toilet."

"But didn't you have a bathroom in your apartment, you know, with a sink to wash your hands and a bathtub to take a bath at night?"

"Sarah, I'm explaining, I'm telling you. The bathroom, the toilet, it was in the hall, just a room big enough for a toilet. We shared with four families, that toilet. And you had to be quick there. Four families. Of course, if you needed in the night, we used the chamber pot. And paper was the newspaper, ripped into strips." She looked at me sitting there with my mouth open, and laughed at the memory.

"Newspaper in strips?" I whispered.

"A bath was in the kitchen. I had there a tub, with a cover. And once every week, was a bath for each. Avram went to the baths, public baths, you know, the shvitz. But the kitchen was the warmest place, I told you that already, so that was where the children had a bath. We had heat only from the stove, you know, a coal stove. Shiny, black, every day polished. Your mother used to sit by the stove and read. 'Rivka, you'll go blind! Stop reading so much,' I used to say to her. She never listened. She wasn't like the others, your mother."

I propped myself up, pressing one hand on the table, so I could see out the front window. It had grown dark. A pair of headlights approached, but swung past the house and out of sight around the bend. A wave of nervous nausea swept over me. Could David have died? I shuddered and took a deep ragged breath to dismiss the idea. And then two headlights swam up the driveway and shined through the window. The clunk of a slammed car door propelled me up from my seat, causing me to upset the remnants of my bowl of corn flakes. An apron of milk puddled across the table but stopped before it spilled over the edge. My grandmother reached across the table mopping with the dishtowel she had in her lap, and I yanked open the door as my mother pushed it in from outside.

"Is he going to die? Is David okay? Where is he?" I spewed questions and began to cry in convulsive sobs.

"Die? Who said anything about dying? Mama, what did you tell her?" Rikki's voice was a motley blend of comfort and reprimand. She had brought a whiff of hospital smell into the kitchen. Then my father was at the door.

"And I thought there was carrying on in the hospital! What's all this hubbub about?" His voice was loud, reaching around for humor, but his eyes were pinched, and his skin was gray. He looked so tired to me, like he had been carrying something very heavy and bulky.

"She thinks David might have died. God knows what my mother said to her," Rikki explained scornfully.

"I said nothing," Mary defended herself proudly. "I was telling about 326 Madison Street. But how is David, Rivka?" She was the only adult who seemed correctly focused, I thought.

"It'll take more that a ruptured appendix to stop David," Joe answered proudly of his feisty son, and his normal color flooded back into his face. "He'll be back on the baseball field in no time." I couldn't decide if he was just trying to make me feel better, and making himself feel better at the same time, or if he was telling the truth. I sniffled loudly, and the sound relieved the pressure of the room and made them all smile. Rikki handed her me a wad of Kleenex. "Here, blow your nose, please, instead of snorking it down."

"But how did his appendix get ruptured? Does that mean broken?"

"Yes, Sar, it means broken. David needed an emergency appendectomy. I spoke to the principal of the school who told me the whole story of what happened. At recess today, David was running to catch a fly ball. You know David; he's the star of the field, so he ran right beyond the foul lines of the baseball field and, never taking his eyes off the ball that was way foul, he smashed right into a pole. That pole had been cemented into the ground years ago, and it stuck up just to the level of his belly." Joe rubbed his lower abdomen to show me where he meant. I rubbed my belly sympathetically.

"There was once a picnic table that was chained to it, but it rotted and was carted away years ago, but the pole, that they left there. Stupid. David was being a showman, and the possibility of making a spectacular catch far into foul territory was too tempting for him to resist. He crashed right into the pole and it ruptured his appendix. The school called your mother, Sarah, and she called me in the city. Bubby stayed here to wait for you to get home from school. Did she treat you right, Sar?" Joe winked at his mother-in-law. Explaining to his young daughter what had happened seemed to have calmed him. His color was normal again, and the wink took the tightness out of his eyes.

"You call them stupid, Joe, but I call it malicious. Malicious and negligent. I want to sue the school district!" Rikki was looking for something to put her distress into, I decided. My father was proud of his son's vitality, and visibly relieved that the incident was resolving itself. But my mother wasn't finished yet. "I'm calling a lawyer right away, Joe. I want satisfaction!" She began walking out of the kitchen but called back over her shoulder, "Tell her where I'm going, Joe. I have to get some things."

"Oh, right. Sarah, your mother wants to stay in the hospital with David. So she went to grab her toothbrush." The he lowered his voice and confided in his daughter. "They told her he was fine, you know. But you know your mother, Sar. She made up her mind, and she's not changing it." Then he leaned out the door into the hallway and shouted up the stairs, "I don't agree with that suing thing, Rikki. Let's just calm down about that!"

I heard my mother's voice float down the stairs. "I can't hear you, Joe. We can discuss the case when we're all back home." If she couldn't hear, how could she respond to the exact topic he had raised? I was slightly uncomfortable at this vague disagreement. My father sighed.

"So, Mama," Joe addressed his mother-in-law. "What's there to eat?"

354

"Apple cake! Sarah and I were going to eat dessert first, but instead we ate goose breakfast for dinner. So there's plenty of apple cake for you."

"Goose breakfast?" he laughed. I knew he didn't understand the reference, but I loved that he was laughing. My grandmother shuffled to the pan of apple cake and pulled off the waxed paper cover. She reached for a small plate, but then rejected it for a dinner plate. Father and daughter watched her slice a serving that would normally furnish four people with dessert. She looked at him for approval as she pushed the knife under it to wedge it out of the pan. He smiled and nodded his head conspiratorially toward his wife upstairs.

"Looks like dinner to me," he whispered and took his place at the table.

Thirty-Six

The rooster plaque was a great success. I painted the background blue, and the mosaic tiles I had chosen, mostly yellow and white ones, shone brilliantly along the edge. "This rooster is jaunty and jolly with his red comb," chirped Mrs. Pappalardo as she held it up for the whole class to see. I remember blushing and glowing simultaneously. "He looks like he's dancing the jig in his barnyard, doesn't he? I love how his feet are pointed in two directions, Sarah. You did excellent work." She handed the plaque back to me, and I wrapped it in brown paper so it wouldn't crack on the way home. And that Sunday, Mother's Day, I presented it to Rikki before all the aunts and uncles arrived.

"Oh, Sarah, this is beautiful; I love how the tiles around it shine. We're hanging it right up over the table. Joe, I need you to knock a hook into the wall right here where my hand is," enthused Rikki, climbing up on the yellow bunk seat and holding her hand against the wall. David had come home from the hospital the day before, and Rikki was full of energy now that things had ebbed back into normalcy.

There had been one glitch after Rikki had called her sister Ruthie to report that David was safe at home. I overheard the part of the conversation about suing the school district because of that abandoned pole, and then, after Rikki had hung up, I had heard my father trying to talk his wife out of that idea. "I do not know what that district meant when they left that rusty pole right in the middle of a baseball field, but a lawsuit will clear it all up," she had explained haughtily to her husband. His response was stern and loud. "I don't care what your sisters have told you, Rikki. We're not suing anyone!" So now that they were having an ordinary conversation about where to hang my rooster plaque, I was relieved. That my plaque was the cause of this détente was a source of great pride for me.

"And when everyone gets here, they'll see this beautiful new addition to the kitchen," continued Rikki as she stepped off the bunk seat and stood back to admire the plaque. "And then we'll have a barbecue outside. It's going to be a beautiful day. I'm going to clip a bunch of lilacs. All the ones on our side of the fence are technically ours, don't you think, Joe?"

"I think they are not ours, Rikki. They may be spilling over the fence, but they're not ours. But I also think the Millers will not mind. So go clip whatever you want."

"Sarah, you go tell Bubby she doesn't have to sit with David all day. He needs to rest, not listen to a chatty grandmother." She took a pair of clippers out of the knife drawer and walked out the kitchen door. "The rose vines are half-way up the wall, Joe. Can you tie them to the trellis before they get here?" Her voice faded as she reached the end of the breezeway and turned right into the backyard and toward the lilac bushes along the side fence.

"Hooks, trellises, what next?" Joe laughed and aimed himself for the basement door.

I wandered to the bottom of the steps and called up to my grandmother as I mounted the stairs, "Bubby! Let David rest, my mother says. You can tell me stories instead."

"Shh! He's sleeping now. Help me to go downstairs, Sarah." Mary was coming out of David's room and pulling the door partly closed behind her. I waited for her to make her way to the top of the stairs, and then I turned around and reached for my her hand. "I want to tell you about when your mother went to school. Do you want to hear that story?"

"You mean the one about how she got the point of a pencil stuck in her leg?" I asked as they descended the stairs one by one.

"No. She told you that? I don't remember about a pencil."

"She told me Uncle Morty sharpened her pencil with his knife and she kept it on the shelf under the school desk, and it was so sharp that when she bumped her knee into it by accident, the point went right into her skin. But she didn't tell the teacher because she was too scared." They reached the bottom step and Mary heaved a sigh and straightened herself up a bit. "Should we go outside?"

"Let's go on the porch, my perfect Sarah. We'll sit on the glider together. I think you and your mother are the same scared."

I found it almost impossible to think of my mother as scared, and the story of the pencil point had always puzzled me. "My mother is like me? Are you sure, Bubby?"

"Yes, I'm sure. I never knew about the pencil point. Many secrets are hiding, many secrets."

I got my grandmother installed on the glider and sat down beside her. I didn't understand the remark about the secrets. How did Bubby know that there were things I kept to myself?

"I was a terrible mother, Sarah, terrible," Mary moaned, suddenly changing the mood. I began to protest such heresy, but my grandmother waved me away and went right on lamenting. "Every term, your mother came home with her report card. She read it to me, every time. 'A+ in Reading, Mama. And A+ in Arithmetic. Only A in

Geography. I'm sorry. But here in the end, it says I skip the next term.' And I slapped

her. 'Liar, I don't believe you that you skip a term!' I screamed at her. 'Yes, Mama! It

says right here,' she cried. This happened not only one time. Every term, it was the

same. 'I skipped again,' she would say. 'Liar,' I would say. I never believed her. I

never went to ask the principal, not once. And she would cry, 'Please, Mama, I'm not a

liar.' But I didn't pay attention. And Esther, her I called 'Stupid girl!' And I told her to

stop going to school and get a job. And after I told her so many times she was stupid, she

wouldn't go to school anymore. So I got my wish."

I backed myself into the corner of the glider, as far away from my grandmother as

I could get. How could this same sweet grandmother have said such things? But I didn't

ask.

"Mayshe, him I called a gonif. A thief. He ran away from home a hundred times.

Finally, when he was not yet 14, he stopped coming home altogether. I don't know

where he went. But it was my fault because I told him I never wanted to see him again."

Her voice was full of pain as she continued. "He was 18, I think, when he married his

first wife. I didn't go to the wedding because he didn't tell me about it."

First wife? She didn't go to her son's wedding? Who was this woman sitting

beside me on the porch? My bottom lip was trembling. My grandmother always had the

ability to whip me into quivering misery in three sentences. I whispered, "First wife?" I

didn't even think my grandmother would hear me. But she turned sharply toward me.

"Another secret, Sarah. I told you there were plenty. Mayshe had a wife before

Marly. And he never divorced her, the first one. This is why your aunts don't like

Marly. They say her mother ran a brothel, a whore house." My hand flew suddenly over my mouth. My grandmother shook her head as if to apologize for saying the wrong thing. But I wasn't sure of what her words meant. I only knew her tone was contemptuous.

"Anyway, maybe it's not true about Marly's mother. I don't know." The grandmother and her granddaughter sat beside each other, each staring straight ahead as if she were alone. But then the words continued.

"A terrible mother, I was. I told you. And Rose Aronsky, she was pregnant before the wedding. My Morty, my prince, my miracle, he and Rose together ruined his life, and they did it just to ruin mine." This was too complicated. Uncle Morty's life didn't seem ruined. And neither did Bubby's, for that matter. And the connection between the two was completely obscure.

"Bubby, I can't understand what you mean," I whimpered. But my grandmother had gone into one of her unreachable states, and she just talked on.

"Ruthie had a boyfriend once. Abie Gershowitz. He loved her. He came to the house all the time, and he didn't care if there was screaming there. He sat in the kitchen and drank tea from a glass and talked to Ruthie. He was a college student going for pharmacy, and also very handsome. Blond hair he had, like a German count." She began smiling at the memory of the smart and handsome Abie courting her daughter. Maybe the mood had turned, I thought. But the smile became a sneer. "But she wouldn't go with him. 'Ruthie,' I begged her. 'Go with Abie. You'll have a good life.' But she wouldn't listen. She only wanted Milton, Milt, she calls him. Scrawny, foolish, Milt. They got married before the war, after she sent Abie away. Who knows what happened to him. A pharmacist he became. And Milt, what is Milt? A nothing. That's who my

Ruthie was good for: a nothing." She sounded like she was on the verge of spitting. I scrunched myself even further into the corner. "All because of me. Fie on me, a terrible mother. Cursed from childhood, I was. I never spoke a kind word in my house. I was always angry with Avram because I tricked him to marry me and he never forgave me. No peace, no love, nobody learned to be kind or good to each other. Every day a new anger, and new spitefulness, a new resentment. And each of my children was another reminder of my miserable life and my mistaken evil marriage. Terrible. Horrible. Shameful."

I could barely stand this conversation. I began to wonder what time it was. Weren't all these children of this terrible mother going to be arriving any minute to visit her? Why would they come so much if she were such a terrible mother? And I didn't believe there could be such a thing as a curse on someone. I was about to ask her, to tell her she must be wrong. But when I turned toward her, I saw that her eyes had reddened and were overflowing with tears. She was rooting around in the pocket of her sweater for a tissue. I extended my legs and began to slide forward. "Wait a second, Bubby. I'll go get some tissues."

"No!" Her reaction was a demanding shriek. "I'm not done, so I want you to sit here and listen. No tissues!"

I scooted back into my corner and my eyes widened. My grandmother had never spoken like this to me. Was I imagining it, or did the sky cloud over and darken the porch? I was too upset to answer.

"Jean, my baby, Jean was her father's favorite. I never even touched her. He, after six children, he did everything for her. The others, mostly he couldn't care if they lived or died. He didn't care if they starved. He didn't know if they were home or gone, and he never asked. And I never told him, because I don't think I cared either. I just watched myself get older every day. And I watched the only thing I had, my beauty, slide away day by day by day, until later, a stroke came and ruined whatever was left. . But Jean! She went with Avram to shul, and she went with him to buy clothes, coats, shoes, and earrings even, he bought her. He took her to a jeweler, Morris Krongold on Rivington Street. His wife took a needle and pierced her ears. She was only six years old. And she put gold studs in her ears. Jean. She looked like a gypsy's child. I never said anything to stop him." She stopped then, seeming to think about how to explain to me the next part.

"But he took her with him also to another woman. She told me, Jean did. 'Papa took me to see his friend today. She is more beautiful than you, Mama.' A little girl, she was then, too young to know what she was saying. I turned to him to look in his eyes. 'What woman is this, Avram?' And he stared at me. And then he said, 'Once you were beautiful, Mary, more beautiful than any woman on the earth. I remember when I used to want to stand next to you because your beauty warmed me, and to sleep next to you, Mary, that was a warmth no one in the world knew but me. But no more, Mary. Now you are worn out. Look at you. Your hair is gray now, and your hands are red. Look at the lines you have, Mary.' His voice was tired, like he had no strength to speak. And he reached his hand out and started to touch my face, my wrinkled face. I couldn't believe what was happening." She paused then, thinking about that moment, I supposed. She took a deep breath then, and seemed to fortify herself.

"And then, at that moment, a witch was born in my brain, like a wind that blows around and around and sucks up everything in its way, good and bad. She filled me up in one second, that witch, and I felt her blackness pour out of my eyes. My hand flew out, I didn't even know I was doing it, and I smacked him. Then my other hand turned into a fist, and I began to beat him. His glasses flew off his face. They hit the wall and split into a million needles of glass. A sliver of glass came like an arrow, and sliced right into Jean's forehead. It just missed her eye. The screaming then! He was screaming, Jean was screaming, and I was screaming. And the blood was pouring out of Jean, and also Avram. Everyone in the building heard. They came to the door, banging on the door. 'What's going on?' They cried. I came to my senses. I looked at Avram then, and I spoke very calmly. 'We are moving out from this house this week. I will never speak another word in this house to you or anyone.' And something must have scared him, because he ran out the door, sent the neighbors home, and went right away to the Bronx where he took a big apartment that very day. And we moved that week. I left every stick of furniture, every pillow, every dish, pot and spoon right there in Madison Street. And the next week, I bought all new. Avram didn't say a word. We lived together in the Bronx then, but we never spoke a kind word to each other after that."

My grandmother leaned her head back and closed her eyes, suddenly exhausted. I waited in my corner to see what would happen next. I realized that the dog had been barking and howling in the backyard. He must have wound his lead around a tree. I twisted my head around and tried to see out the window, but my seat on the glider was too low. After a few minutes, I decided that my grandmother had fallen asleep, so I inched forward carefully and slipped off. The barking had stopped. Could he have untwisted himself? Maybe my mother had come? I leaned my hands against the windowsill and searched the yard. No dog and no Rikki. I tiptoed to the door that led into the living room, but just when I thought I had gotten away from my grandmother and her fierce story, I was stopped by a whispered raspy voice.

"There's more, Sarah. More secrets. More ugliness. More about the terrible mother and the poisoned children. Do you think you can stand to hear it?"

My head swam dizzily and I steadied myself against the doorframe, my knuckles white. I could barely summon my voice. I swallowed and licked my dried lips. "Yes, Bubby, I'll try." At that moment, I heard a horn ring from the street. Then I heard my mother's voice call gaily from the kitchen.

"Sarah, the cousins are here! We have to show everyone the rooster plaque! Tell Bubby!"

I looked at my grandmother and shrugged my shoulders. The rest would have to wait. From someplace inside myself, I managed to call inside to my mother. "Here I come."

## Thirty-Seven

"After Mother's Day, Sarah, comes Decoration Day, and then it's a hop, skip, and a jump to Father's Day. And then, it's summer. Daddy and I are thinking about a family vacation during the summer, maybe to Cape Cod. We could stay in a little cottage there by the beach." Rikki was beating eggs for breakfast and her eyes were trained on her springy eggbeater, but she darted them quickly at me as I passed my mother on my way to the bunkseat.

"Will the aunts be decorating the bungalows on Decoration Day?" I knew my mother was testing me for my reaction to the proposed vacation but I ignored the issue. What would be the right reaction?

"Decorating the bungalows? They'll be sweeping out sand, I guess. That's not really decorating." Rikki was smiling, her face somewhere between enjoying a possible joke her daughter had made and laughing at her ignorance. She put a plate of scrambled eggs in front of me. "The things you don't know! That's not what Decoration Day means; it's about remembering the soldiers who died in the wars." I looked at my breakfast, suddenly not the least bit interested in eating.

"But I thought decorating was. . . ." I stopped myself. I felt foolish.

"But what about Cape Cod? Wouldn't you like to go stay in a cottage by the beach?" Rikki didn't seem to notice my embarrassment.

"Okay, I guess." Several questions sprung to mind, but I kept them to myself, unwilling to chance revealing any further ignorance. I forced myself to eat a few bites of the buttery eggs and then, glancing up at the clock, I slid off the bunkseat and left for school.

"Have fun today, Sarah," Rikki called after her daughter who was halfway down the driveway. "And pick up your head," she added. My head jerked up reflexively, but fell again almost instantly. I studied the pavement as I made my way to school, wondering whether Cape Cod was a place where there was only fish to eat, whether a vacation away meant I wouldn't see my grandmother all summer, and wondering when I would know enough to avoid asking any more questions of people who always seem ready to laugh at me.

The rest of the week passed uneventfully. School began to wind down toward its close with review lessons, packing of textbooks into storage shelves, and final testing to measure the year's comprehension. There was planning for the science fair to be held during the first week of June, and practice for the Flag Day Field Day Celebration. The pressure abated slowly like a minute leak in a bicycle tire. There was still a month to go, Miss Sullivan reminded the class, but it was impossible for anyone to ignore the brighter warmer days.

There were no further stories from my grandmother, and I was grateful. Lying in bed each night, listening to my grandmother's nocturnal moaning, I thought how the whole of my grandmother's life seemed to be a series of miserable incidents that spread out in every direction like a puddle of blood that grew under an animal that had been hit by a car. I had seen a raccoon like that once as we sped past it on the parkway. It was an image I couldn't erase from my memory, and it popped up as I considered the various chapters of my grandmother's stories.

It all began with a charmed childhood, I thought, of a girl whose father adored his beautiful daughter. But then it tilted into ugliness when that adoration had turned perverted. And then came the day when that daughter, poisoned with the possibility of rejection from the man she loved, had made a decision that led to a series of wretched incidents that broke her heart over and over again. The decision to go to London and trick Avram into marrying her had ruined her life, his life, and then the lives of the children they had. Which of my aunts or uncles was happy? Who had a calm and peaceful existence? Who was not busy judging everyone jealously? Not one of them. And now, I realized with a sickening awareness, it had spread viciously to my generation, too. My cousins, I thought with a kind of nausea, which of them was free of the same suspicions that crippled their parents? None of them, either, I concluded as I ticked them off one by one in my mind.

The curse that my grandmother had been bewailing lately, maybe she was right about it. There was a curse. But she was wrong about where it came from, I concluded. It didn't come from my great-grandfather, as his daughter thought. No. He never cursed her. He was afraid of her, I realized as I thought through the story. He never spoke to her again after that hot day at the river, and she never spoke to him either. The curse that had created my mother's family came from my grandmother herself, from the exact second she decided to steal her sister's coat and her mother's money and go betray a man who was shallow and vengeful.

But why did she do it? Why did she bring such misery to the world? I turned over the question night after night. What should I think about a beautiful woman who knows her beauty has power and uses it to enrich herself? And then, when she learns that what she gets isn't what she wants, or needs, that it doesn't make her happy, what should I think when she repeats the same error, over and over? When the life she arranges for herself is poison, what kind of a person allows the poison to spread around her like a puddle that grows from a leaky sewer pipe and spreads from one person to another? My eyes grew smaller as the shadows under them deepened. Was the curse oozing into my life too? Into David's? Rikki was different than her siblings, I had always thought. But was she different enough? Was she immune from the curse? Could the curse skip a generation? I lay in my bed chewing my tongue raw with anxiety. I heard the distant train whistle every night when I should have been sleeping for hours. It was such a desolate sound that I felt it was reacting to my own mournfulness. I so identified with it that I had begun to wait for it before I could fall asleep.

The next Sunday was to be the last visit of the aunts and uncles before they took up their summer lives in their Rockaway bungalows. The topic of discussion at the table centered on how Mary would be installed into Aunt Ruthie's bungalow. This was a subject that was repeated each year, and my father had predicted it that morning at breakfast. Uncle Morty was outside washing his car, as usual, and Joe glanced out the window over the sink and watched his progress. "I have a surprise for your sisters and brothers, Rikki," he said with a sly laugh.

"What's the surprise?" she answered warily.

"Well, I might as well tell you before he gets done with the car and comes in for his first cup of coffee," he said pointing with his chin out the window at his brother-in-law. "I have a tape of them having the "who's taking Mama to Rockaway" conversation from last year. I ran the recorder that day. Remember, that was right after we got the recorder? I almost forgot I had saved that recording, but I was looking for some blank space on a tape last week, because I wanted to record some songs. And there it was, Jean screaming at Solly about the kids, Ruthie cackling, all of them. And they were going over how to get your mother out to Rockaway. Today, when they're all here, I'm going to turn it on. Maybe we can avoid the same fight just this once, and I'll get to laugh my head off." Joe was smiling so happily, triumphantly, that even though there was an angle of derision against her family, Rikki joined his good humor.

"Won't this be a riot?" she responded laughing. "I can't wait to see Jean's face when she hears herself screaming like a fishwife."

And just then, Uncle Morty pushed open the kitchen door. "What's everyone doing up so early? Hey, Rivka, gimme some coffee, okay?" There was leftover laughter in the air, but Uncle Morty must have assumed they were laughing at the rakish angle of his straw fedora, because he quickly righted it and sat down on the edge of the bunkseat and cleared his throat.

By noon, everyone was ensconced around the kitchen table. As usual, each person was enjoying a different course of the meal that Rikki had prepared, some nursing a bowl of soup, some gnawing on fried chicken, and some slurping coffee and filling their mouths with forkfuls of Russian bobka. I was positioned at my usual listening post, just inside the living room door, and anyone who chanced to glimpse a look at my face remarked how haunted I looked. "Sarah, you look sick. Look at the circles under the girl's eyes. Doesn't she sleep, Rikki?" Aunt Esther remarked in her usual derisive tone.

"You can mind your business, Esther. I don't see Darlene looking so perfect," retorted Rikki. I smiled quietly. I liked when my mother defended me.

"You have one kid recovering from a burst appendix and the other looking like she lives in a concentration camp. So don't tell me," spat Aunt Esther. Suddenly, everyone was flaring with an opinion of the appearance of various children, and the moment threatened to erupt into chaos. I sucked in my breath and began to sneak away towards the back door. But from the opposite end of living room came the sounds of a duplicate family argument. I looked to where the sounds were emanating, and there was my father, fiddling with his tape recorder that was perched on a broad shelf of the bookcase. He turned the volume higher and higher until it finally penetrated the storm that was blowing in the kitchen.

"Get her away from me, Solly! I'm warning you right now, Melissa: stop whining or I'll crack you right across your face!" It was Aunt Jean's recorded voice. It was overlapped by Uncle Mayshe's voice.

"Hey, Marly, take off that watch and gimme it." And that was overlapped by Aunt Ruthie's voice.

"I'm not coming here for Mama. I have a car full of linens. Where do you want her to ride?" I looked at my father who was grinning as if he had discovered treasure. And from the kitchen, there came silence. I turned from my father to the door into the kitchen. All the squabbling had broken off, and my aunts and uncles were looking at each other and listening to their other selves squabbling.

The taped played on. "I brought her last year," complained taped Aunt Esther. "It's not my turn."

"Well, Solly doesn't drive. He has a goddam plate in his arm," whined Aunt Jean in a tone not unlike her daughter's had been moments earlier.

"Is this supposed to be news, Jean? Alert the papers: Solly has a plate!" announced Uncle Morty.

"Shut up, Morty. And make plans to transport your mother. It's your turn," retorted Aunt Jean.

I trained my eyes on my grandmother who was sitting numbly in her usual chair at the head of the table full of her children. I could only see her in profile, but I could tell that her jaw was clenched, and her eyes were down, studying the dish in front of her. Her shoulders were hunched up, as she seemed to be trying to retract her head like a turtle. Tears sprang from my eyes. But there was no way to stop the past from happening. The silence from the kitchen was proof that Joe's joke had not had the expected results.

Just then, my cousin Daniel burst through the kitchen door from the breezeway. "There's a fire! Around the corner a house is on fire!" And in mere seconds, every one of my relatives poured out of their seats and bolted through the door. I went into the almost empty kitchen. Only my grandmother remained, forgotten in her chair.

"Bubby, I'd better go see what Daniel was talking about. Will you be okay here? David is upstairs in his room. If he tries to go out, maybe you should tell him not to, okay? I think he's supposed to still be resting." I pushed open the door to the breezeway. I craned my neck out the door to see where my relatives had gone, but there wasn't a trace of anyone. Now I could smell the smoke. I turned toward the backyard and the smell grew stronger, more acrid. In a moment, my eyes were stinging, and the back of my throat felt raw like I had tonsillitis. "I'll be right back, Bubby!" I called over my shoulder, and I ran into the backyard and climbed over the fence, taking a short cut to scene of the burning house.

The wail of sirens filled the air as densely as the smoke had. I could see flashes of fire engine red poking through the trees, as I got closer to the site. I ran through my back neighbor's property, climbed another small fence and stepped down into the street that ran parallel to mine. And there it was: a house that looked just like mine, except billows of smoke were pouring out of what would have been my bedroom if it actually had been my house.

Flames had pierced a hole in the roof right above the upstairs bathroom. The shrieking of the sirens waxed and waned as new waves of pumping engines and ladder trucks converged in the street. I counted four police cars parked helter skelter as if their drivers had abandoned them, their lights flashing blue and white beams. There was a throng of onlookers, adults and children, and it was building rapidly as I sidled around the flank to get a better view. Policemen with megaphones held by one hand at their mouths and the other hand out herded the mob backwards up a slight incline and away from the spectacle.

And suddenly, I was terrified. Everyone was craning this way and that to see, rocking up on their tiptoes and boosting themselves up on each other's shoulders. The atmosphere was, to my horror, joyous, like they had all come out to an unscheduled country fair to take in the sights and sounds, and maybe get to see something grotesque like a two-headed calf or a bearded lady. But this was someone's house burning down, the end of everything they owned, their sofa, their beds, their photographs, everything.

My pulse was soaring, and I couldn't see anyone I knew. All my family had emptied out of my kitchen to come here, and everyone who lived in the neighborhood had come, too. But where was even one recognizable face? This rabble was like the people I had learned about in school who would come to the town square to witness, gleefully, a hanging. This horde had a collective life different from the individual lives that made it up, and even if I knew any of these people, including my relatives, I couldn't distinguish them. I was beginning to feel washed over with panic.

And then something even worse came to me: this was like a reenactment of the fire in Ulla that had brought my afflicted grandparents together. I glanced around reflexively, somehow expecting to see them, two beautiful young versions of them, locked into each other's eyes. They would be encircled with a supernatural glow, a kind of spectral light that grew out of them rather than reflected down on them. My eyes swept around the crowd, knowing I wouldn't see them, but still continuing to look. The pulsing roar of the sirens, the choking stink of the burning house, the evil laughing of the mob around me, all these faded back and I felt light-headed and woozy.

I knew I had to get away from this scene, and I began to dart between people, ducking one way, bobbing another, until I reached the thin edge of the crowd. The air seemed cleaner even though I was still very near the fire. But as I walked further away from the tumultuous scene, I felt calmer. My heartbeat slowed, and I started to think rationally again.

At that moment, as I made my way home, ready to tell my grandmother what I had seen, a certain revelation dawned on me. I've thought about it over the years as often as I've thought any thought, and the truth is, I understood my grandmother's life at that exact moment. As I turned the corner onto my own street and saw my own house, the unburned duplicate of the disaster around the corner, everything coalesced and was as whole and pristine as my house. The reason my grandmother had brought such misery onto herself and her descendants came clearly to me, unmistakably the truth. And when I turned it over to examine it carefully I knew that it had been obvious all along, from the beginning of the story to that very afternoon in the kitchen. My grandmother's curse, I decided, had been her beauty, and how it lured her into repeating behavior that hadn't worked, thinking each time, the charm of the beauty will make the outcome different. Her appearance had created a toxic atmosphere around her from her childhood forward. It had prevented her father from treating her like a daughter and it had prevented her from learning normal things, like reading, and crucial things, like coping with life's twists and turns. He was crazy in some way that I didn't understand, but my grandmother ignored his constant abnormal attention and gifts and praise because she thought a beauty like her deserved more than anyone else. She was a victim, but then she used the beauty again to draw a man to her who was attracted mindlessly, like a moth to a candle. Once he had been burned by her beautiful evil, the attraction evaporated and she was disappointed again by her beauty. But trapped by her poisoned decisions, the fix was in and the rest of her life played out unstoppably. She abused her children, of course. How could they have escaped when they were the living result of the trap she had caught herself in? And they grew up to make matches with spouses who could round out their own disabilities. Their children, my cousins, were doomed, too.

I turned up my driveway, dramatically relieved to have worked out the knots that had been tormenting me. I felt like the very air was cleaner, the light of the day clearer. I began to whistle a tune my father had been singing that morning. I skipped up the driveway, gloriously happy. "Bubby! Where is everyone? The fire was so scary, but you know, it reminded me of the fire in Ulla when you met Avram. Bubby?" I called out as I bounced through the breezeway and stepped up the concrete step to open the kitchen door. "Bubby?" I called, but there was no answer. I pulled the door open, and in the relative darkness of the kitchen compared to the bright light of that May afternoon, I found it difficult to focus. And then my pupils closed down enough to bring the whole kitchen into sharp clarity. And that was unfortunate, because what I saw was my grandmother slumped forward across the kitchen table, a dish of potted meat and potatoes smeared half under her like a pillow that had exploded its dark contents.

"Oh, my God," I whispered. "Oh, my God." I sat down on the edge of the bunkseat, put one hand gingerly onto my grandmother's still back, and waited for my mother to come home.

Thirty-Eight

There was a funeral, of course. But I didn't go because Rikki thought it would be too frightening for her children. Mrs. Farrington, the nearly deaf babysitter came to watch us. David was nearly recovered from his appendectomy and might even have gone back to school that day, but he wrapped himself up in the blanket from his bed and ensconced himself on the sofa in the living room. The TV was pointed at him all day, but he didn't look like he was hearing any of the game shows or daytime dramas that were blaring out of it. Mrs. Farrington was perched alongside him, supposedly to watch him as my mother had instructed, but each time I wandered by, I observed that the only thing being watched was the television screen. Sometimes, David would be asleep when I looked into the living room, but he never unwound himself from of the blanket cocoon whether he was awake or asleep. He and I never made eye contact.

I couldn't find a place to put myself. I was awakened early by the sounds of my parents getting ready to leave for the funeral home, and although I tried to go back to sleep to escape from thinking about what was happening, I never made it. The empty bed across the room was echoing with filaments of stories that had been coming from it.

I heard my father's car drive off when he went to pick up Mrs. Farrington, I heard Mrs. Farrington and my mother murmuring in the kitchen, and I heard the screen door close behind my mother as she left. At that final smack of wooden door on wooden doorframe, I gave up trying to sleep and crept down the first few steps so I could see what Mrs. Farrington was up to. She was sitting at the head of the kitchen table in the chair that my grandmother had died in not twenty-four hours earlier. I watched as she lifted the brown coffee mug to her lips, and then I stood up so I wouldn't see any more.

How could she be sitting right in Bubby's chair on the day of her funeral? I considered going right down to the kitchen to ask her. Well, she couldn't know, could she? And it was only a chair, after all.

I walked into my parents' room. It was Monday, so there was no pile of white collar stays on my father's dresser. My mother's closet door was ajar, and I knelt down to look at the shoe rack. The black shoes with the pointy toes were gone. That figured: black shoes to a funeral. The bed was unmade, which was odd, and a hat box had been left at the foot of the bed, its cover just next to it on the floor. I bent to pick it up and place it on the bed. I wandered over to the window, which overlooked the back yard, and there was the dog's run where Bubby had fallen while trying to save the dog from the rainstorm. I sighed raggedly and left the room.

I went into the bathroom to look in the mirror. I wanted to know how I looked when I was this unhappy, but before I managed to boost myself up on the edge of the sink, I saw the glass perched on the toilet tank where my grandmother kept her false teeth at night. They were there, sunken to the bottom of the glass but with the top teeth not quite lined up with the bottom ones. It was a cockeyed grin that I was staring at in the glass, my hands evenly placed on the rim of the sink. I shifted my gaze to the mirror and involuntarily copied the lopsided smile of my grandmother's teeth. It was too strange. I darted backwards out of the bathroom and shut the door against the grinning teeth.

There was nowhere left to go upstairs except back in my room. As I made my way past my grandmother's bed, I raised my left hand to the side of my face, blocking the view, but I peeked through my fingers as if the hand trying to save me from the bleak view of the empty bed was not mine and I could trick it. I opened the closet door and peered inside. There were my school dresses with their white Peter Pan collars and their colorful plaids on the left side of the rod, and there were my grandmother's starched dresses, hanging neatly to their right. No one would ever wear them again, I thought to myself. Then I glanced down, and my breath was stolen away. There were my grandmother's black orthopedic shoes with their pushed down backs and tangled black laces, the right one standing straight on its sole, but the left one knocked over on its side pointing way off to the left. It was just like her twisted crippled body, I thought. Her right side worked fine, even though she was so ancient that she could remember back to before cars were invented, but her left side had stopped working years ago, way before I had been born. It was too much. The tears came then, quiet but torrential. I sunk to my knees and cradled the shoes to my chest and leaned my head down and caressed them with my cheek.

I stayed there until I heard Mrs. Farrington moving around the kitchen and then snapping on the TV. I heard David padding down the stairs with his blanket dragging behind him. Then I climbed back into my own bed, still clutching the shoes. I stayed there except for the few times I went to check on my brother and Mrs. Farrington, but I never let go of the shoes.

The rest of the week was a blur of relatives making noise, plates of food being delivered and consumed, and a constant smell of coffee being brewed. No one spoke about Mary in my presence. In fact, it didn't seem to me that anyone remembered why they had all gathered there day after day instead of going to work or school. My grandmother had just slipped through some crack in the universe, it seemed, and all her descendants acted like the occasion was a convenient excuse to pretend it was Sunday every day for a week. At night, I could sometimes hear my parents talking to each other quietly in sad tones next door in their room. But during the day, there was no sign of mourning except for the sheets covering the mirrors and the big candle burning steadily on the fireplace mantle.

Then finally, it was over. And on Saturday morning, my father stepped into my room just as I was waking up. "Let's go, Sar. Big day today. You and I are going to Coney Island," he announced as if we had been planning it for weeks.

"Coney Island? You mean the rides?" I replied, propping myself up on one elbow.

"Well, yes. But really only one ride," he said with a mysterious smile and raised eyebrows.

"All of us?"

"No, unless you think you and I make up all of us," he laughed.

His mood was infectious. I scrambled out of bed and grabbed the first pair of shorts in the stack in my drawer and a white sleeveless blouse.

"Better take a sweater, Sar. The ride I have in mind might be chilly," my father called as he started down the stairs. He was singing about the moon hitting your eye like a big pizza pie before I could ask any questions.

My father sang along with the songs on the radio all the way to Coney Island. When they were in Rikki's car, the station was WQXR, which only played classical music. But in the little black car my father drove, the radio was tuned to a popular music station. The DJ repeated the most popular songs over and over, and by the time the air coming in the rolled down windows had turned salty, I could sing along, too.

"Okay, Sar, we start with a Nathan's dog and some fries, " directed my father, as if he had a printed itinerary. He knew every nook and cranny of Brooklyn, and even though the crowd at Coney Island was thick, he had found a secret parking lot, deposited the car, and they were, "way ahead of schedule," he claimed happily.

"But what ride are we going on? We drove so far for only one ride?" I wasn't as carefree as I knew he wanted me to be. We walked together through the crowd, passing the Steeplechase building with its track of wooden racehorses suspended high up the outside wall carrying delighted riders.

"Well, this ride is one helluva ride, Sarah," he said, daring to use language that Rikki would not have been pleased to hear.

"What ride is it?"

And then I saw it: the Parachute Jump. A lacy metal tower poked its tip up into the sky, taller than any building. The top was spread open like an umbrella that had lost its fabric, and suspended in a circle around the structure, from each of twelve points was a multicolored parachute. Most were closed, hanging like delicate handkerchiefs held by invisible fingers at various heights. One or two were descending, like open umbrellas that had been dropped off a roof. A few were all the way at the top, still furled tightly. And then, as I watched, my head tilted all the way back, one of the ones at the top seemed to drop from the grip of the invisible fingers, and it fell through the air for a few seconds until it was caught by the wind under it and it opened like a giant flower coming instantly into bloom. I stared with my mouth open as the rest of the parachutes completed their trips upward, paused at the top, and let go, and each bounced open with a sudden jolt and floated downward to the bottom of the metal structure. Only then did I notice that suspended from each parachute was a swing on which was perched a delighted rider or two. Then the screams of glee that were drifting from these riders came into focus, and at the same moment, the realization that my father intended to take me up to the top of the Parachute Jump hit me.

"Oh, no! I'm not going up there," I said, and grabbed my hand away from him.

"Yes, Sarah, we are going together. It's just what the doctor ordered," my father said and scooped back my hand into his.

"But it's too scary! What if the parachute blows out to sea?" I said, my eyes gazing at the vast ocean just beyond the ride.

"Not possible," Joe replied, guiding me closer and closer to the booth at the bottom where tickets were for sale. "Each parachute is attached to the ride with chains. Look up there and you'll see them."

"But what if our chain breaks? We could die!"

"We're done with dying for a while now, Sarah. We're going on the Parachute Jump." His tone was resolute and I knew there was no way he'd change his mind.

The ride attendant strapped my father and me into the canvas swing. My father put his arm around my shoulder, and the swing began to ascend. The chain that held it clattered noisily as we rose higher and higher. I gripped the belt across my lap with terrified fingers, my eyes shut tightly.

"Open 'em, Sarah, and take a look around," instructed my father.

The chain noise continued, but more slowly as our swing seat neared the top. I obeyed by instinct rather than desire. The sight took my breath away. The huge green Atlantic Ocean blanketed the earth in one direction, and the now tiny buildings that made up the amusement park lay scattered around like Monopoly buildings. The roller coaster, which if you stood next to it, towered above you like a huge skyscraper, looked like a prize you could get in a box of Cracker Jacks, and the delighted shrieks of the riders sounded like a radio playing in a far off room. The chain stopped its clickety-clack, and the parachute reached the top and the earth was silent, gloriously silent.

I took a big breath and smiled at my father who beamed down at me happily. I felt every worry lift up off me and I could almost see them float away into the endless blue sky. And then, in that moment of silence, everything in the world paused, and I imagined my grandmother flying off, too. I thought I could see her soaring horizontally in the sky with her arms outstretched like Superman, and then I thought maybe my grandmother lifted her arm, the left arm, the one I'd never seen move, over her head and waved at me, smiling with a mouthful of white beautiful teeth shining in her mouth. I waved back, and my father, somehow understanding what I'd had seen, joined me in waving. I nearly wept with happiness.

And then the parachute let go, released from its perch at the top. For a few endless seconds, it fell straight down, untethered and wild, as if it would hit the ground and plunge my father and me into the sand beneath us. But then the wind shouldered its way into the silk folds of the parachute and was caught with a loud pop. The parachute jerked to a near stop, and floated soundlessly to the ground.

The attendant released us wearing a passive face that told me that he had no idea how wondrous my experience had been. I opened my lips as I stepped away from the swing, ready to try to explain. But a glance at my father changed my mind. He was shaking his head, and when he lifted his finger to his lips, I knew that the whole thing

would be our secret.  No one else needed to understand.

Epilogue

Of course, without some kind of ignition, everything that I had been told would have remained a dusty dried bundle of the straw of childhood, never to create enough light to illuminate anything. The stories would have moldered away, their importance forgotten as if they had been mere dreams that dissolve like wisps and webs in the morning. No one would have considered how one young woman's decision about what to do next her own life would result in painful and poisonous repercussions for four generations. Every so often, my mother leaked out a detail of the dysfunctional household in which she grew up, but these puzzle pieces hung disconnected for years, never falling into their places and showing a clear picture that would have explained her family.

But years later, something did happen that forced me to resurrect the stories and allow them to throw their light. It was after my mother's siblings and their spouses had died, and some were actually forgotten. And it was well after my father had died, and my brother had died, tragically young, and many of my cousins had died, too, or scattered, and even after my own children had grown up and gone to create their own families and stories. It came when my mother, who was born Rivka and became Rikki and lived for more than 90 years, finally came to her end. She had been the absolute last person to have any memory of Mary as a healthy, beautiful young woman, and when Rikki finally closed her eyes for a night of sleep and never opened them again. It was at her funeral that I gained the ignition that was necessary to rekindle the tales my grandmother had told me when I was a nine-year old child, and we had shared a bedroom in the middle of the 1950s.

It was autumn when my mother died, and her funeral was on one of those sparkling days when the air is so utterly clean and crisp that it feels like the very composition of the atmosphere has changed for the better. I had called Stacie, Aunt Ruthie's daughter to let her know.

"The last of them, huh?" she had responded to the news.

"I can't believe we're the elders now. Remember when they all used to sit in my mother's kitchen every Sunday and she'd be turning out potato latkes by the dozens? She must have grated half her knuckles into that mixture every week."

"She grated by hand?" Stacie, like all my cousins, had never paid attention to what went on in that kitchen.

"Yes. She was positively religious about doing it Bubby's way, no matter how many new kitchen gadgets got invented. She was rolling dough and stuffing cabbage until a few months ago." We both paused to consider the past.

"Well, I'll be there for the funeral. But I wouldn't count on anyone else." Stacie was only saying out loud what I knew to be true. The family members had begun to ignore each other right after my grandmother had died more than 40 years earlier, and by the time her last child was dead, hardly anyone was on talking terms.

And now, standing at her grave watching the last of the earth being shoveled in, I considered what had become of all those relatives. Most of them had died without each other's support. Uncle Morty was told he had cancer, but he refused treatment because he said the doctors didn't know what they were talking about. His sisters called each other to rail about why Aunt Rose didn't force him, but no one called him to try to help. Aunt Rose, his ignored and neglected wife, shriveled up quickly after, and died within months, alone in her apartment without calling any of her sisters-in-law. They said she deserved it because she had let their beloved brother die. I have no idea what became of the children.

Uncle Mayshe and Aunt Marly died fighting with each other to the end. Aunt Ruthie and Aunt Esther maintained he had stabbed her just after she had fed him a corned beef sandwich laced with arsenic. Who knows if it's true, but it may as well have been, because it satisfied the family members who heard it. Their son Daniel hadn't spoken to them in years. He had gone to Europe as a young man to re-invent himself, married a Dutch woman, and rarely came back to New York at all.

Uncle Sidney, whom I had thought of as dead throughout my childhood, had emerged from an institution after over 40 years of silence, while I was at college. He spoke in cadences that were vaguely tinged with expressions that had disappeared from the language in the 1930s. He never made eye contact with me or anyone else, although my mother tried desperately to pretend he was fine, cured, and perfectly able to function in a society he could barely recognize. He died of complications from the diabetes he had ignored completely until doctors had to amputate gangrenous feet. My mother and Aunt Jean were his only siblings who came to his funeral. Aunt Esther said, "He's been dead to me for years. Why so I want to go to a funeral now?" Aunt Ruthie and Uncle Milt were taking care a grandchild of theirs whose parents were locked in a bitter divorce in New Jersey, but she promised to visit his grave. I have no idea if she ever went.

Aunt Jean and Uncle Solly stopped living together shortly after my grandmother died. She had a series of boyfriends who accompanied her to various family functions over the years. Every family picture features her on the arm of a different man, but all were interchangeable and undistinguishable from the others in their too youthful hairdos, rows of glinting gold necklaces visible at their open neck shirts, and endless chains of cigarettes. Uncle Solly's face never appears in another picture. The family never spoke to him again after they separated, even though they had been related to him for their whole adult lives. Both Aunt Jean and Uncle Solly smoked themselves into their graves, too young, and in separate hospitals. One of their daughters endured a series of disastrous marriages and finally swore off men. The other married a very rich man, whom she detested from the moment they met, and they led separate lives, both paid for by him. Their children alternated between speaking only to their mother and only to their father, and became young women who suffered from anorexia.

Aunt Esther, clearly the angriest of my grandmother's children, and Uncle Jack, had four children. One became an extremely obese woman who sobbed loudly, like a child who had dropped her ice cream cone onto the sidewalk, when she thought she was the object of some derision, even if it was as minor as being short-changed by a supermarket cashier. One married a woman who clung obsessively to her own mother throughout their marriage, until the mother died in extremely old age, whereupon the daughter moved into her mother's apartment and denied access to her husband, who alternated between making excuses for her and taking out ads in newspapers absolving himself of her debts. One daughter moved to Florida and refused any contact with her mother, no matter how many calls Uncle Jack made begging her to reconsider. The last of the four children is afraid to leave her home for any reason. Aunt Esther's grandchildren are mirrors of their parents, ranging from obsessive crybabies to lonesome neurotics of one stripe or another.

Aunt Ruthie died within a week of falling ill. No one seemed able to look into what she was suffering from in that week, and the days passed painfully as various members of the family weighed in with screaming rants at Aunt Ruthie's immediate family for their supposed neglect. Stacie's brother, having alienated his ex-wife and children thoroughly, followed his mother to his own grave within the year. Uncle Milt's propensity to tell constant awful jokes finally fell away, and he died nearly silent before long.

There are other sorry tales to tell of my mother's family, but they are redundant. Almost no one seems healthy and peaceful to me. Maybe the ones who escaped are better than the ones I know. Just thinking of them all is heartbreaking.

After the funeral, where as Stacie predicted, almost no one from my mother's family appeared, I went home to think. An insistent light illuminated my memories so relentlessly that it forced me to begin to work my way through my grandmother's stories carefully and methodically. Somehow, I think that every thread of the story unwound itself from the very moment beautiful Mary, refusing to be a discarded woman, decided to go to London and redeem a young man's misguided promise. The contagion was released then, and it lodged, one by one, into everyone who followed. What a legacy she left.

I have no idea how much of my grandmother's story was actual hard truth. After all, no one ever spoke a word about any of the accounts of her life. Maybe she invented the whole tale just for me. But why? The only thing that makes any sense is that she saw in me someone she could save from the fallout of the actions she never forgave herself for. She wanted me to be strong, independent, and capable, free from the debilitating suspicions that crippled everyone else. It really didn't matter it the stories were true; what mattered was some bigger truth about how to negotiate my life. She offered this truth to me in the form of a gift, really, the only gift she had.

No matter how much of an outsider I had been back then when they all gathered around that long and crowded oak table presided over by an old broken lady, no matter how twisted the lives of my relatives had been, no matter how appalling the past was, I realized that I was indeed part of it, and lining it all up carefully for a close examination was exactly what I needed to do. My grandmother knew it, and that has been my antidote, my escape route, just as she hoped it would be.

Made in the USA
San Bernardino, CA
26 September 2014